The Feminist Case
Against Bureaucracy

In the series

Women in the Political Economy,

edited by Ronnie J. Steinberg

THE FEMINIST CASE AGAINST BUREAU- CRACY

KATHY E. FERGUSON

Temple University Press

Philadelphia

Temple University Press, Philadelphia 19122
© 1984 by Temple University. All rights reserved
Published 1984
Printed in the United States of America

Library of Congress Cataloging in Publication Data

Ferguson, Kathy E.
  The feminist case against bureaucracy.

  (Women in the political economy)
  Bibliography: p.
  Includes index.
  1. Bureaucracy. 2. Feminism. I. Title. II. Series.
HD38.4.F47   1984   303.3'5'088042   84-221
ISBN 0-87722-357-2

Parts of Chapters 3 and 4 are adapted from Ferguson, "Bureaucracy and Public Life: The Feminization of the Polity," Administration and Society, Vol. 15, no. 3 (November, 1983), pp. 295–322. Reprinted by permission of Sage Publications, Inc. The same article will appear in *Leviathan* (Fall, 1984). Reprinted by permission of the Gottlieb Duttweiler Institute, Zurich, Switz. Parts of Chapter 5 are taken from Ferguson, "Feminism and Bureaucratic Discourse," *New Political Science*, no. 11 (Spring, 1983), pp. 53–73. Reprinted by permission of Caucus for a New Political Science. Chapter 1 epigram is from Alice Walker, *In Search of Our Mothers' Gardens* (New York: Harcourt, Brace & Jovanovich, 1983), p. 283. Chapter 2 epigram is from Samuel Beckett, *The Unnamable* (New York: Grove Press, 1958), p. 52. Chapter 5 epigram is from "Women's Talk," a poem by Astra, in Dale Spender, *Man Made Language* (London: Routledge & Kegan Paul, 1980), p. v.

For my father, Al Ferguson,

and my grandfather, Virgil Sears,

men who could raise a girl

to be a feminist.

Contents

Preface

This book is about modern organizational life from a feminist point of view. It is not a book about how to succeed in organizations, although such books are discussed at one point; "success manuals" for women in bureaucracies are seen here as part of the problem rather than as part of the solution. Rather, this book aims to present a radical argument, identifying the power structures of bureaucratic capitalist society as a primary source of the oppression of women and men, and advocating the elimination of such structures rather than their amelioration. In light of the fact that most women who work outside the home do so in low-paying, routine jobs with little chance of advancement, and in light of the increasing degradation of the labor of most people in this century, and in recognition of the enormous human costs imposed by bureaucracies on their recruits, my main concern is not to assist the relatively small number of professional women in their pursuit of upward mobility in the organizational world.[1] I do not mean to cast undifferentiated aspersions onto women's professional ambitions. As a professional woman myself, that would be offensively inconsistent; further, it would also ignore the fact that at least some professional positions offer the opportunity to do rewarding work and that access to such positions is often the only avenue to decent-paying jobs. Efforts to move up in the organizational world often provide both material and social rewards for individual women; such efforts are understandable, but there is nothing particularly feminist and certainly nothing radical about them. The argument that organizations will somehow be altered simply by virtue of recruiting women into them is, I hope to demonstrate, fallacious. To equate the upward mobility of individual women with the success of feminism is simply to embrace a new and self-serving version of the old laissez-faire myth that the sum of the self-interests of each individual equals the interest of the whole.

Any thorough-going critique rests, ultimately, on a vision of an alternative possibility. It is futile to advocate political struggle against that which cannot, under any circumstances, be different than it is. At the same time, one need not provide a blueprint for change in order to offer grounds for imagining and articulating a different way. In light of this, the goals of this book are as follows:

First, to clarify and render intelligible the structures and processes of power in bureaucratic society and the effects these structures and processes have upon individuals caught within them. By exposing the contradictions and manipulations contained within a bureaucratic society, one can demystify the theory and practice of that society. Since the organizational society is maintained in part by creating and perpetuating the appropriate ideology, one that both reflects and distorts the reality it describes, a different form of understanding is in some ways also a form of action.[2] The truth alone does not set one free, but if one seeks freedom it helps to have the truth of things.[3]

Second, to offer a basis for opposition to bureaucratic discourse and bureaucratic structures. While I do not believe that knowledge is the same as virtue, I do believe that political theory can be transformative, can help us to live well, if it is used to rethink our lives, reshape our possibilities, and resist the official definition of reality. The grounds for resistance, as I see it, are in the typical experiences of women, whose lives constitute a submerged voice within the overall discourse of bureaucratic society. The traditional experiences of women in our society shed light on bureaucracy in two ways—by revealing persistent patterns of dominance and subordinance in bureaucracy that parallel power relations between men and women, and by suggesting a different way of conceiving of the individual and the collective that reflects the caretaking and nurturant experiences embedded in women's role.

Third, to suggest an alternative, nonbureaucratic approach to the problem of organization, one that criticizes and rejects the forms of organization and the terms of self-understanding embedded in bureaucratic discourse and calls instead upon the theoretical and practical terms of a specifically feminist discourse. The bureaucratization of society is not an irredeemable, inexorable fate but is rather an ongoing social and historical process, one that generates its own contradictions, that requires continuous maintenance by those in power, and that *can be resisted*. A radical feminist discourse can be one source of such resistance, naming alternative forms of relations and suggesting different types of organizations.

During the course of my research I have interviewed a number of people about their organizational experiences, and I use this material to illustrate my arguments. I can make no claims to have selected a representative sample; these interviews do not represent a statistically valid or reliable population and are not statistically generalizable. I began by talking to people I know, and was referred to others through them; in all I interviewed twenty people, a few only once but most several times, over a four-year period. My interviewees occupy a range of organizational positions, including those of middle-level professional/managerial personnel, low-level white-collar staff, clerical workers, industrial production workers, and clients. I used an open-ended format, asking each person to tell me about her or his organizational experience. While I am aware of the methodological limitations of my interviews, I believe that the responses of these people shed considerable light on the nature of everyday life in modern organizations. I nearly always came away from the interviews with two feelings: a renewed sense of the degradation of human possibility that modern organizations impose, and a profound respect for the ways that people hold onto their humanity in the face of organizational tyranny.

Two further points need to be made at the beginning: one concerns the nature of feminist theory, the other the nature of organizational theory. First, it is no longer possible to identify feminist theory as theory concerned solely with what happens to or has happened to women, just as it is no longer possible to segregate "women's issues"—for example, abortion, childcare, the Equal Rights Amendment—from the broader issues of politics. Feminist theory is not simply about women, although it is that; it is about the world, but seen from the usually ignored and devalued vantage point of women's experience. Second, most contemporary political and social thought about organizational society, particularly that generated from within the mainstream of the social sciences, serves as apologia for that society, justifying it, defending it, or regretfully arguing that things must be as they are. I do not wish to contribute to what Alvin Gouldner has rightfully called the "mortician's role" of the social scientist, "all too eager to bury men's [and women's] hopes."[4] Put simply, bureaucracies have a tremendous capacity to hurt people, to manipulate, twist, and damage human possibility. I believe that feminist political theory has the capacity to help us resist the steady incursion of bureaucratic discourse, that theory need not stand impotent in the face of the disintegrating public situation, and that an adequate theory can provide us with both clarity and vision.

Finally, a few words are in order about the enormous intellectual debt that this work owes to Michel Foucault. It is always dangerous to take up for one's own use the ideas of a still-living thinker, since that person might well speak up and discredit one's claims. Particularly in the case of Foucault one must tread carefully: his ideas are complex and difficult; they are undergoing constant development and revision; and they are at the center of current intellectual controversy. Since this book is about bureaucracy and not about Foucault, a brief explanation at the beginning about my relation to Foucault's arguments might ward off objections later on.

I agree with what I take to be Foucault's major preoccupation; his belief that, as Herbert Dreyfus and Paul Rabinow state in their excellent commentary, the "increasing organization of everything is the central issue of our time."[5] Foucault's discussions of modernity, particularly his insights into the production of individuals and relationships by the prevailing language and structures of power, provide a valuable means for comprehending the complexities of social control. I have taken Foucault's enormously suggestive ideas about the emergence and maintenance of the "organization of everything" and have applied them in areas that, to my knowledge, Foucault has not discussed and in ways that perhaps he would not accept. For example, Foucault speaks positively about the feminist movement at one point, suggesting that its strength is to "have actually departed from the discourse conducted within the apparatuses of sexuality."[6] But he does not define women's voice as a submerged discourse in the modern episteme, while that is precisely the argument I am making. I am also applying my analysis to education in ways that Foucault has not.[7] Finally, I wish to avoid "overusing" Foucault. Most people who have read the opening pages of *Discipline and Punish*, no matter how convinced they are of the pervasiveness of the disciplines in modern society, are likely to come away preferring prison to public disemboweling. There are some aspects of the discourse of modernity and the claims of subjectivity that I find compelling in ways that Foucault does not. Nonetheless, I believe that he is right to look for politics in language and for domination in bureaucracy, and this is the lead that I wish to follow.

I also have some reservations, or at least questions, about some of the central ideas in Foucault's analysis. Briefly, I question his arguments concerning the role of the subject, the definition of discourse, the uses of theory, and the nature of power. Much of Foucault's work elaborates his position that the modern subject is invented through the operation of the "microphysics of power." By this he means more than the claim that individuality is an ongoing and noncapturable process, as Bergson and other process philosophers argue.[8] He seems to claim that there is no identifiable subject outside of the prevailing productions of power and knowledge, no "I" to match the socially constructed "me." In one of his later essays, however, he departs from this position and actually urges his readers toward subjectivity, saying that "we have to promote new forms of subjectivity through the refusal of this kind of individuality which has been imposed on us for several centuries."[9] So perhaps his position is being rethought. But in the main Foucault's argument seems to be that subjectivity, and inter-subjectivity, are simply the creations of the prevailing episteme.[10] Thus I conclude that Foucault would probably see my efforts to create a feminist discourse, grounding it on the concrete relations with others that shape female experience, as another misguided effort to create meaning and as another manifestation of the historical subjectivizing trends of modern culture. But Foucault is short-sighted here; without a concept of human agency, the promise of resistance that the submerged discourse of outsiders can offer is rendered mechanistic, flat, and empty. I believe that Foucault neglects to explicate a crucial aspect of our experience as both social and temporal beings; as I will try to make clear in subsequent chapters, the view of the self that I adopt sees the individual as the evolving outcome of the interaction of possibility and circumstance. I do not share Foucault's "rejection of all recourse to the interiority of a conscious, individual, meaning-giving subject" because such a position renders much of our day-to-day experience incomprehensible.[11] I see the creation of meaning both as unavoidable and as a potentially ennobling process, allowing us to order our collective lives in light of values we embrace and in a language we make our own.

Further, Foucault's use of the term "discourse" contains a certain ambiguity. In some of his work he takes the term to mean the domain of speech and language; in other places he gives it a larger and more diffuse meaning. In the latter use he succumbs to the "illusion of autonomous discourse," which leads him to stress the impact that language has on institutions and practices while neglecting the parallel impact that institutions have on language.[12] I have adopted the first notion of discourse, confining it to its more common-sense meaning.

Also, there is some ambiguity in Foucault's approach to the activity of social analysis. Foucault explicitly resists the temptation toward "summing up," toward the definitive causal analysis that a thorough totalization would entail. He seems to fear that the complexity, contingency, and layering of our experience is such that any effort to draw grand conclusions would be dangerously distorted. In fact, he specifically warns against my project: "It may be wise not to take as a whole the rationalization of society or of culture, but to analyze such a process in several fields, madness, illness, death, crime, sexuality, and so forth."[13] Yet Foucault does often invoke the "big picture," as when he discusses the shift from the classical to the modern episteme. His analysis often suggests larger conclusions than he is willing to draw, and it is some of those suggestions that I am pursuing here. Perhaps it is indicative of the difference in temperament between the historian and the political theorist that the latter is more willing to blur details in search of a coherent picture of the whole.

Finally, Foucault's politics and his view of power are something of a puzzle. There are many points where his view of power has an anarchist ring to it, particularly in his insistence on localized resistance and his rejection of a centralized, hierarchical seizure of power. I agree with the observation made by Alan Sheridan that Foucault is on the side of the underdog, that "the Foucaldian genealogy is an unmasking of power for the use of those who suffer it. It is also directed against those who would seize power in their name."[14] But to what end is this unmasking? There seems to be no alternative vision guiding this critique; perhaps it is condemned to the problem of Hegel's owl of Minerva, "waiting if it is modest, prophesying if it is rash, but denied the power to rebuild."[15] There is no clear grounding in Foucault's analysis for a view of power as anything other than domination. In one of his essays Foucault warns us that "a society without power relations can only be an abstraction"; he then states that the analysis of the particular power relations in particular societies is "politically necessary" so as to comprehend

> their historical formation, the source of their strength or fragility, the conditions which are necessary to transform some or to abolish others. For to say that there cannot be a society without power relations is not to say either that those which are established are necessary, or, in any case, that power constitutes a fatality at the heart of societies, such that it cannot be undermined.[16]

The conclusion seems to be that, while a society without domination is unthinkable, a society with less domination, or at least different forms of domination, is feasible. This is certainly a coherent position, but the problem of direction remains—to what end does resistance proceed?

In light of these criticisms and reservations, one might well ask to what extent the present work actually utilizes Foucault at all. In answer, I would appeal to one of Foucault's own observations on his relation to Nietzsche: "For myself, I prefer to utilize the writers I like. The only valid tribute to thought such as Nietzsche's is precisely to use it, to deform it, to make it groan and protest."[17] If I have accomplished this in relation to Foucault, I will consider my use of his work a success.

Acknowledgments

The ideas for this book were born out of the intersection of political theory and radical politics with modern organizational life. In each of these areas of my life there are important people to be thanked, people whose voices are present here in various direct and indirect ways. In my meeting with political theory as a student and graduate student I was fortunate enough to encounter two teachers who brought together the intrinsically exciting world of ideas with the critical perspective on political and social life that exists on the "fringes" of respectable academic life. In their very different ways, Michael Weinstein and Mulford Sibley taught me both to think critically about what is and to think imaginatively about what could be. In the world of radical politics, my comrades in the women's movement and the peace movement have helped me to sustain the commitments to autonomy and community that are so antithetical to life in modern bureaucratic organizations. I found that I could not continue to value autonomy and community, or to sustain either critical or imaginative ways of thinking, without turning them to an examination of the context within which most people today spend most of their lives: bureaucracies.

Many people have helped me clarify and develop my ideas. Several people have read and discussed the manuscript in its various stages of development and have offered differing combinations of insightful scholarly criticism and generous personal support: Larry Spence, Mark Bertozzi, Mike Gibbons, Jim Stevers; the members of the Yankee Conference on Political and Social Thought; the participants in the First and Second International Conferences on the Comparative, Historical, and Critical Analysis of Bureaucracy, especially Bruce Berman, Wolf Narr, and Roz Bologh; Ken MacDonald, Ray and Maureen Aumand, and Frank. In particular, Linda Nicholson and Joan Tronto gave line-by-line comments that have been extremely helpful in developing and revising the arguments.

I am very indebted to the people I interviewed, who let me into their lives and shared their organizational experiences with me. Most of my interviewees requested anonymity. Among those who did not, I am particularly grateful to Cindy and Phil Carson, who gave me insights into aspects of factory work that I would not otherwise have comprehended; to Glenn Williams and John Portelli, who recounted their experience in various social service organizations; and to Moe Manghelli for his insights into blue-collar work and union activity.

The editors and readers at Temple University Press have been wonderful to work with. I'm particularly grateful to Ronnie Steinberg and Jennifer Nedelsky for their help in developing the strongest lines of argument and in qualifying or curtailing others. Michael Meilach typed the manuscript with skill and good humor; Cathie Chmura brought those same qualities to her work on the index.

Through my work on this project I have developed a greater appreciation of the working life of my own family. My parents and grandparents were farmers and factory workers, and I understand better now both their fierce pride in their hard labor and their determination that their children would do "better." I also appreciate more deeply the fact that I am the only child, out of a complicated family of nine children and stepchildren, who has neither worked in the factory nor married someone who worked in the factory. I want to thank them all—Mom, Mac, Steve, Diane, Susan, Barbara, Connie, Gary, Roger, and Julie—for their support and their care.

Last of all, I want to thank Siena College. The school has provided me with the financial support necessary to pursue my research; many of my colleagues on the faculty have given both intellectual and personal encouragement; my students in my political theory and women in politics classes have entertained and debated many of my ideas. Bill Baller and the Siena College library staff have been enormously helpful in meeting my research needs. I have also realized, through my study of modern organizations, the uniqueness of the institution itself; feudalism has its drawbacks, but at least it is not bureaucratic.

The Feminist Case
Against Bureaucracy

One What Does Feminism Have to Do with Bureaucracy?

Whether we speak or not
the machine will crush us to bits—
and we will also be afraid

Your silence
will not
protect you
—Audre Lorde

There has always been an uneasy relationship between feminism and bureaucracy. The emergence of a specifically feminist political theory and an organized feminist politics is largely a phenomenon of the late nineteenth and the twentieth centuries. Not coincidentally, the expansion of the bureaucratic organization of political, social, and economic life is also a phenomenon of the last one hundred years. Until recently, however, the relationship between the two has gone largely unarticulated.

Historically, modern feminism and large-scale bureaucracy arose together in the United States. The First Wave of the women's movement coincided with the beginning of the expansion of managerial and clerical work in the mid to late nineteenth century and with the growth of social welfare agencies that marked the Progressive era. During this time women, particularly white women of the middle class, moved into the paid labor force at its lower levels in both the government and the business world. The Second Wave came on the heels of the post-World War II increase in social service organizations and in white-collar work, providing similar opportunity, at similar low pay and low status, for women to work outside the home in bureaucratic settings.[1] Both the appearance of feminism and the bureaucratization of public life can be understood as consequences of massive underlying changes in the economic and technological spheres: the centralization and specialization of labor that marked the transition from market capitalism to corporate capitalism, with its accompanying need for extensive supervision and record-keeping; the growth in scale and complexity of organizations; the reworking of the relation between private (that is, domestic) and public life as paid work moved outside the home and into the factory and the office; the rise of large-scale service industries and service agencies of the state to supply and regulate activities formerly done within the home. In other words, both feminism and bureaucratization can be seen as consequences attendant to massive shifts in the division of labor in society; women's lives changed as their roles as wives and mothers were redefined in the family, and women's and men's lives changed as their roles as workers were redefined in the factory and in the office.

Politically, the relation between feminism and bureaucracy is problematic. The feminist movement is divided internally, as are most major movements for social change, between those who are primarily interested in gaining access to established institutions and those who aim at the transformation of those institutions. The struggles for equal legal status, for equal pay for equal work, and for admission to the more prestigious and lucrative careers, carried on primarily by liberal feminists, are frequently identified in the popular media as representing the entire women's movement. Liberal feminism has appealed to the bureaucratic apparatus of the state and of the corporate world to integrate women into the public sphere through programs seeking equal opportunity and affirmative action. The more radical voices within the women's movement, however, reject the exclusive focus on integration because they see the existing institutional arrangements as themselves fundamentally flawed. It is this latter group that has made bureaucracy an issue on the feminist agenda.[2]

Because the bureaucratic organization of public life directly controls the work of most women who hold jobs outside the home and affects the entire society in a way that is antithetical to the goals of feminist theory and practice, it is a crucial target of feminist concern. Feminism and organizational theory need each other. In order for feminists to construct an adequate theory of domination and liberation, we must deal with bureaucratic modes of power; in order for analysts of modern organizations to develop an adequate critique of bureaucracy, they need to consider a feminist perspective.

A specifically feminist analysis sheds new light on the subject of bureaucracy in two ways. First, understanding the patterns of dominance and subordinance that exist between men and women can help us to comprehend the subtleties of power and control within bureaucracies. Second, revealing the notions of personal identity and social interaction embedded in women's traditional experience can suggest a nonbureaucratic vision of collective life. From the more radical feminist theorists and activists comes an anti-hierarchical orientation that aims at healing the breach between private and public life and that rejects bureaucratic organizational forms in favor of a different vision of individual and collective life. For example, in her analysis of current feminist theory Lynda Glennon argues that "feminism is potentially the most radical social movement today because, in challenging the dualism of private-expressive and public-instrumental selves and worlds, it reaches to the roots of the crises of modern society."[3] By attacking technocracy, rather than simply capitalism *per se*, Glennon initiates a far-ranging analysis of the penetration of instrumental, administrative orientations into everyday life.[4] Similarly, Roslyn Bologh has suggested a feminist interpretation of Max Weber that challenges the inevitability of bureaucratic rationality in favor of a qualitatively different view of what it means to be a rational human being.[5] Jean Elshtain and Sara Ruddick have each looked to feminists to create a public discourse that calls on particularly female experiences for its inspiration rather than on technocratic values and institutions.[6] Robert Denhardt and Jan Perkins have noted that feminism challenges the very heart of modern organizational life in that it "argues that superior domination through hierarchical patterns of authority is not essential to the achievement of important goals but in fact is restrictive of the growth of the group and its individual members."[7] A crucial dimension of feminist utopian novels such as *Woman on the Edge of Time, Herland,* and *The Kin of Ata Are Waiting for You* is their construction of anti-hierarchical, participatory images of human community.[8] Radical feminist organizations make a self-conscious effort to divide work and responsibility in egalitarian, nonhierarchical ways, and even within the more "mainstream" feminist groups such as the National Organization for Women (NOW) and the professional women's caucuses there are efforts to de-bureaucratize in favor of more participatory organizational forms.[9]

Once bureaucracy itself is seen as an *issue*, rather than as simply a fact of modern life or a neutral method of organizing activity, questions about it appear in a fundamentally different light. A critical analysis of bureaucracy entails an analysis of the history and structure of bureaucratic society, a society permeated by both the institutional forms and the language of instrumental rationality. An investigation of bureaucracy—what it is, how it is talked about, by whom, for what purpose, at whose expense—becomes an investigation of both organizational structures and organizational discourse. By "discourse" I mean the characteristic ways of speaking and writing that both constitute and reflect our experiences; in contemporary society, the dominant form of linguistic practice is that of bureaucratic discourse. The feminist project is to seek grounds for an alternative mode of discourse, and to articulate an alternative vision of society, that can both comprehend bureaucracy and allow us to go beyond it.

Defining Bureaucracy

Contemporary bureaucracy needs to be understood both as a structure and as a process. As a structure it can be described as a fairly stable arrangement of roles and assignment of tasks; since individuals in their day-to-day interactions with bureaucracies tend to experience them as static and fixed authority structures, it is the established structural dimensions of bureaucracy that are most readily identified. Bureaucracy is also a process, however, a temporal ordering of human action that evolves out of certain historical conditions toward certain political ends. The maintenance of bureaucracy is an ongoing process that must be constantly attended to; its modes of domination must be reproduced and the opposition it generates must be located and suppressed.

Following Weber, the modern bureaucracy is usually described as an organization having the following traits: a complex rational division of labor, with fixed duties and jurisdictions; stable, rule-governed authority channels and universally applied performance guidelines; a horizontal division of graded authority, or hierarchy, entailing supervision from above; a complex system of written record-keeping, based on scientific procedures that standardize communications and increase control; objective recruitment based on impersonal standards of expertise; predictable, standardized management procedures following general rules; and a tendency to require total loyalty from its members toward the way of life the organization requires.[10] Modern bureaucracies are sufficiently large so as to prohibit face-to-face relations among most of their members. They aim at arranging individuals and tasks so as to secure continuity and stability and to remove ambiguity in relations among participants, but are nonetheless usually beset by a variety of internal conflicts. In fact, bureaucracies are political arenas in which struggles for power, status, personal values, and/or survival are endemic. They are oligarchical (ruled by the few) and recruitment is at least partly done by cooptation (selection of successors by the elite themselves).[11]

While large-scale bureaucratic organizations are not themselves modern inventions—the ancient Chinese dynasties and the bureaucracy of the Russian tsars show that this type of organization has deep historical roots—modern mass society is unique in the extent to which it is penetrated by bureaucracy.[12] In mass society both the private and the public realms are increasingly absorbed into an undifferentiated social arena, in which the formal legal equality of the citizens masks underlying inequities and disguises the pressure to conform. As both a structure and a process, bureaucracy must be located within its social context; in our society, that is a context in which social relations between classes, races, and sexes are fundamentally unequal. Bureaucracy, as the "scientific organization of inequality," serves as a filter for these other forms of domination, projecting them into an institutional arena that both rationalizes and maintains them.[13] The institutions of mass society converge on the individual in ways that induce conformity; in Hannah Arendt's words, mass society "expects from each of its members a certain kind of behavior, imposing innumerable and various rules, all of which tend to 'normalize' its members, to make them behave."[14]

In light of the pervasiveness of bureaucratic language and practice, distinctions between that which is public and that which is private must be carefully made. Older usages of these terms, which equate "public" with government and "private" with the market, are largely obsolete; as discussed in Chapter Two, the two realms are so intimately intertwined that such distinctions have little empirical substance, though they still serve the ideological purposes of bureaucratic capitalism. I am using the term "private" to refer to the set of discursive and institutional practices of domestic life, the realm of personal intimacy, household labor, and reproduction within families, kin relations, or friendship networks. "Public" refers to the outside world of paid labor, of government, and of those institutions of communication, transportation, leisure, culture, and so forth, that are rooted outside the home, in the larger world of strangers.

Similar care must be taken in analyzing the political impact of bureaucracy on the class structure of late capitalism. The increasing bureaucratization of work at all levels of organizations has two related consequences for class relations: it homogenizes the work setting, so that many of the traditional differences between manual and nonmanual labor, staff and line positions, and so forth become less important; and it simultaneously mystifies the class-based authority relations remaining between workers and managers by disguising the adversarial nature of these relations in the language of administration. The problems of capitalism cannot be reduced to bureaucracy nor can the authority relations within bureaucracy be accounted for solely by class analysis. Rather, it is the interaction between them that defines them. The bureaucratization of capitalism creates common problems of dominance and subordinance for employees and clients at all levels of organizations. Bureaucracies are set up to accommodate the needs of certain forms of science and technology as well as to maintain social control, and are staffed by functionaries who can claim expertise in relevant areas. In fact, one indicator of the increasing bureaucratization of society is the increasing variety and scope of the claims made by various experts to knowledge about relevant techniques: in work, politics, leisure, child-rearing, sexuality, marriage, dress, personal mannerisms, and in "relationships" there are ever-growing armies of experts offering diagnosis and prescription. Living in a society invaded by technique requires the mastery of certain social, cultural, psychological, political, and linguistic arrangements by its citizens. These arrangements are much the same in most contemporary bureaucracies, whether they are "public" (for example, the Pentagon, the state service agencies), "private" (for example, the corporations), or some combination of the two (for example, the university).

It thus makes sense to view bureaucracy as a type of social system, one in which certain social acts are established and maintained, certain social objects are valued, certain languages are spoken, certain types of behavior are required, and certain motivations are encouraged. The norms and rules dominant in bureaucracy, as in any social system, are generally those that support the requirements of bureaucratic self-maintenance. Motivations and behavior that are consistent with the needs of self-maintenance are encouraged and rewarded; those inconsistent with it are penalized. Thus the real goals of the organization become those that keep the machinery of the institution running. Bureaucracies proliferate rules as means to their ends, and emphasize adherence to established procedures in order to obtain standardized, reliable progress toward these ends. But the situation is such that the bureaucrats come to see adherence to the rules as itself the goal.[15] Thus the function of bureaucracy comes to be equated with its purpose; whatever it is doing is seen by the staff as what it should be doing, and the continued existence of the institution—and of the staff—depend on the continued workings of the machinery. Institutions thus often have ostensible purposes (for example, saving Vietnam from the Communist menace, helping the poor, or issuing drivers' licenses) that are not the same as their actual purposes (for example, keeping the military or service machinery running, processing forms, employing staff). Therefore the formal and ostensible purpose is only technically, sometimes incidentally, the end goal of the process; the real purpose is to maintain the process itself and, further, to maintain the conditions that are necessary for the stability and expansion of the process.[16]

Bureaucracies continually pursue a stability that eludes them. In the course of seeking stability, both internally and in the environment, and of rendering the behavior of functionaries and clients predictable and capable of rational management, bureaucracies must seek to eliminate uncertainty. The bureaucratic dream is "of a world which is thoroughly reduced to certainty. We can control what we can know."[17] Uncertainty, both in the organization and in its environment, threatens the institutional imperative of bureaucratic self-maintenance and also undermines the diagnostic and prescriptive claims of the designated experts to predict and control the aspect of the environment with which they deal. An understanding of the various dimensions of this search for certainty, the various overt and hidden forms that it takes, the reactions that it tends to elicit from both bureaucrats and clients, takes one a long way toward understanding the conflicts and contradictions built into a bureaucratic system.

Conformity, Contradictions, and the Search for Control

The effort to eliminate uncertainty and assure control creates a distorted political situation in which individuals are isolated, social relations are depersonalized, communications are mystified, and dominance is disguised. The usual defense of the hierarchical division of labor within bureaucracies relies on an appeal to greater efficiency and fuller utilization of expertise within the work process. However, the appeal to efficiency is largely a guise to conceal the control function that hierarchy performs. Considerations of efficiency and effectiveness are at best secondary and frequently irrelevant; they are justifications, rather than explanations, of bureaucracy. The fragmentation of the work process, the isolation of workers from each other, and the expendability of any one worker due to the partiality of her/his contribution to the end product, all operate to control the workers by making them dependent on management within the organization. An illusion of upward mobility is sometimes produced by the cooptation of a few into managerial ranks, while the constant supervision, strict adherence to rules and procedures, and hoarding of knowledge maintain control among the rest.[18] Harry Braverman, Dan Clawson, Stephen Marglin, and others have argued persuasively that the bureaucratic organization of work, with its separation of conception from execution, originally entailed the literal theft, from the worker, of knowledge about the work process. This knowledge was then standardized, taught to managers, and reapplied to the work process so that it was carried out in the interests of the owners: "The social function of hierarchical work organization is not technical efficiency, but accumulation. By mediating between producer and consumer, the capitalist organization sets aside much more for expanding and improving plant and equipment than individuals would if they could control the pace of capital accumulation."[19] The specialization of tasks under capitalism was done initially to ensure the capitalist, or his agents, a place in the production process as coordinator and marketer; the routinization of tasks was imposed to cheapen the worth of the worker and to make the worker replaceable.[20] Much of the specialization and routinization took place before technology became so elaborate and expensive as to require large-scale mechanization or the infusion of fixed capital: "The key to the success of the factory, as well as its inspiration, was the substitution of capitalists' for workers' control of the production process; discipline and supervision could and did reduce costs *without* being technologically superior."[21] Similarly, many contemporary technological developments do not require bureaucracy and central control.

They are often, as Charles Perrow points out with regard to radio and television, "compatible with diversified, segmented markets that reflect diverse cultural styles and interests."[22] It is not technological requirements *per se*, in most cases, that produce forms of organization, but rather it is the control of technology by powerful interests that determines its use.

People whose lives and work are ordered bureaucratically experience both the unconnectedness and the unfreedom of "anonymous social relations."[23] Bureaucracy imposes the simultaneous isolation of individuals from one another and the depersonalization of the channels still linking individuals together. Relations among members of a bureaucracy are impersonal and rule-governed in order to maintain the organization and to "prevent the disintegration of the bureaucratic structure which would occur should these be supplanted by personalized relations."[24] Thus managers who break these rules and seek to humanize, perhaps even democratize, relations within their offices are posing a fundamental threat to the organization; even if their offices function effectively, they are subverting the hierarchy, undermining the official value system, attacking the organizationally defined identity of other managers, and propagating relationships within the organization that are antithetical to the legitimated ones. Small wonder that managers who do attempt such reforms are seldom rewarded and often punished.[25] Both in the factory and in the office, managers who are seen as "soft" on the workers are not promoted further and may be demoted or even fired. One of my interviewees, a woman who worked for seven years on the assembly line of an automotive plant, told of a foreman who was aware that his collegial relations with the workers were blocking further promotions but was unwilling to capitulate to the demands of higher management. Another interviewee, a woman in her late thirties who managed a large and expanding media enterprise, wrongly believed that the high level of productivity of her office would earn her the approval of her superiors, despite her unorthodox practice of treating her subordinates in a humane and quasi-democratic manner and her unwillingness to harass union activists. For these and other reasons (relating to her ob-

clients who fail to understand it will both encounter negative sanctions.

Bureaucracies often generate their own peculiar, semi-secret language in order to allow the personnel to maintain control over their objects and procedures. This secret language performs several related functions. It allows the organization to monopolize information and safeguard the actions of its members from protest or supervision by outsiders. In order to do business with bureaucrats, one must engage in conversation with them; this requires that one learn their language, play their game, and come onto their turf:

> Functionaries are allowed to utter any statement they like from within a repertory assigned them by the organization. They need not see to it that this organizationally approved statement is understood. On the other hand, clients have to bend over backwards to learn the bureaucratic language. Otherwise they suffer the denial of service.[28]

Since the objects and/or services provided by bureaucracies are valuable in that they involve expenditure of resources, it is in the interest of the functionaries to keep the language secret and so to retain control over the resources involved. Bureaucratic language thus functions to increase control; it does not intend to facilitate communication but rather to channel information and directives. "Bureaucracy's inherent lack of a need to explain itself to itself" renders real communication out of order.[29] Bureaucratic language is one-directional, in that it is difficult to "talk back," and it is acausal, in that it is difficult to find out where the directives originated and who is responsible for them. As the public realm is reduced by bureaucratization to a barren network of interlocking agencies, speech is reduced to the sterile interchange of procedural information. The language of technics replaces the language of human action; "feedback," "input," and "output" replace dialogue, debate, and judgment.[30] The linguistic tendencies of technocratic society suppress the processes of open conflict and compromise that constitute meaningful politics. Those who wish to engage in active protest or refusal are confronted with a language in which military assaults on peasant villages are called "protective reaction," massive displacement of poor and middle-income people by government buildings, superhighways, and housing for the wealthy is called "urban renewal," wholesale firings are impersonalized as "reductions in force" (or "rifs"), and workers are referred to as "human resources." The linguistic dimension of depersonalization renders both bureaucrats and clients mute about themselves and their situations, divesting them of the self-articulation that is basic to conceiving and pursuing political opposition.

Further, since one consequence of hierarchical organization is the diffusion of responsibility, the ability to mount successful opposition is further undermined in bureaucracies because there is no clear focus for it. The decision-making process itself becomes "vague and impersonal, the instrument of an anonymous, fragmented intelligence."[31] The complexity and fragmentation of bureaucratic procedures leaves the impression that bureaucracy, in Hannah Arendt's words, is "rule by nobody." Bureaucratic "red tape" thus performs a system-sustaining function in diffusing and confusing potential dissenters: "As bureaucratic space encroaches upon public space, there are fewer and fewer responsible persons to be found. It seems there is no place where one is able to present a grievance, no place where power can be effective. No one seems to be in charge."[32] This is not the same as saying that elites have no ability to command, but simply that their power to command is disguised.

A final dimension of bureaucratic discourse is that, as it attempts to (and partially succeeds in) rendering its victims silent, it simultaneously disguises this effect in its claims to political neutrality. The myth of administration "defines organizations as efficient and effective instruments for the realization of publicly proclaimed goals."[33] By claiming to be the nonideological instrument of technical progress, bureaucracy clothes itself in the guise of science and renders itself "ideologically invisible."[34] Those who accept this version of what Marcuse, following Hegel, calls "the Happy Consciousness—the belief that the real is rational and that the system delivers the goods"—are led to adopt "the new conformism which is a facet of technological rationality translated into social behavior."[35] Those who do rebel against bureaucracy, in protest against personal dishonor, injustice toward themselves or others, incompetency, or generally immoral politics, demonstrate that the official version of reality does not exercise complete control over the bureaucrats and clients who encounter it. But to engage in such oppositional activity one must first penetrate the facade of ideological neutrality that administrative structures claim for themselves and see them as political arenas in which domination, manipulation, and the denial of conflict are standard operating procedures.

Seen in light of the ubiquity and intensity of their control mechanisms, bureaucracies are much like explicitly authoritarian political systems. They share a common goal of regimentation and rationalized manipulation of human life for purposes of rendering it predictable and directing it toward behavior that supports, or at least fails actively to challenge, the established authority structures.[36] Neither provides channels for recognized dissent, and, in the absence of a legitimized "loyal opposition," any opposition is equated with disloyalty and treason. Since bureaucracies, like authoritarian political regimes, are in fact not monolithic, and do indeed witness the periodic rise of internal dissent, their claims to being apolitical are equally fraudulent: "Organizations are not self-corrective and, therefore, are not nonpolitical. They are, instead, seed beds of conflict in which overt struggle is often muted by repression, just as it is in the authoritarian state, which also claims to have dispensed with politics."[37] The terror sometimes used by authoritarian regimes performs a similar function to that of the control structures of bureaucratic organization: "Bureaucracy is the routinization of domination; terror arises when routines of domination collapse in the face of mounting crisis, or before routines of domination have yet developed."[38] Both are ways of dealing with an overtly or potentially resistant population upon whom the ruling group is dependent for some good or service, even if that service is simply an agreement to acquiesce to the claims of the powerful, but whom it cannot otherwise mobilize or eliminate. Both systems of dominance can be aimed simultaneously at administrators within the organization and clients outside of it; Stalinism, for example, both eliminated millions of ordinary citizens who posed a real or potential

or imagined threat to its hegemony and also "reproduced itself structurally as a grotesque persistence of bureaus amid a
chronic execution of bureaucrats."[39] Terror eliminates political
activity that might give rise to active and concerted resistance;
bureaucracy deals with more passive and atomized opposition.
Both bureaucracy and terror depoliticize society by crippling
public life, reducing individuals either to passive agents of the
system or to inmates of it, and denying them the status of responsible actors capable of rationally giving consent and acting in concert toward shared ends.

In the face of this overview of the various dimensions of bureaucratic control strategies, it is important to emphasize that
control of personnel, clients, and the environment is neither
unproblematically achieved nor easily maintained. In fact, it is
the persistence of basic obstacles to the achievement of total
control that renders the continuing pursuit of that control comprehensible. If certainty were readily available to the organization, then the claims to administrative neutrality would be
more accurate and the bureaucracy would not be the politically
interesting, and politically dangerous, place that it is.

There are at least four major overlapping reasons why uncertainty remains in bureaucracy. First, some power must be dele-
gated within a large administrative structure, and with it goes
some discretion over the performance of the task itself. Even
though attempts are made to monitor this discretion, either
through direct supervision or by hiring people who are "reliable" in that they have thoroughly internalized the organization's view of themselves and the world, the existence of discretion entails the persistence of at least some uncertainty.
Second, information that is passed through bureaucratic channels is selectively screened along the way by various persons.
These people may filter the information out of a variety of motives—misunderstanding, or a need to please their superiors
by presenting only welcome or expected information, or a desire to protect clients—but the end result is that "intelligence
failures are built into complex organizations."[40] Thus one common direction for bureaucratic expansion occurs when the officials, in search of better information, turn to more and different kinds of "knowledge specialists" and planners. Third, the

goals of the individuals within the organization do not necessarily coincide with the goals of the organization itself. Even the most willing bureaucrat or obedient client is likely to have an individual interest that is at odds with the interests of the organization, resulting in, for example, struggles over issues such as job security, retirement and welfare programs, standards for promotion, and so forth. More fundamentally, people often act out of a sense of friendship or of obligation to particular others, or loyalty to personal values of honor, or a commitment to truth or justice.[41] Some of the most coercive and restrictive of the bureaucracy's informal norms are those designed to remedy the lack of convergence between individual and systemic goals. Fourth, as an extension of the above, people often resist the demands of the organization. They sometimes resist overtly and collectively, as Clawson's description of workers' struggles against deskilling reveals.[42] More often they resist individually and covertly; because opposition is illegitimate, their evasions are furtive, their resistance is either penalized or coopted, and they face real suppression if they lose. Given the day-to-day compliance that ordinary people usually give to bureaucratic demands, it is important to stress that this is not done merely out of habit or the routinization of choice; obedience is *enforced*. One empirical study of bureaucratic compliance offers, apparently without chagrin, the conclusion that "the clear designation of enforcing agents plus sanctions for compliance are major contributors to the power of bureaucratic rules."[43] In most political contexts it would come as no surprise to learn that people are much more likely to do what they're told when they're afraid not to; in the disguised and mystified politics of bureaucracies, however, the point needs to be explicitly made.

An understanding of these obstacles to the total victory of bureaucratic language and institutions highlights again the point that bureaucratization is a process, a moment in a dialectic of domination and resistance that must be constantly reproduced. It generates oppositions, tensions, and counter trends, which the defenders of the bureaucratic order, those who benefit or who believe that they benefit, must constantly seek to overcome. The enormous force behind technocratic imperialism comes not from the absence of any resistance, or the inherent inability of individuals or groups to imagine alternatives, but from the tremendous pervasiveness of bureaucratization, its capacity to coopt, marginalize, and destroy its opposition.[44] It is difficult to achieve precisely the right balance here, to comprehend both moments of this complex and ever-moving dialectic. I mean both to clarify the tendencies toward bureaucratic totalization and to avoid reductionism. Human beings are more than bundles of stimuli and responses, or internalized need hierarchies, or reflections of the generalized other. These are partial and distorted visions. We are unavoidably and essentially social, temporal beings, created through our relations with others and also creating ourselves as we project ourselves into imagined futures and redefine the received past.[45] Part of the perniciousness of bureaucracy is that, when passed through the filter of personality, it seeks to "tie up our loose ends" and reduce us to a reflection of the organization.[46] Ortega y Gasset expressed this thought in saying, "I am I and my circumstances and if I do not save my circumstances I do not save myself."[47] When our circumstances are increasingly bureaucratic, then the process of creating oneself through interaction with others is debased and the self that is created is simply a rationalized commodity readied for exchange in the bureaucratic market.

Efforts within organizations, and within the larger bureaucratic environment, to deal with the ever-recurring tensions and conflicts reveal the multiple contradictions at the heart of the bureaucratic order. A contradictory situation is one that is "based on premises that cannot be simultaneously realized, so that to pursue one it must repress the other, and thus become self-refuting."[48] Since bureaucracy rests on the assumptions of scientific rationality—namely, that there is a "single best solution" (or at least a managerially defined resolution) to organizational problems—and since it cloaks itself in the myth of administrative neutrality, the very effort to deal with conflict must be disguised even as it goes on. Bureaucracy is anti-political because it cannot recognize the legitimacy of conflict, seeing it as a temporary aberration to be dealt with through elaborated administrative techniques.

Some contradictions are rooted in the internal workings of

organizations. As bureaus exist through time, the search for certainty leads to the development of extensive formalized rules to cover more and more of the situations the staff is likely to encounter. The "desire for organizational memory" causes the bureau's officials to extend these rules even further, to write them down, and to keep elaborate records.[49] The rules make the behavior of the staff more standardized and predictable over time; they also cause the staff to focus more and more on conformity to the rules as the primary goal, resulting in the goal displacement described earlier. They also "increase the bureau's structural complexity, which in turn strengthens its inertia because of greater sunk costs in current procedures."[50] Thus, the longer the bureaucracy is in existence, the more officials invest of themselves in mastering and enforcing the procedures, the more stable and rigid the organization becomes, and the less able it is to adjust to new circumstances or redirect its efforts.

The increasing complexity of organizations results, as was mentioned above, in the delegation of tasks to subsystems. This leads to a different type of goal displacement, as the suborganizations develop and pursue their own interests and needs, not those of the whole organization. Efforts by the central authority to counteract this tendency usually lead to recentralization and increased supervision, thus making even more acute the original overload at the top and the original impetus to delegation.[51] The pressure constantly to increase supervision results in the employment, in most large bureaucracies, of one supervisor for every three-and-one-half workers, and it explains why the managerial component of organizations always grows much faster than either the workers or the clients.[52] Increasing supervision simply means that more and more people are employed doing less and less actual work; thus the main bureaucratic claim to fame, the efficient use of resources, is shattered. Further, the elaboration of the formal rules, impelled by the desire to decrease arbitrariness as well as to cement control and secure organizational memory, gives subordinates more and more detailed knowledge about the boundaries of unacceptable behavior. Workers who have little commitment to the organization can use this knowledge to "get away with" minimal work and minimal conformity. This again leads to decreased productivity and to greater supervision and control from above.[53]

The strict hierarchical arrangement of roles within bureaucracies, and the need to maintain this hierarchy in order to achieve predictability and control, exacerbates the problems of goal displacement and inflexibility. Often those officials and employees closest to the bottom of the hierarchy observe its failings first hand, since they deal directly with the "objects of control" (that is, clients, artifacts, nature). But for those at the bottom, or even in the middle, to try to correct abuses and to improve performance is to violate the hierarchical chain of command and jeopardize the power of the elites. Since bureaucracies are fundamentally authoritarian forms of organization, any effort to air grievances or alter policies from below must be suppressed, and any real effort to create such channels is seen as illegitimate. Political struggles over organizational inefficiencies and abuse go on ceaselessly within bureaucracies, but they cannot be acknowledged as such by the organization because, again, the myth of administrative rationality defines the organization as the rational and efficient instrument for the realization of policy. When the reality of political struggle contradicts the myth of administrative neutrality, bureaucracies generally seek to preserve the myth, even at the expense of organizational goals.

Constructing Feminist Discourse

To seek out and articulate alternative voices it is necessary continuously to recall the two competing dimensions of human experience within bureaucratic society: the dominance and pervasiveness of bureaucratic discourse, the manifold incursions that it makes into daily life; and the incompleteness of bureaucratic discourse, its inability totally to absorb the field of conflicts within which it operates. Its programs and technologies operate upon and through human beings who both succumb and resist, whose identities are both created by the dominant discourse of power and knowledge and simultaneously create themselves in opposition to that discourse. While there are very few individuals or groups today who live completely outside the boundaries of bureaucracy, there are some who are more on the fringes than others, whose lives are less embedded in the linguistic and institutional structures of bureaucratic society. Foucault suggests that one might look to the psychiatric patient for a certain kind of "outside" knowledge.[54] Robert Denhardt notes that the very poor in Appalachia, having never been socialized into hierarchy, are characterized by " a person-oriented behavior accompanied by an ideology of leveling."[55] In groups such as these, Foucault suggests, one might encounter "subjugated knowledges," "located low down on the hierarchy," which are sufficiently outside the mainstream that their "validity is not dependent on the approval of the established regimes of thought."[56]

I believe that women are an important, perhaps the most important, of such marginal groups. In our society, women as a group tend to experience their social worlds differently than do men as a group. In their relations with parents, in the roles that are available to them both in the family and in the larger public world, in their encounters with others and in their knowledge of themselves, women's experience is institutionally and linguistically structured in a way that is different from that of men. But women are different from other marginal groups such as the mentally disturbed or the very poor (both of which, of course, include women) in that, while women have been victims, they have also been more than that; they have been actors, creators, builders of objects and of relations, confined, certainly, to a limited private realm but nonetheless immersed in a world that possesses its own positive merits and is more than a reaction to exclusion from the public world of men.

To be firmly located in the public realm today is, for the most part, to be embedded within bureaucratic discourse; to be firmly grounded in the nonbureaucratic is to be removed from the arenas of available public speech. Having been excluded, historically, from public life, and still occupying largely peripheral and powerless positions when they do enter that realm, women have developed a different voice, a submerged discourse. But the fact of that submergence has rendered women's experi-

ence both inaccessible and distorted by the experience of oppression. The aim of feminist discourse is to move beyond this
dilemma, to penetrate the constraints and limitations of bureaucratic discourse and seek out the submerged discourse, implicit in women's experience but left largely unspoken due to
their severance from public life. To pursue this project is to
take advantage of the marginality of women's position, caught
between the instrumental requirements for entry into male-
dominated public life and the expressive values carried by
their more traditional roles. If successful, such a project might
articulate a feminist discourse that neither accepts the male
public world as it is nor simply abdicates it to men.[57]

To build an alternative political discourse from the experiences of women, and to take from this discourse indications of
a nonbureaucratic way of life, one must look squarely and
clearly at the two opposing dimensions of women's experience.
Women have been and continue to be both active creators
within their own sphere and also passive victims of male dominance. It does us no service to ignore or downplay either of
these sides, nor to overlook or simplify the complex dialectic by
which they are intertwined. To emphasize only women's subordination was an understandable tendency in much early feminist writing, which was concerned primarily with expressing
the outrage that comes from exclusion. However, to continue to
do so is to undermine our collective energies and to close off access to the alternative perspective that women's traditional
experience can offer. Similarly, to emphasize only women's
strength as historical subjects and as agents in their own
world, as does some of the most recent feminist theory, is also
partial; it risks the glorification of traditional role limitations
and avoids confrontation with the unpleasant and ignoble effects of powerlessness on personality.[58]

In its positive, creative dimension, women's experience is one
of caretaking. Women's domain is characterized by "the kin-
and locale-based or *Gemeinschaft* nature of its structure and
the love-and/or-duty ethos of its culture."[59] Women's responsibilities in anticipating, interpreting, and responding to the
needs of others both encourage and require a sensitivity and
empathy toward them, an attitude of nurturance and coop-

eration. Women tend, for a variety of reasons that will be elaborated later, to experience themselves as continuous with, rather than as opposed to, others. Women's experience suggests a way of conceiving of the relation between the self and others that is neither purely self-interested nor purely altruistic and self-sacrificing. Rather, self and other are seen to be attached to and continuous with one another in important ways (even as they are separate and distinct in other ways) making human sociality a fundamental component of the individual. Women tend to assume responsibility for taking care of others as a moral obligation, and to pass judgments that are based more on contextual rather than on abstract criteria and that focus more on process than on outcome.[60]

The values that are structured into women's experience—caretaking, nurturance, empathy, connectedness—carry both the strengths mentioned above and also an enormous weakness. Woman's experience of herself as continuous with others results in a great need for others, a dependency that, in a world of wilful actors, often goes unfulfilled. Even in a just world, the bonds between people can be betrayed or can become stifling. Women's acknowledgment of their need for others, while more honest than men's repressed affiliation, results in a great, sometimes too great, vulnerability. It leads women to be preoccupied with the threat of loss, a fear that in its most extreme forms accounts for most of the clinical depression seen in women.[61] It also often leads women to seek to avoid risk and conflict, to be threatened by the open clashing of wills that an authentic, nonbureaucratic politics requires.

The dialectic between connectedness and vulnerability is an essential part of what it means to be a human being. To uncover it is to uncover a tragic dimension of our existence, to see ourselves as beings constantly seeking a completion that constantly eludes us.[62] That women experience this process more fully than men simply means that men are likely to be out of touch with this aspect of their humanness. Since we are social beings, our self-definitions are rooted in our relations with others; since we are simultaneously temporal beings, able to project ourselves through time in many possible directions, we constantly redefine our sociality, often leaving particular connections behind. There is no political solution to this dilemma; it is an inevitable dialectic of relation and loss.

But added to this dialectic is an explicitly political condition, one which marks the other pole of women's traditional experience. In addition to, and partly as a result of, being caretakers, women have also been and continue to be subordinates to men in both private and public life. Subject to laws she had no hand in making, to economic circumstances in which her labor is invisible and/or devalued, to language in which her experiences are unspeakable, and to daily life in which violence against her is an everyday event, women have been victims. Even in the best of circumstances, women have tended to lack the sense of competence that comes from being able and entitled to act, to *do*, in the larger public world of strangers, and to have one's projects and actions valued in the public currency. Their condition of powerlessness has been closely bound up in their role as caretaker, so that the latter is distorted by the former. Women's traditional role is in part intended to prepare them for, and is easily misshapen by, powerlessness, just as men's traditional role is in part preparation for, and quickly distorted by, the exercise of power. When one is a subordinate, one does what must be done in order to survive in a world largely beyond one's control. Oppression distorts one's abilities and self-understanding, silencing authentic speech. Because women have been subordinate, their ties to others have lacked equality and thus have often become sacrificial or manipulative.

In their role as subordinates, women's experience sheds considerable light on the nature of bureaucratic domination; in their role as caretakers, women's experience offers grounds for envisioning a nonbureaucratic collective life. The remainder of this book is taken up with explanation and elaboration of both of these threads of argument. In this preliminary statement of the main argument, however, three important points remain to be made.

The first takes the form of an addendum. Feminists are not the only ones who have sought to envision and enact a nonbureaucratic form of social organization. Much of anarchist theory and practice over the last two centuries has been aimed at precisely that goal, as the many anarchist experiments in alternative education and in producers' and consumers' cooperatives testify.[63] Similarly, much of the impetus behind the counterculture of the 1960s stemmed from an anti-bureaucratic impulse, a desire to transcend the limited and self-destructive instrumental rationality of technocratic society. Radical feminist theory draws heavily on both of these sources, and the radical branch of the women's movement was born out of the ranks of the counterculture and the anarchist-inspired New Left. However, the feminist case against bureaucracy goes beyond the other critiques in that it constructs its alternative out of concrete and shared experiences of women, rather than out of a romantic vision of pre-capitalist life or an abstract ideal of "human nature." As Roslyn Bologh points out in her critique of Weber, the feminist argument draws upon "the version of the individual and rational action that characterizes the domestic world, the world of informal personal relations based on trust and caring. This other world is the underside of public and bureaucratic life."[64]

The second point takes the form of a caveat. The equation of women's experience with the private realm and men's with the public is a useful vehicle for capturing the two distinct worldviews and for unveiling their political significance. While it is always possible to think of exceptions, the distinction rests on an analysis of the experience of most people, not on that of those who are exceptionally privileged or unique in some way. Sandra Harding has pointed out that "men's and women's experiential worlds each extend through both public and domestic life," and certainly it is true that men as well as women live in families and that most women have some sort of public role, as paid workers, as shoppers and organizers of consumption, as citizens.[65] But members of each gender carry the worldview of their own domain with them into the other realm, and must consciously put it aside to "succeed" in the other world on its terms. Also, I do not wish to exaggerate the differences between the male and female worlds to the point of distortion. After all, it is important to keep in mind that men and women are more like each other than they are like any other species of being; as Dorothy Sayers once well remarked, if women are the opposite sex, "what is the neighboring sex?"[66] Finally, it is a mistake to equate the public/private distinction as it is here argued with some larger metaphysical opposition between nature and culture. The gender-defined parameters of male and female experience are equally cultural products; similarly, both dimensions of women's role, that of caretaker and that of subordinate, are socially created and maintained, not ordained by biology or by some metaphysical invisible hand. To attribute women's distinct worldview to some special creative power associated with female biology is simply to conjure up the old Aristotelian mystification in modern guise. It is not biology *per se* but the web of significance within which biology is embedded and from which it takes its meaning that makes gender differences intelligible. The persistent reappearance of the tired old nature/nurture arguments is getting boring; arguments from biology simply cannot be used to explain arrangements that are historically and cross-culturally variant, as are gender arrangements. Claims to extract morality somehow from biology, whether they are made by the so-called "difference feminists" or by more straightforward reactionaries, are equally unacceptable. In particular, the "it's all in the genes and hormones" claims of sociobiology should be seen as a particular manifestation of a social problem, not as a contribution to social theory.[67]

The third point takes the form of a qualification. Many of the most visible and tangible feminist victories have evoked the apparatus of the state to make good on liberal promises of liberty and equality. Liberal-inspired battles for equal opportunity and affirmative action are important for improving the life chances of individual women, and legal reforms in the area of reproductive freedom are crucial for the same reason. In any important political struggle there are many battles to be fought, many tools to be used. My point is not to denigrate these reforms, but rather to make clear their limitations. Entry into the public world, now almost exclusively a bureaucratic world, is necessary to some extent, if for no other reason than to be able to speak against it; in order to articulate the virtues of female experience, women have to transcend its constraints. But, as Foucault tells us, disqualified knowledges are easily reabsorbed once they are brought to light: "The particular elements of the knowledge that one seeks to disinter are no sooner accredited and put into circulation than they run the risk of re-codification, re-colonization."[68] Radical feminists such as Adrienne Rich have warned before that women do not want to fit in too well, that we need to "preserve the outsider's view and the outsider's consciousness."[69] However, as I mean to make clear in subsequent chapters, conformity and the abandonment of critical consciousness are the prices of successful performance in the bureaucratic world. An exclusive focus on integrating women into public institutions produces a situation that perpetuates bureaucratic discourse rather than challenging it; important questions are not asked, critical arguments are not formulated, alternatives are not envisioned. There is a tricky dialectic at work here. Change emerges out of people's confrontations with the existing social arrangements; coming up against institutionalized limitations in a personal way, not simply in theory or at a distance, opens the way to resistance. But to encounter bureaucracy only on its own terms, to confront it within its own discourse, is to forfeit the struggle. The goal of feminist discourse is to articulate the relations between women's experiences, the forms of speech that can adequately convey these experiences, and the forms of institutions that can encourage and legitimate them. I expect that my attempt at it will be incomplete, but at least I hope to meet the challenge posed by Jean Elshtain: "A first requirement is a feminist framework that locates itself in the social world in such a way that our current public, political realities can be examined with a critical and reflective eye."[70] Feminist discourse can interject into public debate a reformulation of the basic political questions of power and rationality, and can legitimate a concern for community. Feminist discourse can provide a way of thinking and acting that is neither an extension of bureaucratic forms nor a mirror image of them, but rather a genuinely *radical* voice in opposition.

Two   *Social Structure and*
        Bureaucratic Discourse

---

*I am walled around with their vociferations, none
will ever know what I am, none will ever hear
me say it, I won't say it, I can't say it, I have no
language but theirs.—Samuel Beckett*

While bureaucracy has existed in other times and places, the expansion of bureaucratic discourse and institutions is virtually synonymous with the birth of modernity. Students of bureaucracy in the social sciences today are all too likely to view bureaucracy as an inevitable aspect of collective life; in light of such assumptions, it is important to stress that bureaucracy is a historical creation, a mode of organization that emerged with capitalism and the modern regulatory state. Bureaucratic ways of thinking and acting structure social life at both the institutional and the individual levels of experience, but they do not completely dominate our experience: bureaucratic discourse and practice are both pervasive and incomplete. Bureaucracy continues to invade social life without ever completely capturing it, because the very processes of invasion generate points of resistance and opposition. The purpose of this chapter is to cast fresh light on bureaucratic modes of thought and action by describing briefly some important points of bureaucratic expansion in modern history, by analyzing the relations between and among bureaucratic organizations at the institutional level of society, by discussing the role of education, the family, and sexuality in colonizing individual life along bureaucratic lines, and by revealing the politics inherent in the discursive practices of the administrative disciplines.

Historical Roots of Bureaucratic Society

The origin of bureaucratic society in the Western world can be traced to the efforts of weak monarchs in the late feudal period to overcome the resistance of local authorities to the central government's efforts to impose taxes, raise armies, and control and expand trade. The bureaucracies set up by the absolute monarchs survived the demise of the monarchical system and became an integral part of bourgeois society; the administrative system provided "a dual system of force and welfare to establish order in the confusion resulting from the economic transformation of Europe" from feudalism to capitalism.[1] Contrary to the claims of classical liberal theory concerning the independent marketplace, the activities of the state bureaucracy continued to expand, claiming more and more authority to regulate activity in the realms of laws, defense, culture, and social welfare. Foucault traces the rise of extensive administrative regulation—what he calls "the disciplines"—from the seventeenth and eighteenth centuries, describing the complex process in which individuals are made into objects of study and human activity is defined as in need of organization, regulation, and control.

The modern increase in administration coincided with the rise of capitalism in ways that confirmed de Tocqueville's observations about expanding state power, while confounding the predictions of the laissez-faire theorists. Bourgeois ideology entailed an anti-public, anti-community worldview, leaving individuals to their own devices for securing their economic existence. It urged people away from collective issues toward exclusive concern with private gain, while simultaneously impelling legislators toward ever-greater efforts to collect and centralize information and to regulate and direct activity. Thus Henry Jacoby notes that "the growth of bureaucracy in a period of economic liberalism was one of the great ironies of history."[2] Protestantism, as Weber has convincingly shown, further cemented this privatization, directing attention toward an inner-worldly asceticism and a concern with marketplace salvation. Successful operation in the depersonalized marketplace required that both social relations and technical production be rendered calculative, impersonal, and predictive; this asocial world is then held together and given coherence by the formal authority relations and rational accounting practices of bureaucracy.[3]

Great optimism accompanied the rise of the regulatory institutions, which were seen by their proponents as vehicles for inculcating the bourgeois virtues—punctuality, frugality, economic rationality, and so forth—in the hearts of the recalcitrant feudal classes. Scientists, industrialists, and middle-class radicals such as Joseph Priestly (one of the founders of utilitarianism as well as an important scientist), Josiah Wedgewood (inventor of the time clock and founder of the first Chamber of Commerce), John Wilkinson (founder of the great steel fortune), and others epitomized the goals of modernity: to free individuals from the constraints of the Old Regime in order to subject them, for their own good, to the new disciplinary authority of factories, jails, schools, hospitals, and managers.[4] Defenders of the old order such as Edmund Burke fought a losing battle with the proponents of progress, who personified the marriage of knowledge, profit, and power and who announced the dawn of an age that Burke disdained as one of sophistry, economy, and calculation. Foucault shows that the spread of the disciplinary order provided a way of controlling large numbers of people, rendering their behavior stable and predictable, without utilizing the uneconomical and "ostentatious signs of sovereignty" and without rousing people to draw on the forces of their numbers in rebellion:

> Discipline fixes; it arrests or regulates movements; it clears up confusion; it dissipates compact groupings of individuals wandering about the country in unproductive ways; it establishes calculated distributions. It must also master all the forces that are formed from the very constitution of an organized multiplicity; it must neutralize the effects of counter-power that spring from them and which form a resistance to the power that wishes to dominate it: agitation, revolts, spontaneous organizations, coalitions—anything that may establish horizontal conjunctions.[5]

Foucault's analysis allows us to see the connection between the two common dictionary meanings of the word "discipline."

One deals with control: "training that develops self-control, character, or orderliness and efficiency"; "the result of such training; self-control; orderly conduct"; "a system of rules or methods"; "subjection to rule"; "correction." The other deals with knowledge: "anything taught; branch of knowledge or learning." Foucault merges these two meanings. Discipline stands at the intersection of words and things, of power and knowledge.[6] The regulatory disciplines produce "truth," in the sense that they produce "ordered procedures for the production, regulation, distribution, circulation and operation of statements."[7] The knowledge thus produced is a part of the discursive practices by which rules are constructed, objects and subject are defined, and events of study are identified and constituted. "Discipline," as Dreyfus and Rabinow explain it,

> is a technique, not an institution. It functions in such a way that it could be massively, almost totally appropriated in certain institutions (houses of detention, armies) or used for precise ends in others (schools, hospitals): it could be employed by preexisting authorities (disease control) or by parts of the judicial state apparatus (police). But it is not reducible or identifiable with any of these particular forms of power which existed in society. Rather, it "invests" or colonizes them, linking them together, extending their hold, honing their efficiency.[8]

This imposition of disciplinary order onto individual and collective life expanded still further during the Progressive era of the late nineteenth and early twentieth centuries. Various fields of administrative practice—for example, administrative law, policy "science," social work, public administration, and rational planning—brought together a focus on instrumental questions of technique and procedure with a substantive concern for reshaping the lives of clients, especially the poor. Together these fields redefined the relation of citizens to the polity in light of "the administrative approach to political membership," substituting individual therapy and the consumption of services for political action.[9] The Progressives identified the "social pathologies," cultural peculiarities, and economic conditions of the immigrant working class as a threat to the social order. Moreover, the styles of political action popular among the immigrant poor—anarchism, socialism, and syndicalism; spontaneous labor strikes; agitation against militarism and the state; ward politics—were particularly disruptive of the Progressive movement's "scientific" goals.[10] The answer given by these administrative disciplines to the problems of the poor was therapeutic intervention, in which an agent of the philanthropic interests and/or the state brought domestic tutelage into the immigrant household, seeking to normalize the working-class families, to make them behave. Competent urban managers were expected to order public life in a way that provided essential services to citizens without disrupting the class interests of the well-to-do.

The development of the administrative disciplines throughout this century continues the work of the Progressive era. In the post-World War II era the interlocking of economic, political, and scientific institutions has reached a zenith (or, one might say, a nadir) in the form of what Jacques Ellul has called the "technical civilization." The technical civilization is one in which the rule of technique, defined as "any complex of standardized means for attaining a predetermined result," dominates social life.[11] The technical civilization is characterized by extensive deference to and dependence upon a very limited notion of rationality (a linear, rule-governed, instrumental order), artificiality (distance from and opposition to nature), automatism (efficiency and control as self-justifying virtues), and universalism (no distinction between techniques and the use to which they are put). Because technique "refuses to tolerate moral judgement" it is applied as soon as it is available to whatever activity is at hand.[12] The ideological expression of the technical civilization is the modern disciplinary worldview and the managerial mentality. Its organizational expression is the bureaucracy.

While the birth of modern bureaucracy accompanied the emergence of liberal political and economic theory, bureaucracy has in a sense "outdistanced" its liberal companion. In consequence, the power relations of technical society lie out of reach of the comprehension of liberal thought in any of its contemporary forms. In the nineteenth century and early twentieth century, differences in power and privilege were to a large extent stated in the law. Those groups that enjoyed economic and social dominance could also claim a higher legal status, as in laws that restricted the suffrage to whites, to males, and/ or to members of the propertied class, or laws that prohibited women from entering the more powerful and lucrative professions, or the Jim Crow laws that preserved the better public facilities for whites. Since it is possible to generate opposition to constitutional inequality out of classical liberalism's belief in equality before the law, these privileges were eventually attacked by forces representing the mainstream of the American liberal tradition. While the use of legal devices to maintain social and economic inequality has certainly not ended—witness the demise of the Equal Rights Amendment—differential legal status is no longer the most important mechanism for enforcing power relations. Rather, the mechanisms of control are built into contemporary institutions, built into the operation of bureaucratic processes themselves. Legal guarantees of equality and constitutional restraints on power can easily coexist with bureaucratic domination. Disciplinary authority is then disguised in that it stands behind the ostensible neutrality and restraint of the law. As Foucault explains:

> Although the universal juridicism of modern society seems to fix limits on the exercise of power, its universally widespread panopticism enables it to operate on the underside of the law, a machinery that is both immense and minute, which supports, reinforces, multiplies the asymmetry of power and undermines the limits that are traced around the law.[13]

Neither of the major types of liberalism typical of contemporary American politics is able to render the technical civilization comprehensible. The spokespersons for classical liberalism, as embodied in the rhetoric of the Reagan administration and the advocates of the "free market," frequently make antiregulatory noises but offer no analysis of bureaucratization. These voices from the right are interested mainly in defending corporate capitalism from the inconvenience of some forms of state regulation while preserving the monopoly of resources that such regulation in fact supports. Their allies, conservative opponents of "entitlements" such as Daniel Bell, speak out against the politicization of the economy only when it comes from the bottom of the class structure and evince little concern for administrative control of the market when it occurs at the top. Similarly, the advocates of reformed liberalism, as represented by the remnants of the New Deal Coalition in the Democratic Party and related interest groups, are equally incapable of providing an anti-bureaucratic analysis. The response from these groups to the manifest inequalities that characterize corporate capitalism is a half-hearted defense of the tired old liberal programs of the New Deal, the Fair Deal, and the Great Society. Since these programs all rest on the proliferation of further bureaucracies to administer and control the marginal allocation of resources to the dispossessed, their "solution" in fact contributes to the problem.

To arrive at an adequate comprehension of the technical civilization, then, one must go beyond the in-house debates among various versions of liberalism. Through an analysis of both the institutional configurations and the linguistic forms of technical society, one can lay the grounds for envisioning an anti-bureaucratic discourse and imagining a nonbureaucratic society.

The Structural Arrangements of Bureaucratic Capitalism

Because bureaucratic domination penetrates social life along many interrelated dimensions, it is necessary to examine it at multiple levels. In the language of the social sciences, a dual level of analysis is crucial because the dynamic of the technical civilization includes both the macro-level interactions of large-scale institutions and processes and the micro-level activities of individuals. Connecting these two levels of analysis are two structural links: the institutionalized sets of roles and events that bureaucracies make available to individuals and groups; and the linguistic description/justification of these roles and events and of the system that creates them, which constitute the discourse of bureaucracy. The relationship between the roles and events made available in bureaucracies and the language that expresses them is a complex one, since the dominant way of thinking and speaking is one of the factors that structures available roles and events, while the experiences one has within the roles and events shape the thinking that goes on. Together they constitute a "package"—that is, an "empirically available linkage of institutional processes and structures of consciousness."[14] The term "bureaucratization" refers to the invasion of disciplinary technique into both the discursive and the institutional practices of a particular realm of human relations (for example, production, education, medicine), reshaping both the roles and the events available to people, and the language commonly used to describe those roles and events, along bureaucratic lines. Discussion of the roles and events of bureaucratic life is the subject of Chapters Three and Four; the remainder of this chapter outlines the main characteristics of the two levels of analysis and of the connecting bureaucratic discourse.

There is a temptation toward reductionism in discussing bureaucracy, which is often seen in the identification of individuals entirely with their organizational roles or in the identification of the actual functioning of organizations with the organizations' own descriptions and defense of their function. It is important to remember that concrete existing individuals are temporal beings who have complex social histories and multiple possible futures; real people cannot be collapsed into their organizational identities. That the modern organization tries to do precisely that, tries to merge the identity of the individual with her or his organizational role, is a problem to be analyzed, not a fact of life to be taken for granted. Similarly, it is crucial to distinguish the actual activities of institutions from the institutions' own account of these activities. Modern organizations, like all vehicles for the exercise of power, have a vested interest in accounting for their activities in a way that is acceptable to the audience at hand. The official version of reality offered by bureaucracies in their own behalf, or in behalf of other bureaucracies, is, again, part of the question to be asked, not part of the answer.

At the macro level of analysis there is a complex relation between capitalism and bureaucracy as systemic processes. Since Weber, most students of bureaucracy have recognized that advanced capitalism needs bureaucratic administrative structures to impose predictability and stability on the economic realm. Such administrative structures seek to ensure system-stabilizing performances on the part of relevant actors, both the clients who are the targets of administration and the functionaries who perform the administration. System stabilization involves continued maintenance of existing structures and procedures, along with intervention into those grave social crises in which the threat to stability is severe and obvious. The task of organization, with regard to the structures of capital, is to utilize "the most intricate techniques and methods of technocratic administration" in order to allow for "cautious crisis management and long-term avoidance strategy."[15]

But even while corporate capitalism requires bureaucracy, the two stand in tension. Theories of legal equality and contract-based rights provide the foundation for the official ideology of the individual's place in bourgeois society. But these theories mask the coercive dimensions of administrative society, the "closely linked grid of disciplinary coercions" that enforce inequality, normalcy, and control.[16] Simultaneously, the discourse of normalization, based on clinical knowledge and scientific legitimacy, undermines the discourse of law and rights by superseding its claims. For example, during the Progressive era, settlement workers and charity agents used the juvenile court system to adjust working-class, immigrant families to the dominant American standards of normality. Children who were seen as either endangered (neglected or abused) or dangerous ("incorrigible"), or likely to be either, were brought through the courts to the attention of the proper diagnostic experts. Through the child the agents of normalization gained entry to the entire family, so that familial relations and domestic practices came under official surveillance and "scientific" regulation. When the families of the working class were made into "cases" and became clients, the members of these families did not explicitly lose their political and legal rights; such rights were simply superseded and rendered irrelevant. The legal rights to own and control one's property, to raise one's own children, to be judged by one's own peers, to protect one's own privacy, to vote, to express one's opinions, and so forth were never rescinded, but they competed unsuccessfully with the social experts' demands for personal disclosure and regulation. As Andrew Polsky explains:

> Of the many state programs developed under the influence of Progressive philanthropy, the juvenile court best reflected the impact of therapeutic discourse on public authority. The court occupied shadowy ground between legal tribunal and social agency. Upon a judicial framework was engraved a thorough-going human service logic and organization. . . . Hence the critical significance of probation: in place of definitive judgments about a case the juvenile court implicated child and family in a process of unending evaluation.[17]

Today the conflict between these two discourses takes many forms—for example, the claims for prisoners' and patients' rights vis-à-vis prisons and hospitals, children's rights vis-à-vis schools and juvenile courts, citizens' rights vis-à-vis the claims of experts, and so on. Sometimes client groups can appeal to the legal structure to limit the interrogation of the service agencies, as when the Supreme Court ruled that the "man-in-the-house" provision of the federal welfare programs was unconstitutional.[18] But more often the authority of judicial, legal, and political discourse competes unsuccessfully with that of administrative discourse.

The technical civilization is one that is increasingly penetrated with large, complex organizations; the further we move into late capitalist society, the more are our various activities captured within such organizations. Not just the punishment of criminals and the organization of military activity, but the organization of work, of education, of medical care, of nature, of leisure, of intimacy—all are increasingly defined within the terms of bureaucratic discourse and performed within the structure of bureaucracies. Our society is made up of a dense network of interlocking organizations, and each of these organizations constitutes an actual or a potential resource for other organizations. Foucault has shown how, in the case of prisons and other institutions of control, the disciplines become intertwined and mutually supporting. Largely in response to the expansion of population and the extension of capitalism, with its need to control the labor force, the administrative regulation of all areas of life also expanded. Knowledge gained in one area supports power exercised in another, and resources captured by one technical structure match activities undertaken by another. One thinks immediately of the relationship between the knowledge generated by the study of psychology and the power exercised in the workplace, which combined to create the discipline of industrial psychology. Or the credential-bestowing activity of universities in relation to the managerial authority of governments and corporate conglomerates, resulting in the proliferation of departments of public and business administration. With Foucault, we must admit that it is not surprising that "prisons resemble factories, schools, barracks, hospitals, which all resemble prisons."[19]

At the macro level of analysis, then, organizations must be viewed as resources for other organizations in an environment invaded by bureaucratic discourse. This is the key to understanding bureaucratic, as opposed to market, capitalism; class relations are both captured and disguised within bureaucratic organizations and networks. Those organizations that are surrounded by more powerful bureaucracies are, of course, more likely to *be* a resource than to find resources elsewhere, although there is usually some reciprocity. Also, some organizations are included in the interlocking network if they can potentially threaten the resources of other organizations; thus unions became vehicles for incorporating their members into capitalist society, replacing the spontaneous labor unrest that destabilized the economic and political climate. The terms of most collective-bargaining agreements make the relationship clear: unions usually agree to restrict strikes to predictable periods, to accept bureaucratic grievance procedures that remove worker-manager confrontations from the shop floor, and to acknowledge managerial control of the work process and of hiring; in exchange the unions receive guaranteed income in the form of automatic deductions of union dues from the workers' salaries.[20] Unions may also gain concrete advantages for their members in the form of wages and benefits, and occasionally even health and safety concessions, but these are increasingly incidental to the central exchange of resources between the two organizations:

> The modern labor agreement is the principal instrument of the class collaboration between the trade unions and the corporations. It mirrors the bureaucratic and hierarchical structure of modern industry and the state. Its provisions are enforced not merely by law, but by the joint efforts of corporate and trade union bureaucracies.[21]

Or, as one of my interviewees, reflecting on her seven years of factory work and union membership, stated: "The only thing worse than having a union is not having one."

The process by which bureaucracies survive and prosper by serving as resources for other bureaucracies is evident at all levels of technical society. Among the most powerful economic institutions, the relationships are well known: banks and insurance companies provide short- and long-term capital to corporations and agribusiness for investment; "captured" government agencies secure the interests of those whom they are supposed to regulate; states guarantee enormous markets to insurance companies by requiring individuals to own automobile insurance. The big pharmaceutical companies have fended off competition and extended their operations by making deals with other organizations: they secured the cooperation of the federal government in changing patent laws, of the American Medical Association by offering lucrative advertising revenues to AMA publications, and of the medical profession itself by offering career mobility for doctors in drug companies.[22] Clusters of organizations—suppliers, subsidiaries, distributors and research organizers, plus firms providing banking, legal, managerial, advertising, and public relations services, plus relevant state agencies—come together to form loose, flexible, but remarkably stable networks of interlocking institutions. While a certain amount of conflict over particular policies and struggle over scarce resources takes place between and among these institutional complexes, such dissension exists within an overall climate of accommodation.[23]

Relations among contemporary social service organizations reveal a parallel pattern. While they employ a substantial number of people, service organizations do not have direct bearing on the major economic activities of industrial or energy production, foreign policy, international trade, military policy, or the processes of capital investment. They thus do not constitute the most important constellation of organizations at the macro level. Nonetheless, the interlocking relationships among them are similar: by controlling and hiding the various client populations, especially the poor, service bureaucracies help provide both political and economic stability. Elected elites can then claim success in maintaining "law and order" for their administrations, and economic elites are provided with a stable climate for investment, some minimum support for generating demand, and a dependable (that is, pacified) reserve labor force.[24] Thus we see similar patterns of overlap and interaction among the front-line institutions of capital and the secondary control organizations: all are linked together through bureaucratic arrangements, allocations, and accommodations.

Education, the Family, and Sexuality

The links between the macro-level institutional relations discussed above and the daily lives of individuals are found both in the roles and events available to individuals and in the language used to comprehend these roles and events. One's experiences in educational institutions, in families, and in the realm of sexuality all provide crucial connecting links between personal life and the larger public order. By looking briefly at the discursive and institutional arrangements in these three arenas, we can begin to uncover the forces of bureaucratization in everyday life.

Educational institutions generate and reflect both the discourse of bureaucracy and the roles and events that recruit individuals into bureaucracies. At the structural level, educational organizations are closely tied to corporate and state conglomerates. After World War II the United States, following the example set earlier by Germany, linked university research programs to government and corporate goals. Most university research is financed by the federal government and highly influenced, if not controlled, by the needs of private industry, leading to "the transformation of science itself into capital." [25] Kingman Brewster, then president of Yale, defined the relationship as follows: "The academy and business have a joint trusteeship for the freedom of the marketplace, the ballot box, and ideas." At the same gathering of corporate executives, the president of Kaiser Industrial Corporation defined this "freedom of ideas" more explicitly: "Business needs education to reach youth. The challenge to business and education is how to motivate youth to believe the system holds the greatest opportunities for them." [26] In both its internal arrangements and its connections to other institutions, the university today is a tool of industry and the state:

> The vocational university is a knowledge apparatus explicitly designed to create and apply ideas and personnel that are functional to dominant national policies. In external relations, the vocational university is dependent on federal and corporate public research interests, which in turn are sensitive to national foreign and domestic interests. In internal relations, both collegiate and intellectual patterns are replaced by cognitive vocationalism in which young men and women are trained for the needs of organized bureaucracies. [27]

Educational institutions serve as links between organizational complexes and also between levels of society, mediating between the personal experiences of individuals in families and peer groups and the collective political culture at the organizational level. It has long been acknowledged that educational institutions reinforce the class structure, that middle-class schools prepare future managers, that working-class schools prepare industrial employees and service workers, and that lower-class schools perform basically custodial functions and "seem unable to prepare their students for any stable role in the workforce." [28] (This is not surprising, since there generally is no position in the workforce for such individuals; they are being prepared to join the ranks of the administered underclass.) Within the educational institutions there is a vested, administratively defined interest in retaining their "raw material" (children and youth) for as long as possible. Hence the problems of schools are "solved" by more schooling, initiating a revolving door of referrals among different educational bureaucracies, and dropouts are seen as "morally unwholesome" individuals who will probably grow up to be "bad citizens." [29]

Further, the very definition of knowledge has come to serve the interests of other organizations in the technical society. The rationalization of education reduces the importance of more overt forms of control such as grades because it disciplines students through the definition of knowledge itself. For example, at the college level relevant knowledge is increasingly defined in terms of the requirements for entering professional schools; in turn, knowledge at the professional level is that which prepares one for certification; and throughout the school system, from junior high to post-university levels, a ubiquitous career orientation prevails. The examination system, which Marx referred to as "the bureaucratic baptism of knowledge," gradually becomes superfluous as the disciplinary function of grading is transferred to the actual activity of learning and to the subject matter being learned: "Those forms of technology that have proved effective in increasing industrial production are now transferred to education." [30] For example, at the undergraduate level the general liberal arts curriculum is losing ground to courses that only a few years ago were defined as professional and/or technical training: social work, criminal justice, "pre-law," public administration, and so forth. These "fields" are highly specialized, "how-to" training programs with little theoretical or critical content. The knowledge they impart to students is fragmented and discontinuous; seldom is there any effort to supply the "big picture," to place the parts together to make a whole. Nonadministrative goals such as open-endedness, self-expression, or critique are sacrificed to the technical requirements of efficient production; in the case of education the "product" is the administratively socialized and docile future worker or manager or client with the appropriate technical and/or bureaucratic skills.

As the popularity of books such as *The One-Minute Manager, Dress for Success,* and *The Fast Track* indicate, "the good life" for individuals has come to be defined largely in organizational terms.[31] While this is not consistent with the still-existent imagery of the successful individual entrepreneur, it is not surprising; since well-being in capitalist society has always been couched primarily in material terms, it is logical that, as material resources are virtually controlled by conglomerates, individual happiness would also come to be identified with organizational life. This results, as even the defenders of the technical society note with regret, in "the creation of the idea that individual welfare can only be realized through the modern organization and its managerial system."[32] Parents seeking upward mobility for their children increasingly look to education, not simply to provide access to a better job at a higher salary, but to supply an institutional linkage to an established occupational hierarchy. A "lifeboat mentality" prevails among both students and their parents. The search for a secure organizational niche reduces education to a matter of acquiring the appropriate credentials, picking up the correct technical skills, and selecting the right line to stand in.[33]

The typical socialization process in our schools prepares individuals simultaneously to participate in bureaucratically ordered activities and to refrain from comprehending the real place of such activities in the technical society. The pervasive mythology of rugged individualism and the work ethic and the commercially supported concentration on personality and inner space encourage people to view their lives solely in personal terms. While bourgeois individualism is most evident in middle-class education, family, and peer group experiences, an equivalent "ideology of sacrifice" (that is, the belief that individual perseverance is the key to success) is pervasive in the lives of the working class as well.[34] Private troubles, to use C. Wright Mill's phrase, are seen as the result of individual inadequacies, to be righted through individual effort. At the same time, there are strong pressures in our society to accept hierarchy as the natural order of things, to believe that authority is self-justifying, and to accept the organizational network as the inevitable result of "progress." In a study of elementary and high school students in a middle-class school, Herbert Wilcox found that "white, suburban, middle class children acquire knowledge about the forms of behavior appropriate to formal organizations at rather tender years." By the age of eleven, sometimes even by age nine, these children comprehend the workings of hierarchical organizations as well as do college students, graduate students in public administration, and even professional administrators. A large percentage of the children "did not distinguish hierarchy as a characteristic of formal organizations from social relationships generally," indicating that their experience of power in various contexts has a similar form. Wilcox concludes, not unexpectedly, that "such children are well-trained for participation in administrative organizations having the conventional characteristics of the pyramidal form."[35]

One can point to resistance and opposition in the schools as well. For example, Stanley Aronowitz notes that the various illicit activities that go on in the school restrooms make them the "locus of resistance of students to total administration."[36] And the increase in violent attacks on teachers indicates opposition of a different order. Recent studies by the National Education Association and the National Institute on Education show that nearly .5 percent of public educators, or about one in every two hundred junior and senior high teachers, were physically attacked at school by students during a one-year period.[37] Most such attacks occur in high-poverty, high-unemployment neighborhoods, not in the schools that Wilcox studied. The response of the schools is to become even more like prisons by increasing hall monitors, locking the schools' doors from the outside, installing security devices, providing therapy, and so forth. Both the affluent schools and the poor schools are, in their own way, preparing students for a lifetime of hierarchy and domination—the middle class kids as bureaucrats and managers, the poor kids as inmates and clients.

A second crucial link between the macro and micro levels of analysis is the family. A brief look at the history of the family in America both reveals the evolution of discourse about the family and makes clear the increasing incursion of administrative rationality into daily life. The evolution of the family from a producing unit to a consuming unit in capitalist society entailed extensive reorganization of private life. Historically, there have been three kinds of "women's work": production of goods and services within the family, for consumption by the family; household production for exchange on the market; and work for pay outside the home.[38] In pre-industrial America, the first category predominated, the other two becoming more important over time. The realms of production and reproduction, of work and family, overlapped. The public and private spheres were more integrated, and, generally, the greater integration and overlap there are between the two, the greater is the equality between the sexes and the higher the status of women.[39] By the mid to late 1800s production of goods was mostly of the third type, and done outside the home. At least for the middle class and among whites, families stopped making consumer goods and started buying them. "Real work" became redefined as that done outside the home, for pay; domestic labor, excluded from the marketplace, correspondingly declined in status. The realm of the household shrank in scope as well as in stature: with declining fertility rates and infant mortality rates, and increasing longevity, women had fewer children and spent a smaller proportion of their lives caring for them. The expanding service industries took over the education of the young and the care of the sick and aged, tasks formerly performed by women at home. Thus, by the latter nineteenth century the realms of work and of family had become segregated. Simultaneously, white middle-class women were being removed from the paid labor force. The dwindling of unsettled land meant fewer jobs in agriculture, and the waves of immigrants took many of the jobs formerly held by white women and also filled the new jobs in industry and commerce. Middle-class women, in short, were increasingly confined to a private realm in which there was less and less to be done.[40]

The needs of the traditional family and the demands of the market converged to produce a new discourse about women and families. As capital became increasingly dependent on the domestic consumer-goods market in the early twentieth century, the management of the consumption patterns of individuals and families became as important as the management of production, and was pursued in similar ways. Knowledge possessed by the emergent social sciences was enlisted to extend rational bureaucratic control into family lives, as well as into communities and into recreational/leisure activities, in the same way that it was invoked to rationalize production in factories and offices. Progressive era reformers sought to discredit the social customs and familial practices of working-class families, to "normalize" personal life, and to surround families and communities with a "permanent network of services."[41] Primarily through advertising and through the offices of the new "experts" in various aspects of daily life, including health, childcare, nutrition, physical fitness, aging, and sexuality, the practices and habits of individuals and families came to be increasingly ordered and administered to meet the needs of social control and the mass consumer market. The net effect on both the family and the workplace, as Barbara and John Ehrenreich point out, has been

> the fragmentation of work (and workers) in the productive process, a withdrawal of aspirations from the workplace into private goals, the disruption of indigenous networks of support and mutual aid, the destruction of autonomous working class culture and its replacement by "mass culture" defined by the privatized consumption of commodities.[42]

In a society in which both the instrumental values of control and autonomy and the expressive values of nurturance and community are eliminated from the workplace, the burden on the family to provide these needs correspondingly increases. Thus the family carries a highly contradictory burden. It is the seat of whatever residual power over others most adults retain, and thus is often an arena of conflict and violence; at the same time it is the main vehicle for the satisfaction of interpersonal need and desire. The traditional role of women as both loving caretakers of, and willing subordinates to, their mates has been the main vehicle for the resolution of this contradiction.

In the nineteenth century the "cult of true womanhood" provided the mythic guidelines for women's role. Women, at least those of the appropriate class, were expected to shape family life so as to provide a safe domestic haven for the harried male worker, to "cheer the weary breadwinner." The man who had to follow orders all day at work could take comfort in coming home to a well-ordered domestic harmony in which his ruling status was unquestioned; after all, "a man's home is his castle." Men who came home to less than castle-like privilege could at least salve their frustration by taking it out on their wives. Simultaneously, women's role as guardians of morality and the hearth required them to save their men from disseminating precious energy in drinking, gambling, and carousing, and to save themselves and their families from the impoverishment that would follow. The enforcement of dutiful work habits in men, and in the children who were to be the next generation of workers, reflected the convergence of the religious virtue of self-restraint with the bourgeois virtue of frugality. In the words of a San Francisco newspaper editor, women were "God's own police."[43] Women's loving devotion to their families was supposed both to supply intimacy and nurturance and also to reconcile women to the dominance, frequently the abuse, exercised over them by men.

While the values and beliefs of the cult of true womanhood continue to lurk under the surface of contemporary gender roles, changes in women's role over the last half-century have undermined its force. Increasingly claiming the rights of citizens, and occupying the position of paid workers, women have begun more openly to resist the role of loving subordinate in the home. Conservative critics of the feminist movement decry this trend and urge women back into the "haven in a heartless world," but such nostalgic longing for an alleged pre-feminist domestic bliss misses the point. The cult of true womanhood was a discursive strategy that served both to disguise and to perpetuate the contradictions inherent in the family, and did so at the expense of women's individuality and autonomy. Foucault reminds us that to comprehend any discursive strategy one must

> make allowance for the complex and unstable process
> whereby discourse can be both an instrument and an effect
> of power, but also a hindrance, a stumbling block, a point
> of resistance and a starting point for an opposing strategy.
> Discourse transmits and produces power; it reinforces it,
> but also undermines and exposes it, renders it fragile and
> makes it possible to thwart it.[44]

The cult of true womanhood was an instrument and an effect of power, an element of a discourse that structured the experience of women around the needs of the traditional family and of emergent capitalism. It was produced by two sources: the new experts in the women's literary industry, and the old experts on daily life, the clergy, recast in a revised role as the guardians of sentiment rather than of immortality.[45] Foucault suggests that, with regard to the relation of discourse to nondiscursive relations, or institutions, we examine the level of their "strategic interaction," "looking at what conjunction and what force relationship make their utilization necessary in a given episode of the various confrontations that occur."[46] The cult of true womanhood mediated more or less "successfully" between the contradictory demands on the private realm for a time, but it became a stumbling block and a source of resistance as it came increasingly into conflict with the evolving economic, political, and social situation of women at the turn of the century and particularly around World War I. The utility of the reification of domesticity as a discursive strategy declined, and it became as much a springboard for an opposing strategy, a feminist strategy, as an agent of established power. The early feminists had to deal with the ridicule that the enforcers of the standards of womanliness, male and female, dealt out to them, but the first feminists also rebelled against those standards. They did so by creating the beginning of a feminist discourse that, in its most radical forms, leveled total criticism at the dominant institutions of church, state, family, and marketplace.[47] In the end, the First Wave turned to liberalism for its ideas and program, and the more radical voices faded as pursuit of the suffrage came to dominate the movement. But the beginnings of a discourse of opposition had been made.

The growing refusal of many women to accept the family role exemplified by the cult of true womanhood has not, however, resolved the contradictory demands within the family for both instrumental and expressive satisfaction. In fact, the demands on private life to satisfy both the needs for autonomy and control and the needs for intimacy and connectedness are amplified in the technical society because the sterile public space provides neither. In sum, the bureaucratization of daily life has confounded and undermined the relation of public to private life in late capitalism. The ideology of bourgeois society claims that the greatest rewards for individuals are material rewards, that material security in private life is in fact a refuge from the requirements of public life. Thus the consumption of commodities within the family is praised in bourgeois ideology, and this activity is seen as fundamentally separate from and unlike the institutional and behavioral context of the public world of production and government. The tendency to seek refuge in private pursuits is amplified even further as bureaucratization intensifies, because the routinization of work and the absence of avenues of participation and self-expression in bureaucracy further encourage individuals to seek refuge in off-work satisfactions.

But this privatization is self-defeating. It generates a level of self-absorption and concern with the personal that puts too great a burden on private life. As Richard Sennett forcefully argues, the world of personal intimacy and self-examination loses its boundaries when it is not contained by and contrasted with a genuine public realm of speech and action.[48] The absence of a vital public space where one can come together with peers, acquaintances, and strangers to deliberate on common issues, undermines private life as well by destroying the balance between private and shared concerns, between individual and collective action. Thus the incursion of administrative rationality into family life has come to serve, along with the continuing traditional role of women, as the vehicle for both perpetuating and disguising the family's contradictory role in technical society. By extending and refining the objectification and commodification of life, the bureaucratization of the family and personal life siphons both work-related discontent and po-

tentially disruptive personal needs and desires into channels
that are harmless to administrative and capitalist hegemony.
The search for both autonomy and community becomes a flight
into a series of administered and commodified activities. Decisions about how to act and how to live are replaced by decisions
about what to buy and what to join. "A man's home is his
castle" and "woman's place is in the home" have been replaced
by a unisex version of "let's make a deal." The personal consumption of cosmetics and romances by women in the 1920s
evolved into the domestic consumerism of the 1950s; then the
focus shifted as housewives, particularly married women with
small children, entered the paid labor force in large numbers.
To be sure, many cultural messages are still sent to women re-
inforcing the traditional domestic role, since even women who
work outside the home also do most of the work in the home as
well.[49] But in addition to this message, corporate America is
now selling a different, more elaborate, image: *success*, life in
the fast lane, bureaucratic upward mobility for husbands *and*
wives. Since, by definition, the fast lane can't hold everyone (or
else what would it be faster than?) there is a residual category
for the losers and for the less privileged classes and colors—
survival.[50] But success is the goal, and it is defined in terms of
a carefully orchestrated convergence of organizational participation. Singles bars, special leisure-oriented housing developments, athletic centers, encounter groups, "stress and re-
laxation" classes, and various social clubs are directed at an
alienated and atomized population. These activities offer both
an essential, if commodified, human contact and an opportunity to achieve through concrete action. The current physical
fitness boom owes at least part of its popularity to the fact that
physical activity allows a kind of personal achievement denied
to most people in their work.

The penetration of administrative discourse into personal
life signifies the ascent of the "cult of rationality." By cult of rationality I mean the subjection of very intimate aspects of human relationships, emotions, and identity to the reign of commerce and technique. A clear example of the homogenization of
the personal and the public that the cult of rationality entails
is found in the situation of workers such as the flight atten-

dants who sell the public security and service on commercial airlines. The flight attendant engages in what Arlie Russell Hochschild calls "emotional labor"; like approximately 25 percent of male workers in America, and over half of employed women, she (for nearly all are women) manages and presents her feelings, and her facial and body expressions, to shape a countenance that produces the required response in the consumer.[51] The flight attendant's smile is like her make-up; it is on her, not of her. The rules about how to feel and how to express feeling are set by management, with the goal of producing passenger contentment. Company manuals give detailed instructions on how to have a "modest but friendly smile," how to provide a "sincere" and "unaffected" facial expression, how to seem "vivacious but not effervescent." In most companies, applicants are required to take an "animation test," not unlike the screening process required of potential contestants on Hollywood game shows, wherein they are judged on their show of expansiveness, bubbly conversation, active body language, and so forth.[52] Emotional laborers are required to take the arts of emotional management and control that characterize the intimate relations of family and friends (for example, the ability to suppress envy or anger, to refrain from expressing love, to offer approval, or to suppress judgment) and package them according to the "feeling rules" laid down by the organization:

> What was once a private act of emotion management is now sold as labor in public contact jobs. What was once a privately negotiated rule of feeling or display is now set by the company's Standard Practices Division. Emotional exchanges that were once idiosyncratic and escapable are now standardized and unavoidable. Exchanges that were rare in private life become common in commercial life. . . . All in all, a private emotional system has been subordinated to commercial logic, and it has been changed by it.[53]

The "transmutation of an emotional system" that Hochschild so convincingly presents demonstrates the invasion of the cult of rationality into personal life. The flight attendant's situation is an extreme and explicitly rule-governed example of the incursion of technique into the private realm of affect. Of course emotion has always been a social experience, but only recently has it become an *administered* experience. The flight attendant is required to rationalize and commodify the most personal feelings, moods, attitudes, and stances, to take an instrumental stance toward "a source of self that we honor as deep and integral to our individuality," to engineer and administer this intimacy along bureaucratic lines and for commercial purposes. The costs to personal identity are enormous: like prostitutes, flight attendants often estrange themselves from their work as a defense against being swallowed by it, only to suffer from a sense of being false, mechanical, no longer a whole integrated self.[54]

In the cult of rationality questions of sexuality and of affect, transformed into questions of commodity and technique, reproduce the administrative mode of being in intimate relations. Foucault's argument in *The History of Sexuality* reveals that sexuality is "an especially dense transfer point for relations of power."[55] In the eighteenth and nineteenth centuries a new discourse on sexuality redefined sex from a question of "sin" to one of "health." The force of pedagogy, law, medicine, economics, and demographics combined to transfer sexuality from an ecclesiastical to a secular context. At stake was the lineage of the ruling class; the threat of "sexual perversions" (homosexuality, pederasty, even adultery) menaced the bourgeoisie's line of descent. The modern techniques of sexuality were first applied to the bourgeoisie to maintain the "health of the class," then were later extended to the working class when the development of industry required a docile labor force.[56]

In technical society the discourse on sexuality has undergone a "tactical shift."[57] What was punished as a matter of sin in the feudal days, then treated as a question of health in the modern period, is now packaged as an item for sale. Along with the treatment of sex as a medical object, today the commodification and bureaucratization of sex defines sex as a commercial product. What Foucault, Sennett, and others who note this shift fail to see is that all these redefinitions of the discourse of sexuality have been largely at the expense of women. The rules of the religious discourse on sexuality were more restrictive for women, the penalties for nonconformity harsher; if even some

of the women killed as witches were being punished for sus-
pected sexual deviance, it was a large number indeed.[58] Similarly, the medicalization of sex was more thoroughly produced
through the bodies of women, and of children, than of adult men.
Campaigns against childhood masturbation, against "hysteria"
and "perversion," affected both sexes but affected women more
acutely, if for no other reason than that women as bearers of
children were the preservers of purity and property in the race
and in the class.

The religious discourse on sex is still an audible voice in our
society; it stands behind the medicalization of sex and the current commodification/administration, which is not completely
new but is emerging as a dominant mode of speech and conduct.
Advice to lovers goes back at least to Plato's *Symposium*, but
today technical guides to sex and intimacy (along with their
twins in discourse, diet books and exercise manuals) clutter the
best-seller list. Similarly, pornography is not new, but its status
as a multibillion-dollar industry is a post-World War II phenomenon.[59] Books and articles on how to masturbate, how to find
your G spot, how to use a vibrator, and so forth command huge
readerships. Popular magazines such as *Cosmopolitan*, *Esquire*,
Playboy, and *Self* encode, standardize, and broadcast the "rules"
of intimacy. For example, people who have substituted for traditional marriage a series of intense relationships ("serial monogamy") can read about the dangers of "love on the rebound";
women confused about their sexual response can find explicit
instructions on how to have an "explosive" orgasm as opposed to
a "humming" orgasm.[60] Some of the new experts on sex, such as
the pornographers, are not fully recognized by all subjects; some
of their products, such as child pornography and the most bla-
tant violence against women, meet with some resistance. But
the themes dominant in pornography—male violence and self-
obsession, female degradation, cruelty, anonymity, and above
all an "absolute, unchangeable, omnipresent, eternal limitless
power over others"—permeate the softer and more acceptable
packages as well.[61] The glossy newsstand magazines, the Playboy Clubs and their clones, the fantasies of sex, wealth, and
power on the popular daytime and nighttime soaps, the ubiquitous, expressionless women whose bodies sell products on bill-

boards, commercials, and printed advertisements—all are part of the same sexual discourse of commodity and technique.

Ralph Hummel points out that bureaucratic socialization prepares people well for the substitution of technique for connectedness: "The entire training of human beings subjected to bureaucratic life is (1) not to attach affect directly to any person, (2) to attach affect only to their own functions, successfully performed according to systems standards, and (3) to attach affect only to the exercise of power." [62] Through the ministrations of sex therapists and counselors, at the behest of "how-to" manuals offering the secrets of sexual prowess, in light of standards of attractiveness established by television, movies, and advertisements, administrative rationality serves up a pale and diluted version of desire. Tim Luke has aptly captured the flavor of the unholy union of scientific rationality, pop psychology, and sex:

> In sexuality, the individual as self-manager can plan his [sic] own needs, program his own goals, acquire the most efficient techniques and realize his own paying-off potentiality after investing the necessary time and energy. . . . Sexuality itself ultimately is submitted to a Taylorist logic of time-motion-energy analysis to maximize one's orgasmic potential and realization. [63]

Happily, desire resists taming in some ways, even as it submits to it in others. It is important to remember that the bureaucratization of society is an inherently two-sided process: it is invasive and pervasive; it is also uneven and incomplete. Foucault continually reminds us that the dominant discourse and structure of any society is never a fixed object but always a *process*, one that invades and conquers at the same time that it engenders the resistance it meets. Capitalism is particularly vulnerable to bureaucratic penetration in that the image of social life that the marketplace provides is one in which individual entrepreneurs continually seek to maximize their utilities in competition with others like themselves, and social relations are reduced to the bare minimum necessary to conduct commodity transactions. Because capitalism provides no meaningful fabric of social relations for its members, the terms of administrative discourse come to substitute for community life. Murray Bookchin states this point well:

> Under capitalism, today, bureaucratic institutions are not merely systems of social control; they are literally institutional substitutes for social form. They comprise the skeletal framework of a society that, as Greek social thought would have emphasized, edges on inherent disorder. However much market society may advance productive forces, it takes its historical revenge not only in the rationalization it inflicts on society, but the destruction it inflicts on the highly articulated social relations that once provided the springboard for a viable social opposition. The most disturbing feature of modern bureaucracy is not merely the coercion, regimentation and control it imposes on society, but the extent to which it is literally *constitutive* of modern society: the extent to which it validates itself as the realm of "order" against the chaos of social dissolution. . . . Capitalist society becomes bureaucratized to its very marrow precisely because the market can never provide society with an internal life of its own.[64]

Thus, both private and public life have been rendered vulnerable to bureaucratic penetration by the transformation of "all of society into a gigantic marketplace."[65]

At the same time, the penetration of the cult of rationality is uneven and partial. Unmediated personal anxieties, continued personal and collective economic crises, and the more positive wellsprings of resistance located in the individual's capacity for creativity, spontaneity, and immediate joy in connection and action—these facts and others point to the incompleteness of the bureaucratic capture of desire. If this were not so, if personal life were easily entrapped in the flashy and boring channels of administration and commodification, then the various sex industries would not need to continue pumping their polluted products into the marketplace.[66] Just as the cult of true womanhood had to be continously produced and disseminated through various cultural channels, most notably through literature and the churches, the cult of rationality also requires continuous maintenance. And just as women resisted or circumvented the demands of domesticity in various ways—for example, through the First Wave of the feminist movement, or through the concrete resistance of working-class and poor women to a model of family life that was unavailable to them—so can individuals resist or evade the infiltration of the bureaucratic ethos into daily life. For example, the ethic of spontaneity, immediacy, and hostility to authority characterizing the counterculture—expressed in slogans such as "Make love, not war," "If it feels good, do it," "If it's possible, it's natural"—is an expression of just such resistance. Cooptation of such ideas into the commodity sphere, as in the bastardization of the word "natural" to describe every sort of spurious, artificial, and even dangerous product from hair color to breakfast cereal to low-level radiation, is one possible outcome. But continued resistance is another. The counterculture also served as an inspiration for much of the radical feminist movement and other community-oriented grassroots political activities. Further, the choice between resistance and conformity is usually a question of degree, and people often do some of each. Colin Gordon makes this point well in his commentary on Foucault:

> The binary division between resistance and non-resistance is an unusual one. The existence of those who seem not to rebel is a warren of minute, individual, autonomous tactics and strategies which counter and inflect the visible facts of overall domination, and whose purposes and calculations, desires and choices, resist any simple division into the political and the apolitical.[67]

For example, the flight attendants that Hochschild studied often found ways to resist the demands of emotional labor. Sometimes they resisted by withdrawing from their work, offering "a thin crust of display" in place of "genuine" personal service.[68] Such defiance is costly, in that it substitutes alienation from one's image for alienation from one's feelings, but it is defiance nonetheless. Sometimes, they go further, as when company "speed ups" (efforts to get more work from fewer attendants) elicit "smile wars" from the workers, who break the appearance rules outright by refusing to conform. The fact that most airline companies require yearly "recurrent training" for all flight attendants, and impose constant policing and self-policing on attendants, suggests that the managers are aware of the fragility and partiality of the organization's control over the workers. And the fact that some attendants form unions, bring suits against their companies, and otherwise assert themselves indicates a willingness to "break the rules."

In sum, the activities and attitudes of daily life can resist rationalization just as they may also succumb to it. The creation of a feminist discourse of protest and vision is one step in the fostering of such resistance.

Understanding Bureaucratic Discourse

Bureaucratic discourse is the speech of the administrative disciplines. Like the language of other regulatory disciplines, bureaucratic language is expressive of certain political activities, activities in which the distribution of power is both expressed and hidden within the discourse itself. Discourse, following Foucault, can be viewed as a form of practice, a manifestation of the structure of social relations represented in it. The speech of those who function within the context of some administrative discipline or managerial setting—public administration, business administration, educational administration, health care administration, corrections administration, social services administration, et cetera, et cetera—is embedded within a politically laden field of meaning. Administrative discourse both creates positions for persons and events and also represents the positions of persons and events; that is, it both expresses and reflects a particular structure of institutions and practices.

Bureaucratic discourse operates as a kind of verbal performance, placing people and objects within the "network of social, political and administrative arrangements." The study of the rules governing word-object relations allows one to "raise questions about how those social, political, and administrative relationships in a society give rise to rules in accordance with which various kinds of objects emerge as a focus of attention for particular disciplines, professions, and other, similarly, bounded collectivities."[69] An analysis of administrative discourse allows one both to elucidate the institutional context that gives rise to the disciplines and to enlarge the realm of the political by "retrieving the politics within which we reside unreflecting as we construct our worlds of domination and submission with our utterances."[70]

The discursive relations of the administrative disciplines reveal power at the "latent ideological level of political culture."[71] Power is not "added on" to the activities at hand but rather is coextensive with them; it consists of the multiplicity of power relations that are immanent in the discursive relations themselves. To comprehend power at this level is to look for what Foucault calls the "tactical polyvalence of discourses"—that is, to look for the

> multiplicity of discursive elements that can come into play in various strategies. It is this distribution that we must construct, with the things said and those concealed, the enunciations required and those forbidden, that it comprises; with the variants and different effects—according to who is speaking, his position of power, the institutional context within which he happens to be situated—that it implies; and with the shifts and reutilizations of identical formulas for contrary objectives that it also utilizes.[72]

Language serves as data for the investigation of the strategies of power immanent in the institutions and the claims to knowledge that constitute the administrative disciplines. By viewing language "as *constitutive* of political phenomena rather than as merely *about* political phenomena" one can comprehend speech as an ongoing social process into which individuals enter when they become participants in social activities.[73] In a very real sense, language can be said to "have" people rather than people "having" language, since our participation in speech consists in joining an already existent flow of activity rather than initiating new activity.[74] Given the enormous pervasiveness of bureaucracies in all areas of contemporary social life, bureaucratic discourse invades and encompasses more and more of our personal and collective lives, presenting us with a "metaphor for living" that is reflective of the values and assumptions of the administrative disciplines.[75]

A *"Case Study" in Bureaucratic Discourse: Public Administration*[76]

The field of public administration, analyzed in Foucauldian terms, offers a useful window onto the general bureaucratic episteme. Adopting a term from Thomas Kuhn, public administration can be seen as a particular "disciplinary matrix," a set of shared knowledge claims, skills, techniques, and ideas of discrimination and relevance. The disciplinary matrix is "'disciplinary' because it refers to the common possession of the practitioners of a particular discipline; 'matrix' because it is composed of ordered elements of various sorts, each requiring further specification."[77] Public administration is a peculiar sort of discipline. The most visible offspring of the unholy marriage between political science and the state, public administration draws on interdisciplinary sources for its organizational discourse. In fact, its interdisciplinary standing is a source of some concern to its practitioners, who fear they will be engulfed by other disciplines and be unable to maintain their disciplinary boundaries.[78] Since it is very closely related in both its theory and its practice to its cousin disciplines of business administration, sociological organization theory, industrial psychology, and so forth, public administration can be taken as representative of contemporary bureaucratic discourse.

Bureaucratic discourse is created both within the corporate and government organizations that manage activities and resources and within the university programs (themselves bureaucracies) where the administrative disciplines are defined and studied. Such a school is, in the technical civilization, a "carrier," "an institutional process or a group that has produced or transmitted a particular element of consciousness."[79] The schools engage in what Foucault calls "social appropriation" of discourse: "Every educational system is a political means of maintaining or modifying the appropriation of discourses, with the knowledge and power they bring with them."[80] The schools are the carriers of what Alvin Gouldner has called the metaphysical pathos of bureaucracy—that is, descriptions and analyses that, by the language used, assumptions made, and values accepted, engender an attitude of positive acceptance toward the subject matter.[81] The dissemination of the metaphysical pathos of bureaucracy via the schools serves the function that Jacques Ellul names "integrative propaganda." In contrast to "agitational propaganda," which is "used to incite people to a frenzy of loyalty or animosity," integrative propaganda is directed "toward the resolution of conflict and the promotion of consensus" within a given setting.[82]

Administrative discourse expresses and reflects the managerial mentality both by what it *says* (which is also a form of acting) and by what it *does*. What it says, both by its statements and by its silences, is that bureaucracy is inevitable, necessary, and/or good. What it does is to prepare recruits for organizational life by training them in managerial skills and beliefs. The producers of administrative discourse claim for their utterances the status of "serious speech acts," those which have some "systematic, institutionalized justification" for their claims to truth.[83] These truth claims are dispersed through the society in part by the students of administration who go on to staff organizational hierarchies:

> Modern organizations are run by managers who are all schooled in the same organizational values, based upon the universal behavioral techniques. It is largely through the personae of the managers that the values of the modern organization have pervaded society. The national managerial system is a vast complex of interlocking management systems, sharing a common set of values, which control modern organizations and which provide order and stability in our national life.[84]

The schools, in short, provide a sort of spring training for the bureaucracy, both in the subject matter they teach and the ways in which it is taught.

The evolution of organizational theory reveals a history not of progress toward greater elucidation and clarity or toward more humane forms of organization but of continuing extension and integration of techniques of control. Foucault's description of the modern discourse on power can be applied word for word to the construction of the theory and practice of public administration: "It is the production of effective instruments for the formation and accumulation of knowledge—methods of observation, techniques of registration, procedures for investigation and research, apparatuses of control."[85] His analysis of the appearance of psychiatry can be appropriated to cover the appearance of public administration: the appearance of public administration as a discipline in the twentieth century was made possible by a shift in the relations between education, technology, the bestowing and evaluating of credentials, the role of the state, the degradation of labor and separation of work from the control of work, the rise of corporate capitalism and the service economy, the eclipse of the family, "in short, a set of relations governing a discursive formation."[86]

Accounts of the emergence of public administration, while differing in emphasis and scope, reveal common central themes. Robert T. Golembiewski divides its history into four phases, three paradigms, and one new perspective. The four phases are: the analytic separation of politics from administration; the concrete separation of politics from administration; "value free" scientific management; and public policy. The three paradigms are: the traditional, centralized, hierarchical model with a focus on efficiency, also referred to as Theory X; the social psychological, human relations model emphasizing participation and group decision-making, also referred to as Theory Y (or, more derogatively, as "cow sociology"); and the humanist/systemic model, a merger of the first two that seeks to put systems theory at the service of human needs. The one new perspective is the "new public administration," which takes on an "anti-positivist," change-oriented approach, emphasizing "relevance."[87] It is unclear how the four phases, three paradigms, and one new perspective relate to each other, but the new public administration, which Golembiewski calls a "miniparadigm" to show its theoretical modesty, has much in common with the third paradigm, which must be part of the fourth phase since it doesn't fit into any of the others. Golembiewski's own favorite "miniparadigm," organizational development

(OD), is presumably part of the fourth phase and the third paradigm as well, although this is not clear from his account. Golembiewski notes that the new public administration was a response to the challenges the discipline received in the 1960s: "For public administrators, the 1960s were like a war." [88] While this is gratifying news for those who identify with the counter-culture and the New Left, it does not hide the fact that the "new P.A." is simply a thinly disguised and warmed-over version of the old.

Charles Perrow's account of the emergence of administrative discourse takes a more limited frame of reference, but makes similar arguments. He traces the main trends in organization theory from their origin in Chester Barnard's *The Function of the Executive*.[89] Barnard emphasized cooperation as the essence of organization and assumed that organizations are functional for all of their members. Pointing out that Barnard's book is still widely used today, Perrow notes that, while it is primarily an apology for management, it fathered three schools of organizational theory: the institutional school, which looks at the whole organization rather than at its parts and stresses the harmonious penetration of the organization and the community; the decision-making school, which looks at individual rational actors calculating their costs and benefits within the context of organizational controls; and the ubiquitous human relations school.[90] Later elaborations on established themes have been contingency theory and environmental theory. Since advocates of contingency theory say that it means that "the best way to manage employee behavior is through the systematic control of the environmental events, both antecedents and consequences, that surround the employee," contingency theory, which also emphasizes technology, seems to be similar to environmental theory.[91]

These two examples are illustrative of mainstream accounts of the emergence of administrative discourse. They share a common discursive universe. They both assume that the emergence and development of organizational theory reveals a progressive evolution from less adequate to more adequate analysis. There is a "truth" that is "out there" in organizational life, and organizational theory is coming closer and closer to grasping that truth. Even when particular organizational analyses are acknowledged to represent the interests of managers (as Perrow says about Barnard, for example), the disciplinary project is a more or less scientific pursuit of the truth. Most overviews of organizational theory share this view of progress: the "bad old days" of Taylorism and scientific management are gone; more enlightened acknowledgment of the needs of employees as people have triumphed; even some tentative moves toward worker participation have been made. Like Priestly, Wedgewood, and the other early spokespersons for modernity, organizational theorists are generally enamoured with their contributions to progress. Blau *et al.*, for example, believe that the deskilling of labor at the turn of the century was a more or less accidental consequence of technological development rather than a control strategy and that it is currently being reversed:

> As education expands further and growing proportions of the labor force acquire technical and professional competence, the adaptation of computer technologies to production and office work will undoubtedly take these higher skills into account. While it is possible to automate many operations without raising the skills workers use, a highly trained labor force makes this increasingly unnecessary. Hence one can expect the growing automation of factories to raise the level of skill and responsibility of workers.[92]

Aside from the fact that "the growing automation of factories" raises the level of poverty and unemployment of workers rather than their level of skill and responsibility, what Blau *et al.* miss is the purpose of deskilling as a control strategy. It is not in the interests of owners or managers to end deskilling, and technological changes do not alter this fact. Similarly, Warren Bennis naively argues that organizations must become democratic and decentralized in order to survive in the face of the increasing professionalization of management, the turbulent organizational environment, and the rapidity of technological change.[93] Like their predecessors in the Progressive era, organizational theorists are the professional mediators between owners and employees, bringing the tools of social engineering to the pursuit of rationalization. Those who see themselves as reformers, out to correct the "pathologies" and malfunctions of organizations, proceed from an expression of faith about the ability of administrative theorists, if they pool their knowledge, to provide more adequate guides to reform.[94]

Within the administrative literature, discussions of personnel problems and practices are the central concern, since it is primarily other people that managers manage. Because the personnel "subfield" deals directly with the relation of the organization to its employees, it announces the human costs of bureaucracy very clearly. Also, personnel activities have tended to be among the least prestigious or powerful of administrative functions, so academics and bureaucrats in this area have launched a major campaign to establish their "turf" and to define their "objects" (people) and "events" (work) of study in such a way as to be able to claim a monopoly on relevant knowledge. They have been assisted in this task by the proliferation of federal regulations regarding racial and sexual discrimination, worker safety, collective bargaining, pension plans, and so forth. Knowledge of these regulations is important to bureaucracies. The job of screening the enlarged pool of candidates, and justifying employee selection in light of the threat of costly discrimination suits or strikes, falls to the personnel department.

A note of clarification is needed here. This is a rather dangerous argument to make because, as soon as one criticizes affirmative action, occupational safety, and similar goals, one risks being equated with the "anti-regulation" voices on the right. I wish to make my position clear. In the absence of genuine equality, legal provisions such as these are necessary; they are often the only recourse for individual employees seeking jobs or justice. My point is not to reject them but rather to show their utter inadequacy.

Personnel administration has a revealing, if unsubtle, history. Early conglomerates such as the Ford Motor Company first sought to normalize their recruits by employing investigators (called "advisers") "who visited the workers' homes to ensure that their homes were neat and clean, that they did not drink too much, that their sex life was without tarnish, and that they used their leisure time profitably."[95] Such overt regulation is usually unnecessary today, since people increasingly manage their dress, their leisure, their intimate relations in light of the demands of the organization. Advertising tells us how and television, movies, magazines, and books set the example: what to wear when jogging, playing tennis, or doing aerobic dancing; how to style one's hair, face, and body; what to eat and drink; how and with whom to be intimate. In the words of one representative column in *Esquire*, one is urged to take as one's "individual style" the same image that everyone else is adopting.[96] Personnel administration continues the work of the early investigators in more subtle fashion: both share the organization's conviction that control of the "human element" is "the very best investment" the organization can make. The goal is still to form "proper work habits," to control and direct emotional energy, to reduce conflict without acknowledging it, and to "improve morale."[97]

In *Classics of Personnel Management*, editor Thomas H. Patten, Jr., defines personnel administration as "the recruitment, selection, placement, development, conservation, compensation, accommodation to justice for, and provision of human resources in a socially responsible manner by work organizations in both the private and public sectors of the economy."[98] He goes on to claim that the activities subsumed under personnel management require the application of immense amounts of new knowledge ("the problems of managing the human resources of an organization must be approached comprehensively"), that offices of personnel management can fill a vital need within work organizations (personnel departments should "assume their appropriate mission is the maximum utilization of their organization's human resources"), and that, while this need has gone largely (and inexplicably) unrecognized, aspiring personnel administrators can take advantage of it to establish their importance ("while organizational units have operating responsibilities, including the management of financial and physical resources, organizations seldom have units specifically accountable for the maximum development of the organization's human capital. The personnel department can fill this void if it has a will").[99] Similarly, the authors of *Personnel Man-*

agement in Government bemoan the "netherworld" of personnel administration, but see hope for its increasing importance
in efforts to professionalize it and thus acquire a monopoly on
relevant information.[100] In their article "The Reasons for a Personnel Department," Ordway Tead and Henry C. Metcalf argue
that personnel administration is increasingly important because bureaucrats have discovered that the objects and events
they manage (human beings and human labor) are decidedly
different from the other kinds of technology or raw material
that the organization utilizes, and thus call for different administrative techniques:

> The fundamental reason for the development of a separate
> administrative division for the direction of human relations
> is a growing recognition that people are endowed with char-
> acteristics different from those of machinery or of raw mate-
> rials. And if people are to be affected in ways which give
> best results, that direction must be specialized just as direc-
> tion in the other major fields of management has been
> specialized.[101]

The power relations expressed in this language are indicated
both by what is said and by what is not said. As Foucault makes
clear, authorized discourse indicates and legitimates power both
in its statements and in its omissions; silence is "an integral
part of the strategies that underlie and permeate discourse."[102]
The personnel administrators reveal both the visible and the
invisible aspects of their discourse in four important ways.

First, the workers in an organization are seen as objects to be
manipulated and directed according to the needs of the organization. Despite claims to the contrary, Taylor's principles of scientific management coexist with and are complementary to the
"human relations" school. Both are part of the "adaptation of
labor to the needs of capital."[103] "Scientific management," taken
up by engineers, work designers, and top management, deals
primarily with the organization of the production process itself. "Human relations" is found among personnel departments
and their academic spokespersons and aims at adjusting the
"manpower" to the work process. Human relations strategies
work better on people with middle-class educational and cul-

tural backgrounds, who are more responsive to cooptation than to direct coercion; such strategies, as Richard Sennett notes, operate to "soften" the demands of authority without changing them, to "mystify what the boss wants and what the boss stands for."[104] Liberal feminists who praise human relations management as somehow liberating for women are revealing either their naivete about bureaucratic discourse, or their willingness to embrace it, or both.[105] As Braverman makes clear, "Taylorism dominates the world of production; the practitioners of 'human relations' and 'industrial psychology' are the maintenance crew for the human machinery."[106]

The turn toward "quality of life" and "job enrichment" programs is yet another step in the evolving managerial strategies of control; it gives the workers the illusion of participation without challenging the bureaucratic arrangement of the workplace.[107] Many workers are well aware of the emptiness of these company-sponsored "quality of life" programs; one factory worker attributed worker acceptance of such programs, even when the strategies the programs represent are a threat to the union, to straightforward economic motives: "Everyone believes they are saving their jobs." The quality of life programs are usually designed to camouflage the authority relations of the organization, not to challenge them. This man described his experience to me as follows: he and his foreman were paired as roommates and "growth partners" for a week of small-group activities, centering on communications games, in a pleasant rural setting. "You're warned the first day that you're there, you're supposed to be open, sensitive, the whole bit." The facilitators labeled those who objected to the setting as "snipers," and discounted resistance as "dysfunctional behavior." The object of the game was to pretend that labor/management relations do not exist, not to alter those relations. This worker concluded: "Once you're back on the [shop] floor the split [between labor and management] is apparent. A few meetings don't replace ongoing relationships. . . . They have to get you into a neutral setting for that to work."

The superficiality of these programs is made clear by those times when experiments in bourgeois self-management have actually succeeded and were discontinued for that reason. Da-

vid Jenkins cites a worker participation program at Polaroid
that was ended by the company because it was so successful it
showed the managers to be unnecessary; as the training director said, "Management decided it just didn't want operators
that qualified."[108] In an eye-opening interview in the *Harvard
Business Review*, Thomas Fitzgerald, then General Motors' director of employee research and training at a Chevrolet Division, argues against job enrichment with the "give 'em an inch,
they'll take a mile" line of thinking:

> Once competence is shown (or believed to have been shown)
> in, say, rearranging the work area, and after participation
> becomes a conscious, officially sponsored activity, participa-
> tors may very well want to go on to topics of job assign-
> ment, the allocation of rewards, or even the selection of
> leadership. In other words, management's present monopoly
> [of control] can in itself easily become a source of
> contention.[109]

American managers enamoured with the Japanese design of
work are drawn to it in part by its application of employee participation to management purposes, not by any willingness to
share power.[110]

Second, the personnel bureaucracy carves out its turf and es-
tablishes its claims to resources by becoming a resource for
other bureaucracies. To do this, personnel management must
be defined as a profession with a monopoly on a field of knowledge that is both necessary and otherwise unavailable to other
bureaucracies. Claims to new knowledge are often primarily
ceremonial in their function; that is, they elaborate and affix
labels to rituals and techniques, legitimated by claims to the
latest breakthrough in expertise, in order to define the new
knowledge as both scarce and valuable.[111] Patten expresses the
hope that the new knowledge of personnel managers

> can not only revitalize many segments of the employer in
> private industry or of its host organization in the public sec-
> tor, but can also expand its responsibilities to include those
> of an in-house group of applied behavioral consultants. This
> expansive role will hopefully not only reduce the cost of the

parent organization's operations, but will have a revolutionary [sic] effect on the content, processes, and personnel of
the personnel management profession.[112]

It thus becomes clear why anxiety over professional status is
pervasive in the personnel administration literature, as it is in
administrative discourse generally. One author anguishes over
whether or not public administration is a "true profession" like
law or medicine.[113] Warnings that public administration is a
field in "drift" and "crisis" are common, and concern over improperly maintained disciplinary boundaries seem to be at the
heart of these anxieties. Another set of authors calls for the
"further institutionalization of personnel processes" so that
only individuals trained in personnel management would have
access to hiring decisions and so that the "knowledge" this
training imparts would be clearly differentiated from other
knowledge. Invoking the seriousness of a quasi-metaphysical
commitment, these authors solemnly proclaim that personnel
administration used to be just a job but now is becoming a "professional calling."[114]

Third, the discourse of personnel management views the
problems of organizations as primarily, even exclusively, problems stemming from the malfunctioning or misallocation of
individuals within the organization and not from the structure
of the organization itself. The institutional arrangements of
bureaucracy are accepted as given, or, rather, they are not
even spoken of at all. They are not, in Foucault's terms, objects
of study within the administrative discourse. If organizations
have problems, these problems can be solved by personnel
changes; the language allows for no other conceptualization.
For example, Martin Gannon states that organizational problems often denote the lack of a "comfortable fit" between the
individual and the organization, but that this can be remedied
"through the proper use of job orientation, training, and selection techniques." He recommends "interviewing candidates to
be sure the individual's personality as well as his or her background suits the job's requirements"; this can be accomplished
by using the "weighted application blank," which selects individuals who are like those already "successfully performing"
in the organization in education, marital status[!], work ex-

perience, military experience, grades in school, and so forth.[115] (One would think that selecting on the basis of marital status would be illegal.) Gannon simply makes explicit what other writers of this genre disguise: in technical society the rhetoric of merit provides a thinly veiled rationale for a process of organizational cloning that calls for scrutinizing the soul.

It is hopefully clear that the devotion to examining the individual while remaining blind to the power structure of the organization is not simply an omission made by managers out to abuse workers. While organizations do routinely abuse their employees, many of the people who write about personnel practices are quite clearly well intentioned, sensitive to such abuse, and anxious to alleviate it. For example, Golembiewski's embrace of OD aims at cultivating humane values such as openness, communication, and trust. In the end, however, his goal is no different from those less concerned with psychic suffering: to change people's behavior toward one another without altering, or even naming, the political context within which that behavior is produced.

Fourth, the terms of this discourse make any talk of altering the work process absurd; issues such as genuine workers' self-management would never arise because by definition workers are objects to be managed and the work process is an event to be directed by others. Relations among workers, and between workers and their labor, are referred to as "human capital," and "revolution" refers, as in the above quotation from Patten, to expanded power for personnel offices. By appropriating the arena of approved statements, the makers of administrative discourse have disqualified the workers from the realm of serious speech acts. Calls for genuine workers' control are seldom confronted in the administrative discourse; they are simply not spoken of at all. The experience of the subordinates, articulated from the point of view of the subordinates, "flickers out of focus through the lens that organizational theory would have us use."[116] Warnings that the workers themselves may not conform to the definition of themselves that bureaucratic discourse offers are warnings couched in administrative, and not political, language. For example, one set of authors acknowledge that there is "evidence that employees are no longer willing to accept authority unquestioningly or refrain from expressing their dissatisfaction with management's personnel policies and practices."[117] But they then hasten to add that personnel officers can alleviate such dissatisfaction by proper human relations techniques. Another author notes that workers today are often dissatisfied with their degraded labor, but attributes this to "management's inability to design suitable jobs that adequately utilize an organization's human resources" rather than to the inability of the workers themselves to design their own work process.[118] Patten warns that "personnel must respond to the fact that human resources will increasingly demand freedom of action in the work setting and more opportunities to be innovative; appropriate psychological space will have to be found for them."[119] Thus protest is seen as unruliness among the "human resources," and the answer is in the managerial provision of "psychological space." No conception of rebellion is possible in this language, nor is it thinkable that workers could participate in the direction of their own work. The definition of the "best results" of bureaucratic activity can be defined only from the point of view of the bureaucracy itself; "human resources" have only a function, not a point of view.

Even organizations that have a conscious and serious commitment to an egalitarian, nonbureaucratic form of operation find their political goals imperiled when they enter into bureaucratic discourse. Since the bureaucratic world controls the distribution of crucial resources (grants, loans, "contacts"), alternative organizations, if they are not self-supporting, frequently must seek entry into discursive relations with bureaucracies in order to survive. While the terms of bureaucratic discourse do not explicitly forbid all experimentation, they simply leave no room for it. The goals of the organization become increasingly focused on the maintenance of the flow of resources that bureaucratic discourse makes available, and the discourse of egalitarianism and participation dies.[120]

Much of the personnel administration literature is taken up with the exploration of relevant techniques. This is in keeping with the evolution of all disciplinary activities, since they all rest their authority on the proliferation of standardized devices to measure, regulate, and control activities. Patten defines the

relevant techniques as "work group behavior, output restric-
tion, supervisory training, personnel research, interviewing
methodology, employee counseling, socio-technical systems
theory, small groups incentive plans," and related strategies.[121]
A fascination with technique, combined with a penchant for
acronyms, plagues most public administration literature; for
example, *Dynamics of Public Bureaucracy*, an introductory
undergraduate text, concentrates almost exclusively on intro-
ducing the student to such strategic tools as decision analysis
forecasting (DAF) to forecast "manpower" and organizational
needs; performance evaluation and review technique (PERT);
critical path method (CPM) for project management; individual development plan (IDP) to assess career goals and
"manpower" needs; planning-programming-budgeting systems
(PPBS); management by objectives (MBO); and zero-based
budgeting (ZBB). A warning that these techniques can sometimes be used to "provide an analytic gloss that can be used to
justify politically motivated decisions" is appended as an after-
thought and has no impact on the presentation of the technical
information.[122] The explicit medicalization of the "personnel
problem" is proposed by writers who claim to be the most concerned about the mental health of employees. For example,
while Golembiewski notes that he is vulnerable to accusations
of "cooling out" opposition, he quickly ignores this insight in
order to elaborate an extensive and incredibly complex array
of techniques that are in fact composed of highly dubious personality tests, tests of affect, and so forth. Calling on the pop-
psychological jargon of T group therapy, sensitivity training,
and role playing, Golembiewski's OD techniques marry the
strategies of EST-like self-help groups to the bastardized language of administration. (Part of OD calls for intense three-
day, twelve-hour-a-day seminars; he doesn't mention whether
or not members are allowed bathroom privileges.) His book is
full of org-speak phrases such as "low-discrepancy respondents
might profit from a more impactful design." Echoing the "creative divorce" jargon of the "I'm OK, you're OK" set, OD practitioners recommend T-group therapy for people who have been
demoted and note that demotion can be "just another learning
and growing opportunity." (By this logic, people who have been

fired should probably also be institutionalized.) Despite its intentions (or perhaps because of them) OD is simply a strategy to derail employee hostility toward the organization, to allow the organization to exercise power more effectively over personnel by manipulating their emotional needs at vulnerable times, and to discourage any effort at collective action, which is condemned as the "formation of cliques."[123] Dissatisfied workers, in this view, need therapy, not justice.

An excellent example of the control function performed by the strategic tools of administrative discourse is found in Richard E. Boyatzis's *The Competent Manager.* Ostensibly "liberated" in that examples are used in which women are managers and men are subordinates, this book suggests methods for applying Taylorism to personality. Boyatzis breaks down various dimensions of personality and role into different "job competencies." Each job competency, defined as "an underlying characteristic of a person which results in effective and/or superior performance in a job," then becomes a category of evaluation for bosses to use in assessing subordinates.[124] Basic interactional traits such as self-confidence, articulateness, and openness to others are formalized into technical-sounding subdivisions such as "positive regard," "use of socialized power," "managing group process." Elaborate language and complex statistical techniques are used to generate much form and little content. These techniques are presented as "neutral" tools for bosses to "help their organizations effectively use their human resources."[125]

Three important control strategies emerge from Boyatzis's discussion. First, because these performance categories are so far removed from actual human interaction or concrete human labor, they lend themselves to arbitrariness. Managers being evaluated in these terms would be hard-pressed to distinguish one category from another or to understand what concrete form of behavior is meant by each. Since these techniques could so easily become "covers" for other, hidden, criteria of evaluation, the vulnerability of the employees and their need to cultivate the good will of superiors is increased. So-called "objective" standards for evaluation in fact invite the most "subjective" kind of abuse.

Second, these performance categories take the basic human

abilities to take the perspective of the other, to empathize, to treat others with dignity and respect, and break them down into minute subcategories, thereby transforming them into nonhuman categories. The parts, in short, do not add up to the whole. Like the work situation of the flight attendants that Hochschild studied, interpersonal relations in the workplace are codified and standardized, divided and subdivided, broken down and controlled. Human interaction is reduced to the implementation of standardized procedures; real people and real relationships are lost.

Third, Boyatzis's description of the managerial environment reveals the perniciousness of the bureaucratic setting. Bureaucracy is a form of social organization that isolates people from any real human interaction while chaining them to the half-empty categories of organizational roles, rules, and language. If people simply *lived*, interacted with others as whole persons, engaged in common projects, they could learn the skills of self-assertion and communication that these categories attempt to capture. The claims of knowledge of the administrative disciplines reflect bureaucratic efforts to compensate for the absence of real community and genuine autonomy in bureaucratic capitalism.

The authors of *Personnel Management in Government* note with satisfaction that the rapidly expanding schools of public administration are busy providing techniques such as those Boyatzis invented; while these schools also pay passing attention to the "ethics" of administration, their more important function is the invention of technical skills that will guarantee to personnel managers the appropriate authority, status, and respect: "But more significant than all of the ethical considerations is the simple fact that the public personnel function is rapidly growing to include a variety of new skills in such areas as human resources, planning, productivity measurement and bargaining, job design, and test validation, among others."[126] In separate chapters on each of these techniques, the authors indicate a consistent preference for the most technologically sophisticated apparatus. Don Hellbriegel and John W. Slocum's popular graduate text *Organizational Behavior* allocates two pages to the discussion of "ethical considerations" in which they warn that some people object to the words "manipulate" and "control" but that there are ways to reduce such fears, one of them being to "emphasize the development of self-control."[127] Other authors appeal for a marriage between behavioral social science and personnel management, seeing in the first an important source of authority for the second. The personnel manager is urged to "become an applied behavioral scientist, using the principles and methods of modern psychology, sociology and economics to help management and workers optimize the total system that is the business organization."[128] The status anxiety of the personnel administrators and their academic spokespersons is again evident; since personnel administration, compared to finance, marketing, production, or engineering, is more precarious as an organizational function, the personnel staff needs to discover "the proper use of behavioral knowledge [which] can enable the personnel manager to have a more significant role on the management team."[129] Personnel administration is thus following in the well-trodden footsteps of all disciplinary discourse by marrying social science and administration, turning to "intellectuals turned technocrats" for the recruitment of theory, even theory rooted in a critical heritage, to the cause of social control.[130] Knowledge is reduced to information, and "thinking" is limited to that which is "routine, useful, perfectly predictable; a machine in which each part has a place and a function and a master operator who sets it in motion and makes whatever adjustments are necessary to keep it going, with no end in mind but the turnings of the machinery in the prescribed orbit."[131] The outcome of scholarship that serves these ends is as routinized and predictable as the outcome of the bureaucracy that is under study; the criteria of knowledge are standardized around the terms of the administrative discourse. The narrowness of professional education, in which "the real world is seen as by a submarine through a periscope whose direction is fixed and immutable," and the recurring reinforcement of the administrative outlook through examinations, screens out most of those potential recruits whose thinking might constitute a challenge to administrative discourse.[132] One experienced bureaucrat with some background in public administration, commenting on the relentless confinement of bureaucratic discourse to prescribed channels, lamented, "Bureaucracies survive by boring people to death." Administrative training increasingly penalizes students who seek a broad and diversified background and rewards those who specialize early; according to one administrator with several years' experience, a liberal arts background such as her own is no longer a common trait of those recruited into her agency. Those who have highly developed technical skills (in her words, who "do their numbers right"), who emulate the mannerisms and attitudes of superiors, and who seek "violent" solutions (who compartmentalize problems and try to solve them in a single managerial stroke from above) are the typical products of administrative training programs. Their career emphasis is encouraged in many texts; for example, Gannon includes special sections in his book in which he addresses students on topics such as "Your Career in a Changing World" and "Preparing for a Managerial Career," where he includes such useful information as how to tell if one is in the "fast track."

The creation of bureaucratic discourse reflects the nature of the links between the university and the public and corporate bureaucracies. The universities provide the training grounds for the professions, and the professions are able to control recruitment and "through their educational programs, examinations, accreditation, and licensing, very largely determine what the content of each profession is in terms of knowledge, skills, and work."[133] The government and the corporate bureaucracies then employ these professionals, supporting their professional activities through subsidies for research and education, protecting their autonomy, expanding their boundaries, legitimizing their monopoly on knowledge, and upgrading their rewards. This link reveals what Foucault calls the "tertiary relations" embedded in discourse, the linkage between the professional boundaries and occupational roles that is implicit in the conceptualization of the objects and events named in the discourse. Thus the meaning of public administration lies in the social relations that legitimize its concepts; the issues that come to the attention of those who write the administrative literature are those issues produced in the discursive relations among mutually supporting bureaucracies. Bureaucrats study bureaucracy not to know it but to strengthen it internally and externally.

The emphasis on technique elevates the values of obedience and predictability above any other possible table of values, and urges individuals to eschew conflict through the utilization of mechanisms for "resolving inconveniences in the smooth and efficient running of human affairs."[134] While those who write about organizational management occasionally recognize that there are conflicts built into the structure of bureaucracies, these insights are usually relegated to the periphery of analysis and have no central place in the discourse. As Perrow points out, "organization theory is shy of the word power, preferring to mystify it by calling it authority."[135] In his very perceptive book *Democracy and the Public Service*, Frederick Mosher explains how this mystification of the politics of bureaucracy affects the manager's activities:

> He [sic] is likely to seek and to find technically correct solutions to problems, even though the problems may themselves involve elements not contemplated in the technique—that is, political or social or interpersonal. Where the solution is patently non-technical, his instinct is to withdraw from open disagreements, hostility and aggressiveness in his associations with his colleagues; internal confrontations threaten both the system and its individual members.[136]

Since there is no language available to speak of conflicts of interest or to conceptualize bureaucratic relations as a struggle for power, managers do not and frequently cannot acknowledge that such things exist.

Bureaucratic Discourse and Political Theory

Administrative discourse is guilty of a "radical deafness" toward any nonapproved questions, and thus is hostile to many, perhaps most, of the usual concerns of political and social theory.[137] (This does not, unfortunately, mean that one can necessarily look to political theorists to resist bureaucratization; as residents of bureaucracies themselves, they often have the same organizationally induced deafness as other bureaucrats.) The literature of public administration is theoretically impoverished, politically dangerous, and, all too frequently, morally bankrupt. Hellbriegel and Slocum can be taken as a representative example of the formula for a "successful" administrative text: start with a chapter of watered-down systems theory; add a superficial treatment of learning behavior that centers on behaviorism and an equally superficial gloss of personality theory with passing nods toward authorities such as Jung and Piaget; sprinkle liberally with case studies and "problems" to be defined and solved from the managerial point of view; then fill the remainder with elaborate discussions of all available techniques and statistical strategies. Some writers, such as Golembiewski, simply dismiss theory as "counterproductive" because it shifts attention away from the "failure of will and skill" in the administrative literature toward abstract and unproductive analytic questions.[138] Others stumble onto the most elementary insights of political theory with great fanfare, reinventing conceptual wheels such as Edmund Burke's notion of unintended consequences with greatest enthusiasm. If "contingency" theorists and "environmental" theorists had ever taken Marx seriously, for example, they would not be so surprised to discover that capitalism affects organizations.[139] Similarly, advocates of "public choice theory" might be less enamoured of cost/benefit analysis and rational actor models if they had even a passing acquaintance with debates among Jeremy Bentham and his critics.[140] Spokespersons for the "new public administration" might be less bold about announcing the abandonment of the "old fact/value dichotomy" in favor of a "normative public administration theory" if they could see such simple pronouncements in light of the last thirty years of debates in the philosophy of science.[141] The more thoughtful pieces in this literature sometimes deal with situations and issues that would be useful to managers, but even then they are frequently simply formalizing and packaging information more easily learned on the job.

The "debates" that commonly go on within the literature on administration center on small questions, questions that beg the larger issues of coercion and control. Authors habitually and endlessly discuss the merits of different administrative ratios, of overlapping versus exclusive jurisdictions, of more or less centralization, of mechanistic versus organic organizations. The "touchers and feelers" argue with the "pushers and shovers" over how best to control people; no one argues against control itself. The more scholarly voices within the literature engage in seemingly endless classifications of organizations: Parsons, in terms of what organizations try to do; Etzioni, in terms of types of resources and compliance structures; Woodward and Perrow, in terms of types of technologies and "raw materials."[142] The more respectable of the academic typologies are useful in distinguishing among types of organizations, but still take the terms of administrative discourse for granted and stay carefully within the boundaries necessary for legitimation of that discourse. Specific bureaucratic abuses are frequently noted and decried, but never bureaucracy itself. For example, from William H. Whyte's classic *The Organization Man*: "The fault is not in organization but in our worship of it." From Scott and Hart's *Organizational America*: "The modern organization is value neutral in the sense that the uses to which it is put depend upon the values that guide it." From Charles Perrow's *Complex Organizations*: "The sins generally attributed to bureaucracy are either not sins at all or are consequences of the failure to bureaucratize sufficiently." And from Elliot Jacques's *A General Theory of Bureaucracy*, the claim that not only is bureaucracy innocent, it is natural: "Social systems cannot endure in the way the bureaucratic system has endured if they are not closely attuned to man's nature."[143]

That professional students of administration should defend bureaucracy and protect it from radical criticism is not surprising. In the terms of this argument, they constitute one more organizational elite using other organizational structures as resources to build careers, to gain lucrative consulting fees, to establish and fund undergraduate and graduate programs, to attract students, to receive grants, and so forth. To put the matter crudely, they know who they work for.

In sum, the proliferation of administrative discourse threatens the project of genuine political theory in at least three ways.

It is hostile to speculative thinking, to rumination on the perennial questions of human life. Such thinking raises questions that are not answerable by appeals to technique, perhaps not answerable at all, but are the epistemological and ontological foundation upon which instrumental knowledge rests. It is the kind of thinking Hannah Arendt likens to Penelope's weaving—unwoven at the end of the day and begun again. There is no appropriate managerial or technical response to such dialogue, and thus no room for it within bureaucratic discourse.

Second, administrative discourse is hostile to the rigorous self-scrutiny that underlies the task of political philosophy. Socrates's injunction that we know ourselves serves ill the goals of managers. Ruthless self-examination, the ability and willingness to scrutinize and judge ourselves in our own concrete lives, requires a commitment to self-knowledge that is simply not possible in bureaucratic language.

Third, bureaucratic discourse rebuffs the project of social criticism and political change. There are discourses of resistance, such as the one I am trying to create out of the experience of women, and they are found in the language of the oppressed, the excluded, the renegades, the critics, and the "losers." These are discourses that are capable of struggle and vision, but they are not welcome in an arena dominated by administrative discourse. Political theorists who are willing, for whatever reason, to function as appropriate bureaucrats may find a home in technical society, but political theory will not.

Three   The Bureaucrat as
the Second Sex

*Let us treat the men and women well, treat them as
if they were real—perhaps they are.—Emerson*

The radical feminist hostility to bureaucracy is
based on a well-founded, if not yet well-articulated, opposition to the consequences of hierarchical domination for both individuals and the
collective. The expanding bureaucratization of
the polity carries severe consequences for meaningful participation in public life for both women and men. Foucault's description of Bentham's panopticon serves well as a paradigmatic example of the bureaucratic domination of both the employee
and the client; following Weber's mechanistic analogy, he describes the panopticon as "a machine in which everyone is
caught, those who exercise power just as much as those over
whom it is exercised."[1] There are, certainly, positions of supremacy and privilege, but they stand within a context of universal domination. This chapter will look at the various positions of employees, both managers and workers, while the next
will look at the situation of clients. In both cases my argument
is that members of bureaucratic society are embedded within a
political situation similar in many respects to that in which
women traditionally find themselves, and are subject to a parallel set of forces and pressures through which subordination is
created and maintained. Thus the illusion that liberation will
result from the integration of women into existing economic,
political, and social organizations has implications that go far
beyond the familiar charge of "selling out." Such an approach
only expands the process by which women and other subordinate populations have been removed from active and authentic
participation in public life by extending it to increasingly larger
sections of the population.

The Organizational Class Structure

In Chapter Two I suggested that the linkage between the complex and multidimensional lives of individuals and the network of interlocking organizations comes primarily in two forms: in the definition of roles, activities, and events that are made available to individuals, and in the discourse that explains and justifies these roles, activities, and events. The different roles available in what one critic calls "the organizational caste system" parallel the general stratification system of late capitalist society. Beyond division among tasks and occupations, which would be a general characteristic of any complex society, the organizational caste system imposes a minute division and subdivision within tasks and occupations, a division not just of work but of the people who do the work. The organizational class structure divides the population into the elite, consisting of directors and top executives, who make policy; the "new working class," made up of highly skilled technical, managerial, and professional employees, who occupy the middle level of organizations; and the industrial and clerical working class, whose positions generally have low educational requirements and involve highly routinized, fragmented work. At the bottom are the marginal workers who occupy the "casual jobs" of the secondary labor market, whose relationship to large organizations is tangential and insecure, and who move back and forth between the roles of worker and of client.[2] In organizations whose "products" are people, the clients occupy the most starkly dependent role in relation to organizations and their resources.

There is a vast and confusing literature in the social sciences about the relations among the various strata of the organizational class structure, with particular controversy surrounding the concept of "new working class."[3] While many of these disputes provoke valuable discussions concerning the shifting class relations in late capitalism, the various claims and counterclaims about the "true nature" of the professional, managerial, and high-level technical strata are not particularly illuminating. The "in-house" debates among Marxists and neo-Marxists over the true definition of class disguise the fact that the appropriate definition of class changes in response to the particular dimension of class experience being examined. Looking strictly at the relation of a group of people to ownership of the means of production, as does Richard Edwards, leads one to see nearly all employed people as part of the new working class since they are all dependent on capital for employment.[4] Focusing on the self-definition of the individuals involved or on the type of work being done would result in different emphases. My concern is with the organizational context within which work is done, and in light of this concern there are both significant similarities and substantial differences between and among the work situations of individuals at the different levels of the organizational class structure.

The differences in the work context at different levels in organizations are particularly evident with regard to both occupational health and safety and to the level of task autonomy and corresponding intensity of organizational surveillance. The much publicized concern for the stress-related health problems of managers and professionals is cast in a different light when considered alongside the much greater risk of those same health threats, primarily heart disease, among those who do deskilled work over which they exercise little or no control.[5] Few white-collar workers ever experience anything approaching the daily work situation of people like Cliff Shields, who works in the foundry of a large automotive assembly plant. Describing the intense heat and constant oil mist in the air—"It's nothin' but a blue haze"—he commented mildly that after working there for a time "you could tell a big difference in your health." Pointing out the relatively high pay and the provisions for early retirement that his foundry job offered, he noted that there is a waiting list of people trying to get into the "hell hole" of the company: "They're paying me for five years off my life . . . but it's worth it. What the hell." He's willing to give up those five years because it allows him to avoid holding two jobs and gives him some time to spend with his wife and children. "I'm just a common man-on-the-street blue collar worker. I don't have nothin' to look forward to except my family."

Even in the somewhat less extreme conditions of the ordinary assembly line, the physical danger of the dirty, noisy, mind-dulling work is a qualitatively different situation than that encountered by the most alienated of the new working class. A laid-off auto worker captures some sense of this in her poem "Before the Robots":

> You say, "quickly tell me
> Before the robots came,
> What was it like to work the line?"
>
> I close my eyes.
> Onslaughts of noise split the air.
> Filth drives deep into my pores.
> Smells. Fumes. Foremen scream.
> Clothes glue to flesh and stink
> of mindnumbing exhaustion.
> Muscles melt. Eyes sting.
>
> No time to do things right.
> They don't want it right
> They just want it
> Now
> Fast
> Jobs roll to me
>   by me
>   past me.
> Turn. Run. Grab. Reach. Slam.
> Rivet. Fumble. Ache. Next job. . . .
>
> What was it like? It was my life.
> I cannot tell you all my life
> quickly. I can tell you only this:
>
> Robots
> always
> worked the line.[6]

At the very least, most professional/managerial/technical jobs are not dangerous in the sense that Doris Delaney's or Cliff Shields's jobs are dangerous. In 1970, 14,200 workers died from accidents on the job; 10–20 million were injured; and more than 100,000 died from occupationally related diseases.[7] Few white-collar employees face any imminent possibility of "cashing in" on the workmen's compensation benefits for loss of body parts: $2,222.50 for a lost ringfinger; $20,891.50 for an arm; $4,445 for a testicle.[8] The compulsory overtime, the graveyard shifts, the tenuous job security, and the brief and fixed vacation time and sick leave are all aspects of traditional blue-collar labor that the "new working class" does not experience, and in light of these differences it is almost insulting to lump the two groups together under the heading of the "post-industrial proletariat."

The levels of surveillance and direct organizational control are also different for the industrial and the clerical workers than for the managers, professionals, and skilled technicians in organizations. At the lower levels of organizations the amount of direct supervision is extensive and the amount of distrust and suspicion is high. (In fact, one of the advantages of foundry jobs like Cliff Shields's is that the work environment is so dangerous that supervisors usually keep a safe distance, compared to the close and constant supervision of the assembly line.) The vast, open, windowless expanses of desks and files in the "clerical factories," while less dirty or dangerous than the industrial plant, are similarly characterized by the more direct and tangible forms of control, because "when everyone has each other under surveillance, sociability decreases, silence being the only form of protection."[9] At the higher levels of organizations the controls are less obtrusive and thus more easily mystified, in that they are embedded in the work process itself and in the organizational vocabulary through which the work is defined. Unobtrusive controls operate without direct application of the rules by supervisors; like professional socialization or informal group pressure, these latent control measures are effective not because they directly coerce workers but because they narrow the possible universe of discourse to a small number of options. Schools, for example, often minimize control and supervision over teachers, and construct ritual categories of activities and events "to avoid inspecting the actual instructional activities and outcome of schooling."[10] Such organizational "slack" increases the commitment of the employees to the institution, while avoiding the difficult task of measuring "output" (teaching and learning) and sidestepping potential clashes among competing norms and values such as those between liberal arts values and career preparation. Schools can afford to exercise less obtrusive controls on teachers because, for organizational purposes, it doesn't really matter what the teachers do; it matters only that the school offer the appropriate institutional linkages to other organizations and operate according to the required legitimating ideology. Thus

> in educational institutions, feedback concerning the work and output of teachers and schools tends to be eliminated, even if it happens to exist. Participants employ the logic of confidence, and overlook observations of actual work and outcomes. Feedback on the categorical status of teachers, schools, students, and programs tends to be retained.[11]

In sum, bureaucracy tends to damage people in different ways at its different levels. There are very real distinctions between traditional blue-collar work and traditional white-collar work in terms of their respective physical settings and types of organizational surveillance. One can acknowledge these differences, however, and still address the important similarities in the organizational context of *all* the participants in bureaucracies. Excluding the top elites, who benefit from and to some extent exercise control over the organizational network, the remaining levels—the professional/managerial/skilled technical workers, the industrial/clerical workers, the secondary laborers, and, in service organizations, the clients—are embedded in a system that so automatizes, disindividualizes, and objectifies their activities and relationships that the power relations therein are synonymous with the activities themselves. The administered environment, as Foucault tells us,

> arranges things in such a way that the exercise of power is not added on from the outside, like a rigid, heavy constraint, to the functions it invests, but is so subtly present in them as to increase their efficiency by itself increasing its own points of contact. The panoptic mechanism is not

simply a hinge, a point of exchange between a mechanism of power and a function; it is a way of making power relations function in a function, of making a function function through these power relations.[12]

The more thoroughly the environment is penetrated with the mechanisms of administrative discipline, the more totally are individuals bound into the techniques of observation, regulation, and distribution. The power relations of bureaucracy are coextensive with the activities which they organize, whether they are educating, producing, incarcerating, treating, or consuming. This is power that is "not above but inside the very texture of the multiplicity that they regiment."[13] Control of work through control of the technological aspects of production, through the design of machines, the direction and pacing of work, and the architecture of the workplace emerged first in the factory and was later applied to the office. First the clerical function was "proletarianized," then the deskilling process invaded the technical, managerial, and even professional activities, robbing them of their autonomy and subjecting them to increasing levels of external control.[14] Conversely, bureaucratic control emerged first in the office and was later applied to production; the social and organizational structure of the institution—its job categories, wage scales, promotion and grievance procedures, disciplinary mechanisms—complemented and extended the original routinization of work. The traditional distinction between blue- and white-collar labor, while still salient in the ways noted above, is largely defunct as a description of the organizational context of work: "In post-industrial society the ideologies of professionalism and privilege on the one hand and consumerism on the other uphold [in the office] a social division of labor no less hierarchical and a structure of authority no less repressive than those among factory workers."[15] The system of control via the routinization and degradation of work produces the same disciplinary problems in the office that have plagued the factory; the organization's response to absenteeism, lateness, and sabotage, predictably, is to increase the supervisory function and thus both increase the resentment of the workers and their willingness to turn to collective bargaining, and also to decrease the efficiency of the organization by diverting more and more resources away from the actual doing of work. Barbara Garson sums up the problem well:

> The problem for management is that they must simultaneously suppress and yet rely upon human judgment. They need human beings and yet they fear human beings. They respond to that fear with an intensified division of labor and increasingly costly supervision.
>
> Eternal vigilance is the price of taking away other people's liberty.[16]

It is important to remember the complexity of bureaucratic domination, its ability to both *suppress* and *produce* its victims. Human beings are simultaneously pliant "raw material" in some ways even as they are resistant in others. Bureaucratic power is certainly repressive in clear and definable ways: it does cognitive and affective damage to its victims, rendering them "less responsive to themselves and their environment, more restricted in the scope of their actions, more cautious in their aspirations and rigidly narrow in their cognitive structures."[17] The incumbents in the higher levels of organizations lose greatest sensitivity to and flexibility in the arenas of concrete action, while the incumbents in the lower levels are made more insensitive and rigid with regard to abstract thought, but in both cases genuine cognitive damage has been done, rendering people less than they could otherwise have been.[18] But bureaucratic power is not simply negative; it is also positive in the sense that it actively produces the knowledge and the individuals that it requires. Foucault makes this point with uncharacteristic clarity:

> If power were never anything but repressive, if it never did anything but say no, do you really think one would be brought to obey it? What makes power hold good, what makes it accepted, is simply the fact that it doesn't only weigh on us as a force that says no, but that it traverses and produces things, it induces pleasure, forms knowledge, produces discourse.[19]

Historically, the emergence of administered subjectivity required a reversal of the individualization process characterizing feudal society. There individuality was the privilege of elites, whose deeds were lauded in oral and written histories while the masses of people lived lives unrecorded for either posterity or authority. In modern society the reverse is the case—the rituals of separation and objectification are descending, characterizing most starkly those in the lowest rungs of the social hierarchy: "The ritual of examination produces dossiers containing minute observations. The child, the patient, the criminal are known in infinitely more detail than are the adult, the healthy individual and the law-abiding citizen. The dossier replaces the epic." [20] As bureaucratic penetration of private and public life increases, the rationalized production of the bureaucratic subject correspondingly expands. Various forms of resistance persist in bureaucratic capitalism but they take place within a field of struggle in which partial and wounded individuals stand against the immensity of administrative absorption. Given the degree to which bureaucracy and society have become coextensive, to remove oneself from administratively defined roles, or to refuse to grant them importance in one's life, is to a large extent to forfeit most social connections. One may be free of the constraint of administrative conventions, but one has also lost the sociality (although it is a diluted sociality) that institutional participation entails. To embrace the administrative roles would be to lose those dimensions of oneself that do not coincide with one's organizational roles. While it is possible to try to resolve this dilemma by embracing one or the other option, it is more likely that the individual would try to balance the two positions, moving uneasily between them. Roberto Unger argues persuasively that this dilemma has given rise to the two main moral sentiments of persons in technical society:

> To the extent they sacrifice the private self to the public one, they surrender their individual identities. When they try to cast off convention and to follow their own course without definite roles, they undergo the disintegration of the unity of self. To suffer at the same time from resigna-

tion and disintegration has become the ordinary circumstance of moral life.[21]

Thus the cost of conformity is resignation, while the cost of resistance is disintegration; like other oppressed people, the victims of bureaucracy find that, whatever course of action they choose, the range of possible choices is determined by the organizational environment of bureaucratic capitalism.

Femininity as Subordination

Just as bureaucratic and technical power within organizations produces bureaucrats, workers, and clients, male power within families and interpersonal relations produces women. More accurately, it produces certain traits of character, styles of interaction, and patterns of thinking and speaking that are generally thought of as typically "feminine" attributes. However, these traits have very little to do with being biologically female, as the literature from anthropology and from studies of gender misassignment shows; but they have a great deal to do with being politically powerless, and with learning to play the role of the subordinate in social relations.[22] Since the traits of femininity are related not to biology but rather to politics, one would anticipate finding a similar set of traits in other subordinate populations; as Elizabeth Janeway has noted, "The weak are the second sex."[23] Any subordinates who are in frequent or constant contact with their oppressors have need of the skills of "femininity." This point has frequently been made with regard to the "Uncle Tom" role for blacks. Lionel Trilling has noted a similar connection between femininity and class among those whose aspirations outdistance their opportunities for class advancement.[24] The same analogy applies to the role of bureaucrats and clients, who find themselves in an organizational situation parallel in many respects to the situation that women have traditionally occupied, and who are called upon to respond in ways very like those conventionally used by women to deal with subordinate status.

As administrative control increasingly invades social life,

the incumbents of bureaucracies undergo a process I am calling "feminization." It refers to the spread of those individual
and group characteristics that are traditionally associated with
the female role: women are conventionally said to be supportive, nonassertive, dependent, attentive to others, and "expressive," while men are seen as analytic, independent, rational,
competitive, and "instrumental." [25] In the political context of a
male-dominant society, the expressive role is primarily a support role, one that allows women to negotiate the dangerous
terrain to which they are assigned, but that does so at enormous political and psychic costs. "Feminization" involves the
extension of the depoliticizing, privatizing aspects of women's
traditional role to the sectors of the population who are the victims of bureaucratic organizations, both the administrators
and the clientele. Both groups of individuals are placed in institutional situations in which they must function as subordinates, and they must learn the skills necessary to cope with
that subordinate status, the skills that women have always
learned as part of their "femininity."

It is crucial to define the term "feminization" with great
care. I am using it in much the same way as does Ann Douglas
in *The Femininization of American Culture*.[26] Looking at the
proliferation of the cult of domesticity in Victorian America,
Douglas uses "femininization" to refer to the spread of sentimentalism in mass culture, a sentimentalism that elevated the
values of purity, gentleness, nurturance, sympathy, patience,
and dependency to a higher moral plane than that occupied by
the more powerful expansionist ethic of laissez-faire capitalism. Feminine sentimentalism preserved crucial values that
were denied in the larger public arena, but did so in a way that
rationalized the cruelties endemic to that arena without hin-
dering or effectively challenging its "progress." Brought into
the twentieth century, feminization refers to the spread of similar traditional feminine traits to bureaucratically defined subordinates.

There is a careful line to be drawn between those aspects
of women's traditional experience that possess an integrity of
their own and thus provide a base for constructing a feminist
discourse, and those aspects of women's experience that reflect

their accommodation to the power of men. Further complicating the picture is the relation between these two dimensions of womanhood, since neither exists in isolation from the other. Compassion, generosity, solidarity, and sensitivity to others are crucial values; that they are more often found in the oppressed than among the oppressors indicates that it is the dominant social order that devalues these traits and that distorts them to serve the interests of the powerful. The distortion of powerlessness affects women's deepest psychic structures and cannot be dismissed as artificial externalities confining the real person. We would not object so strenuously to oppression if it did not in part accomplish that which it is intended to do, to elicit the complicity of the oppressed in their oppression and to produce subjects appropriately readied for subordination.

My critique of feminization does not therefore mean that the "masculinization" of the polity, the organizational extension of character traits traditionally associated with the male role, would be sufficient to ensure liberated individual and collective life. Women will not be liberated by becoming "like men" but rather by abolishing the entire system that allocates human potential according to gender. Nor does it necessarily mean that women are better prepared to operate as bureaucrats than are men. Bureaucrats use their "feminine" skills to imitate their superiors, while women use similar skills to please men, but not to imitate them. Women entering organizations are usually required to put aside the person-oriented values of women's traditional role in order to embrace the organization and prove themselves "one of the boys." Career advice to upwardly mobile women directs them to retain the form of feminine interactional skills but to abandon the content.

The main point of this feminization argument is neither to praise masculinity nor to allocate bureaucratic traits to women. The point, rather, is that the political consequences of male dominance are such that women learn the role of the subordinate, and that the role can easily become self-perpetuating. The skills that one learns in order to cope with secondary status then reinforce that status. The feminine role is inherently depoliticizing, in that it requires women to internalize an image of themselves as private rather than public beings. Women have largely been spectators rather than participants in public life, and the more firmly they have been integrated into the feminine role the more removed they have been from the public realm. Women are not powerless because they are feminine; rather, they are feminine because they are powerless, because it is a way of dealing with the requirements of subordination.

Many of the traits of conventional femininity can be subsumed under the heading of "impression management." [27] Women are often credited with being more responsive to other people than are men; their "women's intuition" allows them to sense other people's needs and motivations, and they can hold social interactions together by "managing interpersonal relationships." [28] For example, recent small-group studies have found that women are generally more responsive to nonverbal cues from others than are men. Men are more likely to initiate and control interactions than are women, even when the discussion concerns intimate topics; men are also likely to fail to respond to topics initiated by women, to listen more or less politely and then resume the conversation at the point of the last male comment. [29] Yet women are expected to be more personable, to display more emotion, and to volunteer more self-expression:

> Women in our society are expected to reveal not only more of their bodies but also more of themselves. . . . Self-disclosure is a means of enhancing another's power. When one has a greater access to information about another person, one has a resource the other person does not have. Thus not only does power give status, but status gives power. And those possessing neither must contribute to the power and status of others continuously. [30]

Further, men talk oftener and at greater length than women, and men are more likely to touch women (in nonintimate situations) than vice versa. [31] Women maintain more eye contact during interactions than do men, in order to obtain nonverbal cues and evaluate the male response. Women are more likely to back down from eye contact, however, once "the look" becomes a gesture of dominance. [32] Men interrupt others more often than do women, while women are more likely to *be* interrupted. Men tend to have more latitude in demeanor than do women, not simply because they are bigger but because they tend to spread out more, to move with less restraint (women's clothing often inhibits them in this regard), and to claim more space as their own.[33]

Women also tend to use language differently than do men. Women are more likely to imitate the speech of men than vice versa; for example, there are many exclusively "female" adjectives such as adorable, sweet, charming, lovely, and divine that heterosexual men are unlikely to use since to do so is to cast doubt upon their masculinity.[34] Women are more likely than men to use tag questions such as "It's a nice day, *isn't it?*"; such appendages make their assertions more tentative and less threatening, and give the listener an easy way out. Women also use voice inflection to make statements into questions, thus seeking approval or confirmation from the listener: Q: "When's dinner?" A: "Six o'clock?" Such practices render women's speech more "polite" and proper; they also avoid direct assertions or claims, leaving decisions open and avoiding the imposition of one's views on the listener.

Our culture's definition of femininity is such that one cannot know if she is being successfully feminine unless she has a response from another person.[35] The feminine role is one that requires continued recognition from males as the sign of success. Women are expected to provide support for others through a process Jesse Bernard has dubbed "stroking"; they are expected to maintain solidarity within groups by offering reassurance to the members, praising them, and raising their status.[36] Women are the providers of the support work of conversations as well as of relationships, restricting their own opportunities for expression in order to be "linguistically available" to men.[37] Most women are well skilled in the art of pleasing others. As Elizabeth Janeway has noted, this is a politically important skill: "The powerful need not please. It is subordinates who must do so—or at least it is subordinates who are blamed if they don't—and especially subordinates who live at close quarters with their superiors."[38]

Since women's use of impression management strategies is a situational response, one would expect it to change as situations change. The research on small-group interactions cited above is usually research on white women and men, and some black scholars have argued that gender outlooks and style of interaction are different among black women. For example, Joyce Ladner argues in *Tomorrow's Tomorrow* that the heritage of slavery, and the exigencies of ghetto life, have required an independence and self-reliance on the part of black women not usually seen in their white counterparts.[39] The slaveholding South made few distinctions between "men's work" and "women's work" for blacks, and survival required enormous physical, psychic, and emotional resources. In contemporary times, the chronic unemployment and underemployment of ghetto men makes the chances of a stable breadwinner remote; as one young black woman noted, most black girls know that Snow White is white, and that there will be no man coming to their rescue.[40] In this situation dependence and passivity are not effective stances toward the world, and they are not highly valued. Other studies, drawing on middle-class samples, show similarly traditional attitudes among both black and white women, suggesting that it is a particular *class* experience that constructs the context within which impression management skills are needed.[41] Certainly the traditional place of middle-class women in the nuclear family has contributed to their dependency. The nuclear family structure is one that leaves housewives isolated from other adults and from the on-going life of the community. Woman's traditional family role does not teach her to become self-assertive, self-confident, or independent. The most common types of employment for women outside the home—the pink-collar jobs, the service occupations, and the "helping" professions—may involve women in outside activities, but they also further reinforce the conventional role.

Variations in women's organizational experience, like variations associated with race and class, also alter the use of impression management skills. Until recently most studies of women in organizations and groups concluded that women are most concerned with maintaining satisfying personal relations, while men are most concerned with furthering their career goals.[42] A 1930s study that purported to examine personality requirements for women in business and professional life, but was in fact heavily skewed toward clerical work, found that the most highly valued traits were courtesy, responsibleness, and the ability to handle people. Careful attention to details, a pleasing appearance, and the ability to follow directions were also highly rated. At the bottom of the list were traits associated both with power, such as "forcefulness" and "analytical" ability, and with creativity, such as "artistic" ability, creative imagination, and originality.[43] More recent studies of women in organizations have produced mixed results, reflecting the changing situation of women in bureaucratic life. Women placed low in organizational hierarchies continue to value personal relations over career goals.[44] Given the fact that they are dependent on the approval of others, their concern for positive group relations is a realistic response to the demands and constraints of their situation. The powerless are always well advised to attend to the wishes of superiors; when one depends on the good will of those whom one does not control, it is important to be carefully attuned to their moods and attitudes, to present oneself in an approved way, to sustain the right image, and so forth. Women at the managerial level increasingly take the same career-oriented approach as do male managers. This does not mean that managers, male or female, cease to need the skills of impression management; on the contrary, as I argue below, such skills are vital, but they are directed toward somewhat different ends.

Bureaucratic power creates an arena in which the "feminization" of subordinates is encouraged. The victims of bureaucracy—both those who are the targets of control, especially the poor, and those who administer the control—have many of the attributes of femininity. They are isolated from one another, and as recipients of services (the poor) and approval (the bureaucrats) they are dependent on the good will of the powerful. Thus they are in need of the right image so as to impress their superiors favorably; the poor must present the right image to their social workers, and the clerks and bureaucrats must employ the appropriate image for their bosses. They often find it difficult to organize against the powerful, both because they lack resources (in the case of the poor, both time and money) and because they are separated from one another by the complex rules and regulations of the system. Neither group is encouraged or allowed to develop the skills necessary for political confrontation, which involve perception of and organization around a common interest. If bureaucracy, following Hannah Arendt, is "rule by nobody," then presumably domination exercised through bureaucracy is "oppression by nobody," difficult to locate and thus difficult to oppose effectively. This leaves subordinates even more helpless because, should they risk rebellion, there is no visible target. As society becomes more bureaucratized, there are increasing numbers of people who live lives perched precariously in this position; we are seeing the feminization of the polity through increased administration.

Genuine political activity, as opposed to bureaucratic manipulation, is ideally a creative process by which individuals order their collective lives. It requires an open public space in which common interests can be defined, alternatives debated, and policies chosen. It engages individuals in an active, self-creative process involving both cooperation with and opposition to others. Politics in this sense entails the empowerment of individuals and groups, so that they are able to do things collectively that they could not have done alone. The institutional arrangements of a bureaucratic society make this kind of politics virtually unavailable to its citizens, and the accompanying feminization process makes it more and more difficult for us even to imagine that such politics might exist.

The Manager as Subordinate

Many analyses of bureaucracy have generated typologies of bureaucratic behavior in order to describe, and sometimes to explain, the various kinds of career patterns that characterize the administrative process. Most of them differentiate among administrators on the basis of the attitudes the individuals hold toward the bureaucracy itself. In *The Organizational Society*, Robert Presthus divides the population into three personality types: the upward-mobiles ("those who react positively to the bureaucratic situation and succeed in it"); the indifferents ("the uncommitted majority who see their jobs as mere instruments to obtain off-work satisfaction"); and the ambivalents ("a small, perpetually disturbed minority who can neither renounce their claims for status and power nor play the disciplined role that would enable them to cash in such resources").[45] Anthony Downs offers five categories of bureaucrats, differentiating between those who see the system as a source of personal advantage and those who mix this motive with allegiance to some larger goal. The categories of purely self-interested actors are the climbers, who continually seek increasing power, income, and prestige, and the conservors, who seek convenience and security. Those with mixed motives are divided into the zealots, who are dedicated to their own "sacred policies," the advocates, who are dedicated to a broader set of functions or to the organization itself, and the statesmen, who are pledged to the "public interest."[46] Generally, it seems that the climbers and the upward-mobiles include the same type of individuals, as do the conservors and the indifferents; the three types of mixed-motive actors can be seen as variations on the ambivalent theme. Harold Wilensky's account of bureaucratic personality types suggests three not dissimilar categories: the professional adopts a service orientation and identifies closely with colleague groups outside the organization; the careerist identifies completely with the organization and its rewards, eschewing other ideological commitments or nonorganizational goals; the missionary holds visions of social change through organizational innovation and identifies strongly with some outside political movement.[47] Wilensky's careerist corresponds to Presthus's upward-mobile and Downs's climber, while Wilensky's professional and missionary categories are split between the anxious ambivalent, who both resists and fears authority, and Downs's three mixed-motive actors.

The considerable overlap among these typologies suggests that there are indeed common patterns of behavior to be witnessed among the participants in bureaucracies; however, this should not be taken to imply that all members of organizations fit automatically into some mold, nor should the relative ease with which these categories can be caricatured allow sarcasm to substitute for analysis. The structure of hierarchical organizations shapes the behavior of the members by facilitating certain kinds of activities and motivations and by discouraging others. Bureaucratic behavior is often a very rational response to the constraints that the system imposes on its members, just as feminine behavior has been a rational response to the constraints of female powerlessness. The various bureaucratic types can be seen as stances chosen by individuals to solve "the problems created in the network of organizational relationships."[48] Analyses of various bureaucratic personalities tend to overlook the very real struggle for personal dignity, autonomy, and recognition that often lie behind these patterns of behavior. It thus becomes all too easy to substitute simple castigation of bureaucrats for radical critique of bureaucracy. Just as bureaucracy pressures its members to merge their identities with that of the organization, so many of the incumbents struggle to avoid this outcome, as the categories of ambivalents, zealots, and missionaries indicate. It is important to recall continually that bureaucratic conformity is constantly produced by the organizational setting, where the lines of penetration between the individual and the institution carry a machinery of power that "questions, monitors, watches, spies, searches out, palpitates, brings to light."[49] The continuous maintenance and extension of bureaucratic power would be unnecessary if it were not being exercised on and through beings who are resistant in some respects, while vulnerable in others. The techniques of disciplinary power treat individuals as both their objects and their instruments; it is a "modest, suspicious power"; it "compares, differentiates, hierarchizes, homogenizes, excludes. In short, it *normalizes*."[50] The pressure to conform is the logical consequence of the recruitment process of bureaucracies, which continues the normalizing process of the educational system described in Chapter Two. As Frederick Mosher explains,

> The actual selection process, conducted normally under the direction of experienced career system members, should weed out those who are unlikely to conform; indeed, in

some fields that is its primary purpose, for knowledge and ability are taken for granted on the basis of college degree and passage of professional exams.[51]

A recruiter for one of the major airline companies makes this point well:

I had to advise a lot of people who were looking for jobs, and not just at Pan Am . . . and I'd tell them the secret to getting a job is to imagine the kind of person the company wants to hire and then become that kind of person during the interview. The hell with your theories about what you believe in, and what your integrity is, and all that other stuff. You can project all that when you've got the job.[52]

The companies, however, are apparently aware of such strategies, as their lengthy training program and mandatory annual recurrent training programs indicate.

This is not to say that there are no "deviants" in bureaucracies. Some nonconformists slip through, and generally they do so by being so good at their jobs that their deviations in manner, dress, and style are overlooked. They occupy the role Presthus describes as the artist, one who rises above the organization's values through exceptional productivity and whose nonconformity is accepted as merely idiosyncratic.[53] One experienced bureaucrat, describing the strategies she used to disguise her insurgency and retain her liberal values, said, "I live as close to the edge as I can get." Others resist by consciously or unconsciously forfeiting upward mobility; by remaining at the lower levels of the organization they avoid at least some of the pressure to conform. Nevertheless, these deviants act within an environment in which the behavior of the upward-mobile/careerist/climber is the most highly valued behavior. As organizational controls tighten, especially during economic crises when resources are scarce, there is greater and greater pressure on all bureaucratic incumbents to adopt the strategies of the upward-mobile simply to survive. Behavior and attitudes that might be tolerated as idiosyncratic when there is greater "slack" in the organizational setting then begin to be seen as unacceptable, as evidence of untrustworthiness or unpredictability on the part of the employee. Another interviewee, a white man in his mid-thirties, formerly the director of a large government research program, described the process by which his superiors made him into a "non-person," stripping him of tasks and responsibilities until resignation became the only honorable course left open. This man had initially "gotten by" through his ability to deliver on difficult assignments on short notice, but even his productivity became a threat because it was not controlled by his superiors: "If they [higher management] don't understand what someone is doing, he's a threat." Those who would be indifferents or ambivalents in a less restricted environment, one less penetrated with interlocking organizational linkages and instrumental rationality, have little latitude to stray from the careerist pattern of deference to those above and detachment from those below.

In order to comprehend the ways in which the structure of bureaucracy shapes, and ultimately victimizes, its participants, it is necessary to examine the various organizational norms and rules that are utilized in the search for certainty and stability. The successful construction of goal consensus among the members of an organization is one method for reducing uncertainty. Goal consensus is said to reduce the frequency and intensity of conflict among the staff and to enhance the reliability of the authority channels.[54] The phrase "goal consensus" is a common one in the organizational literature, and the very words suggest the linguistic mystification inherent in bureaucratic discourse. Those unfamiliar with the particular bureaucratic uses of language might believe that "consensus" would involve unanimity or agreement arrived at by some process of mutual consent in which the individuals who are party to the consensus had some voice in defining it. In bureaucracy, however, goal consensus is merely a shorthand term for the enforcement of the official definition of reality. Individuals recruited into the organization are subjected to a socialization process in which they learn to embrace the goals of the organization, or to give the impression that they have done so, or both. Anthony Downs makes this point well:

> If recruiting is done only at the lowest levels, all top offi-
> cials have to work themselves upward through the hierar-
> chy, presumably by repeatedly *pleasing* their superiors. Su-
> periors usually approve of continuous development of their
> policies, rather than sharp breaks with tradition. Therefore,
> the screening process of upward movement tends to reject
> radicals and create a relatively homogeneous group unless
> the bureau operates in a very volatile environment.[55]

In order to please superiors, the bureaucrat must develop the
skills of impression management; she/he must learn to present
the appropriate image, to anticipate the requirements of superiors and/or of the organization in general, and to comply with
those requirements in order to earn approval and promotion.
The personnel of bureaucratic organizations are thus encouraged to become like David Reisman's other-directed person,
who is "attuned to personal nuances, moulding himself in the
image of those above him.[56] This internalization of control
aims at convincing others, and oneself, of one's appropriateness
for the organization; one's self-image becomes a commodity
marshaled in pursuit of organizational advantage. As William
Whyte points out in his classic study *The Organization Man*,
bureaucracies make explicit "demands for fealty" from their
members; "the organization man" is one who identifies primarily with the organization and the group, who suspects the
outsider, who is often "rootless" geographically, following the
company via transfers, and who has a taste for the "regularized
life"—in his residence (suburbia), his family (nuclear, patriarchal), and his dress (conventional).[57] For the integrated bureaucrat, rationality is identified with the organization's goals:
"The rationality of the organizational member is not defined in
terms of the full range of the individual's interests, but only in
terms of a contribution to the accomplishment of organizational purpose."[58] Thus, in an article in *The New York Times*
entitled "How to Be a Good Subordinate," businessman Roy C.
Smith advises junior personnel not to have "too many 'new
ideas'"—that is, don't make suggestions that challenge the organization's established way of doing things.[59] When recruits
have been properly molded into "team players," it becomes

very difficult for them to define their own interests apart from, or in opposition to, those of the organization. Lamenting over the barriers that this loyalty to the organization poses to unionization, one organizer noted that "catastrophe, crisis, and militance are scare words to white-collar workers. They want to be dignified, professional, and loved. They want to be promoted; they want to be secure; and they don't want to have to fight."[60]

An excellent example of organizational efforts to elicit impression management skills from workers is shown by the Hochschild study of flight attendants. Since they are "frontline" workers, dealing constantly with consumers, flight attendants are trained in extensive image management vis-à-vis passengers as well as superiors. Attendants are trained by their companies to embrace unequal power relations and to attribute difficulties in their work to their own unsuccessful management of feeling and personae rather than to the conditions of work or the expectations of customers. They are taught "anger desensitization" wherein they learn to imagine acceptable reasons for unacceptable behavior and to distance themselves from offensive situations. Actual confrontation with the causes of their anger—obstreperous customers, belittling training programs, or objectionable company policies—are taboo because the attendants have no acknowledged right to be angry. They are paid, in part, to forfeit that right. In the organizationally approved language, passengers are "irates" or are "uncontrolled"—never obnoxious. Planes have "incidents," not "accidents." Attendants are taught never to "blow off steam" with fellow workers, since that might provide the collective support for anger and a sense of grievance of which unions are made. Rather, they are taught to identify wholeheartedly with the organization, to rid themselves of their anger through psychic self-manipulation, and, above all, to smile.[61]

The higher one moves in organizations, the more important impression management skills become; relationships become less rule-governed and more personal at the top, where there is more intense loyalty to and involvement with the organization. Here individuals have more of an impact on decision-making because decisions at this level are often not covered by existing rules and thus require personal judgment. At the top levels officials require more demonstrations of loyalty to the organization and to each other in order to compensate for the relative absence of formal rules.[62] Successful image management requires subtlety of word and gesture and acute attention to the nuances of interpersonal relations:

> Facial expressions, verbal responses, subtle unspoken expectations, provide the cues. . . . The upward-mobile reads the signals his behavior evokes in others. Although the skill will vary among individuals, the distinguishing mark of the upward-mobile is that he *thinks* in such strategic terms and is able to modify his behavior accordingly. Such behavior is essentially rational and requires an ability to avoid passionate value attachments that might inhibit one's versatility.[63]

The skills of impression management allow subordinates to shape their images in such a way as to approximate their supervisors. Given the impersonality of the bureaucratic setting, outward manifestations of trustworthiness take the place of direct personal knowledge and managers fall back on social similarity as a basis for trust.[64] The more similarity there is in outwardly identifiable characteristics, such as race, sex, dress, language, and style, the more likely is an aspirant to be seen as the "right kind of person" and given access to positions of discretion and power. Thus the patterns of racial, sexual, and class stratification of the larger society are reproduced in the organization. Frederick Mosher candidly points out that the public bureaucracy has always mirrored the class structure, and even defenders of the administrative system recognize that "most bureaucratic jobs, especially those in the higher ranks, are middle class in nature and require middle class literacy and educational credentials."[65] But educational credentials are only part of the requirements; the bureaucratic environment also requires the application of certain "cultural resources" that come with middle-class socialization and that provide the communications skills and mannerisms that allow one to perceive and emulate the nuances of behavior and attitude of one's superiors.[66] One of my interviewees puts it most succinctly:

"You have to learn the vernacular and emulate the vernacular. When you're working internally [that is, within a large organization] the internal communication is the most important. A lot of energy goes toward covering your ass."

Lower-class individuals, blacks and Hispanics, and women all encounter immense difficulties in breaking into the administrative ranks because they are identifiably different, they clearly do not "fit in," and their efforts to fit in are stymied by their lack of familiarity with bureaucratic discourse. Their lack of familiarity with the discourse is seen by the organization's elites as evidence of lack of "managerial potential"; one student of bureaucracy has gone so far as to suggest that those who have difficulty with the impersonal and universalistic authority patterns of bureaucracy—blacks, Hispanics, women, and the poor—are "childlike," while those who operate successfully within such a climate, those whose "basic personality inclinations coincide with the patterns of operation of formal organizations," are properly "adult."[67] Those who do not "fit in" tend to cluster at the points of least uncertainty within the organization—that is, at those positions that are more routinized and rule-governed and that require less stringent demonstrations of trustworthiness to gain admission. Since these positions also require less independent judgment and involve less authority, their occupants have less access to opportunities to demonstrate competence and thus to prove that they do indeed "fit in." As Rosabeth Moss Kanter shows:

> There is a self-fulfilling prophecy buried in all of this. The more closed the circle, the more difficult it is for "outsiders" to break in. Their very difficulty in entering may be taken as a sign of incompetence, a sign that the insiders were right to close their ranks. The more closed the circle, the more difficult it is to share power when the time comes, as it inevitably must, that others challenge the control by just one kind. And the greater the tendency for a group of people to try to reproduce themselves, the more constraining becomes the emphasis on conformity.[68]

The pressure toward conformity creates particular problems for the token, one who is visibly different from the mainstream in sex, race, age, language, or some other salient trait. The token is highly visible and thus stands out, getting attention from superiors, subordinates, and peers that both creates performance pressures and also exaggerates the contrast between the token and the ordinary personnel. Both the pressure and the perception of social distance isolate the token, and his/her performance is taken as the basis for generalizations about the token's "type." Those higher up in the hierarchy have a difficult time identifying with the token, and are less likely to serve as mentors for her/him. Thus the token, who needs sponsors even more than his/her peers in order to negotiate the hierarchy successfully, has more difficulty finding them.[69]

In sum, subordinates are required to learn to take the role of the superior, internalize that perspective, and apply it as a guide for behavior. Like women in their relations with men, the bureaucratic subordinate must learn to please, to "sense the moods and prejudices of his superiors," and to "adjust readily to accommodate their needs."[70] Subordinates are well advised to learn to anticipate demands, to understand the problems that superiors face and act to alleviate them, and generally to "help a superior to perform well and look good."[71] One of my interviewees, a young white woman in a responsible managerial position, viewed her anticipation of and accommodation to her boss's needs as a prerequisite for keeping her job: "I see her making gross errors and I know that I'm going to have to clean up. . . . She knows I see all of her flaws and I've never nailed her on them." This woman protects her boss from the consequences of the boss's own incompetence, knowing that the supervisor is "blaming me for the things that go wrong, taking credit for the things that go right." The worker's own competence is both a resource and a threat to her boss, and thus the worker must tread carefully, anticipating and deflecting problems that might turn the balance to her disadvantage: "I'm regarded by some to be very good and she [the boss] takes that as a feather in her cap. But then she is frightened by the thought that she could be replaced and she tries to discredit me."

Those who can utilize image management successfully can both defend themselves against the personal claims of others by appeal to the standards of the bureaucratic self-image and pursue advantage over others by presenting the appropriate face.[72] Successful impression management also benefits superiors because it provides reassurance that the goals of the lower-level members coincide with their own, makes the organization more efficient, and decreases the "relative amount of authority leakage."[73] It also may provide certain psychological benefits to the powerful; as one defender of bureaucracy has noted, "an aspiring bureaucrat who shapes himself in the image of the boss will enjoy immediate advantage. . . . A top executive will find comfort in being surrounded by a hundred likenesses of himself."[74] This process of "homosexual reproduction," in which "men produce themselves in their own image," does indeed help to minimize uncertainty within the organization, but it also undermines independent speech, thought, or action, discourages innovation, and closes off access to the decision-making levels for those who do not or cannot present the appropriate image.[75]

The emphasis on conformity within bureaucratic hierarchies is aimed both at the official rules and the unofficial norms. In his famous essay on the bureaucratic personality, Robert Merton points out that the process of goal displacement encourages the official to direct primary loyalty toward conformity with the rules themselves, as seen in the example of the "bureaucratic virtuoso, who never forgets a single rule binding his action and hence is unable to assist many of his clients."[76] The lower-level personnel are particularly vulnerable to this manifestation of goal displacement, for they are both accountable for their own actions and also dependent for proper results on the actions of those over whom they have no control. Thus "the powerless inside an authority structure often become rules-minded in response to the limited options for power in their situation, turning to 'the rules' as a power tool."[77] The simultaneous need to please the powerful while being relatively powerless oneself tends to create a great deal of anxiety within the individual. The need to please is intensified by the fact that the bureaucrat has no criteria to judge her/his performance outside of the response of her/his supervisors in particular, or of the organization in general:

Bureaucratic conditions, moreover, reduce the opportunity for achieving status at the same time that they stimulate the desire for it. The separation of the worker from his tools and his impotence in a big organization tend to reduce the opportunity for individual independence and self-realization. At the same time, the minute gradations in bureaucratic income, skill and seniority intensify the desire to assert one's uniqueness.[78]

Like women who need the approval of men in order to judge their success or failure at femininity, bureaucrats need the approval of superiors or of the organization in order to know if they have succeeded or failed.

Subordinates in bureaucracies, like subordinates in gender relations, often turn to rumor and gossip as a resource to gain information that would not otherwise be available. Anthropologist Susan Harding has shown that the traditional exchange among women in information, observations, and opinions, derogatively referred to as "woman talk" or gossip, is an important political resource in that it effects reputations and images.[79] But while rumors may serve as a resource, they simultaneously operate as social control devices in that they enforce conventional behavior and warn members of the consequences of social disapproval.[80] John DeLorean gives examples of both aspects of the rumor mill in his account of his career in General Motors. As he states, "Rumors were a way of life." Rumors were useful in allowing subordinates to anticipate the bosses' preferences; he gives many examples of the extreme lengths to which subordinates would go to accomplish this and thus ingratiate themselves with their boss. He also furnishes some telling examples of times in which rumors about personnel changes intimidated other managers and had the effect of punishing those perceived as "mavericks." The high status given to rumor, innuendo, and hearsay is illustrated in his claim that the managers habitually took notes on and kept records of personal conversations, thus contributing to a climate in which the least individual deviation could spell disaster and "management by intimidation" was the norm.[81] In such an environment ability or experience count for little compared to the all-important need to *please*, to be only what one is expected to be, to forego imagination, creativity, or risk in favor of that which is stable, predictable, and safe.

The Industrial and Clerical Worker as Subordinate

The ongoing deskilling of labor inherent in bureaucratic capitalism has erased many of the traditional distinctions between "blue-collar" and "white-collar" work. In fact, the increasing mechanization of production and the replacement of workers with robots may erase the category of "blue-collar" labor entirely; many of the factory workers I interviewed believed strongly that "their kind" is a "dying breed." The application of Taylor's scientific management principles to clerical work has resulted in the creation of "clerical factories" where the skills of the secretary are fragmented and reassigned to the members of the typing pool, the steno pool, the filing pool, and so forth. Similarly, the use of sophisticated computer and word-processing technology, and the fragmentation of human relations in the workplace, increasingly reduces the skills of middle management to those of simple technicians. The bureaucratic "atrophy of competence" affects work at nearly all levels of organizational life."[82]

In clerical work the deskilling entails an interesting shift in the relation of the worker to her work. (Since these jobs are overwhelmingly held by women it is empirically accurate to use the female pronoun. In fact, the office efficiency literature commonly refers to key punch operators as "girls.")[83] The traditional secretary-boss relation is in many ways a feudal relation; bosses exercise patrimonial authority over secretaries in that they can

make demands at their own discretion and arbitrarily, choose secretaries on grounds that enhance their own personal status rather than meeting organizational efficiency tests, expect personal service with limits negotiated privately, exact loyalty, and make the secretary a part of their private retinue, moving when they move.[84]

In her excellent analysis of the position of the "office wife" in the organization, Kanter shows that the secretary's position requires the utilization of typically feminine strategies of image management in order to please those in authority. The secretary's working conditions encourage parochialism (a close identity with the boss and a corresponding narrowness of concerns), self-effacement and timidity (little chance to develop further skills and an accompanying lack of confidence in the ability to develop them), praise addiction (and a corresponding fear of taking on tasks that might evoke criticism from others), and an attitude of assumed helplessness and emotional manipulation.[85] Successful performance of the traditional secretarial role requires skills of impression management identical in many respects to those characterizing male-female relations generally. The shift to the clerical factory redefines the relation from a feudal to a modern context, replacing the personal secretary-boss relation with the more impersonal employee-manager relation. The constraints and rewards of personal, face-to-face supervision and service are replaced by the more diffuse and impersonal controls of the organization itself.

Since the paradigmatic example of deskilled labor continues to be the factory, the impact of routinized labor on the worker is most starkly revealed there. Because there is so little latitude or room for variation in the tasks, there is little room to demonstrate creativity, enterprise, or initiative on the job. A worker can be either reliable or unreliable from the point of view of management, but it is impossible to be excellent. Further, the pressure on workers to produce a large quantity of products and to meet the established quotas means that there is little real attention paid by management to the quality of the product (even though there are endless exhortations to the workers to do so). As Doris Delaney's poem stated, "They don't want it right/they just want it/now/fast." Two of my interviewees, a husband/wife team in which the wife, with seven years of factory experience, was laid off indefinitely, and the husband, with twenty-two years, expected to be laid off soon, explained that the structure of the work process in the auto assembly plant where they worked undermined quality in favor of sheer quantity of output. The people in charge of quality control are assigned to inspect a certain percentage of the parts that come off the line and to "red tag" those with a significant number of bad parts. But the foreman on the line has a quota to meet and will frequently change the "red tag" to a "green tag" so that the part can be sent on. Since the quality control personnel are regular factory workers who want to retain their relatively easier job assignments, the change of tags usually goes unprotested or unnoticed. In other words, both the foreman and the quality control workers have an interest in placing quantity over quality.

The frustration of the worker who tries to do quality work is emphasized both in the literature about blue-collar workers and in the interviews I conducted. One response to the frustration and abuse of the assembly line (that most often emphasized by management) is sabotage. A young mechanic told me, with obvious relish, a perhaps apocryphal story that illustrates the grim satisfaction to be had from creative sabotage. He worked for hours on a mysterious ailment in a new and expensive car brought in by an irate owner, and eventually traced the problem to a small plastic bag hidden inside one of the parts. In the bag was a note that read: "So you finally found this, you rich bastard." In the clerical workplace sabotage is also common; in my own experience in a large clerical factory, missing files were frequently discovered by maintenance people in unused closets, behind file cabinets, and under furniture.

But despite management efforts to attribute low-quality products to defective workmanship, deliberate sabotage seems to be surprisingly rare. More persistent is the near heroic effort of many workers to find ways to make their mind-numbing work more interesting and to stave off boredom. Barbara Garson reports that "whatever creativity goes into sabotage, a more amazing ingenuity goes into manufacturing goals and satisfactions in jobs where measurable achievement has been all but rationalized out."[86] The routinization of work involves the simultaneous denial that the workers have skills and the deliberate effort to minimize the opportunity for the workers to develop skills. Thus Cliff Shields, the foundry worker cited above, is prohibited by the company he works for from fixing the machine he works on, even though he knows how to fix it and the repair crew does not. His machine is frequently "down" for hours or even days at a time; when he does do his own repairs, management chastises him for it and sends in the repair crew to undo his work and reset the machine improperly again. He is acutely aware that this is not simple stupidity on the part of management, but is instead a deliberate effort to avoid acknowledging his skills and to remove from his task the aspects of it that are enjoyable and fulfilling. Reflecting that "I despise factory work. I enjoy working with machinery," he expresses the widespread resentment by factory workers against a work organization that prefers a loss of profit to a loss of control.

Workers are treated like children in both the industrial and the clerical factories. John DeLorean notes the "outright contempt for the working person" that permeates the organization.[87] The Tayloresque view of workers is much like the traditional view of women: that they have their own jobs for which they are uniquely suited, but that they are too stupid to learn to do the labor of men or of managers. Another young factory worker reflected that workers who do simple and routinized tasks are treated as though they were simple people: "It's like going back to high school. . . . You've got your dean, your principal, your teacher . . . only now it's your general foreman, your superintendent." Whenever the actual doing of work is divorced from the making of decisions about work, the decision-makers' claims to competence are upheld by a parallel set of assertions about the incompetence of workers. Hierarchical social control at all organizational levels is maintained by ritualized assertions of the inability of subordinates, accompanied by concerted efforts to make such assertions come true:

> The price of social control is the continual and mundane demonstration of the citizen's inadequacy and error. Thus stability is purchased at the cost of the continual degradation of the members of the organization. Life is possible in such contexts of control, but living in them means learning not to see, not to feel, not to judge, not to discriminate. The

resulting schizophrenic responses to such contexts represent a derangement of human theoretical capacities.[88]

The self-fulfilling nature of the deskilling process reaches its logical conclusion when assembly line workers, especially those accustomed to the relatively high pay of unionized shops, not only accept the mindlessness of their jobs but begin to see it as a benefit; they have to put their time in, but at least they don't have to think about it. An unemployed auto worker who desperately needed a job to support herself and her teenage daughter told me bluntly: "I don't want any kind of job where I have to use my mind." She viewed her work as a form of highly paid incarceration, not unlike that of prisoners or soldiers; symbolically, the phrase "how much time you got?" could be used in any of the three institutional contexts to inquire about seniority. Truly, with Foucault, we can see the echo of the prison in the factory.

As the deskilling of work penetrates further and further up the organization, the experience of manual workers will be increasingly illustrative of the overall context of the workplace. Industrial workers are traditionally more aware of the organizational controls exercised over them than are white-collar employees, who have more of the trappings of respectability in their jobs. A white man in his late thirties, who had recently moved to an office job in the union after many years as a laborer, saw little difference between the two jobs with respect to organizational controls: "Everybody's being worked. Shoot, I'm worked every day in the factory. It's just another way of being worked." As deskilling penetrates up the organization, the use of impression management techniques penetrates down; upward mobility through excessive conformity to the norms and rules of the organization often characterizes the factory as well as the office. A worker on the assembly line who seeks promotion to foreman becomes an exemplary worker; since the routinization of tasks makes it impossible to demonstrate outstanding or unique ability, the aspirant must instead manipulate his/her appearance and behavior in conformity with managerial norms. Such individuals begin to dress more formally, replacing assembly line "grubbies" with casual leisure clothes for men and the "tailored look" for women, despite their inappropriateness for the hot and dirty factory environment. They emulate managerial behavior by, for example, swearing less and by joining appropriate outside groups such as the country club or the Masonic Lodge, often dropping their unapproved Catholicism to do so and thus demonstrating their fealty and fitness.[89] Other workers on the line observe that the aspirant has become more friendly with the foreman and that she/he gets preferred treatment from the foreman. They also note that the foreman possesses information about the remaining workers that he/she does not usually have, showing that someone has "squealed."[90] Thus the promotion process screens for applicants who are the most pliant, the least resistant to pressure to conform, and the most willing to police former colleagues. (Or, as my interviewees more bluntly stated, it selects for the "biggest assholes.")

The character traits outlined in this overview of bureaucratic behavior—impression management, need to please, conformity, identification with the organization, dependency, and so forth—are a double-edged sword for those who work and live within bureaucracies. On the one hand, learning such skills may be a necessary precondition for economic and professional survival, since they are strategies for learning to protect oneself from the exercise of power. Given the structure of bureaucracy, a structure in which most individuals, as individuals, are at a disadvantage vis-à-vis the organization, such survival tactics may be avenues by which the powerless make the best of an unhappy situation. However, the tactics serve to further bind the individual to the organization and to further cement his/her dependency upon it.

Women and Organizational Resistance

Those who resist organizational oppression do so from within the very structure that creates that oppression. Embedded within bureaucratic discourse and institutions, resistance is carried out in bureaucratic terms by people whose subjectivity has been shaped and distorted by the requirements of technical society. But since resistance is a political act, bureaucracy's claim to be nonpolitical mystifies the very act of resisting. Bureaucratic experience mystifies political action both by inhibiting the process of totalization (the creation of a coherent picture of the whole) and by obliterating alternatives. The ability to totalize one's situation, to root it in its social and temporal context, is hampered by the fragmentation of tasks and the isolation of roles; it is difficult to construct the "big picture" when many of the pieces are not visible. The minute division of tasks distances each individual participant from the end result, obscuring each person's contribution to the whole and permitting her/him to feel uninvolved and devoid of responsibility for organizational outcomes. Similarly, the ability to imagine alternatives is blocked by the pervasiveness of technical definitions of problems and solutions; the debased language, the absence of public debate and of shared channels for collective action, and the intolerance of uncertainty and diversity result in what Murray Bookchin has called "the mute society," one that is "divested of self-articulation." [91] Bureaucratization further inhibits alternatives by its constant encroachment onto other organizations; efforts at nonbureaucratic organization frequently fail because they must appeal to conglomerates for resources, requiring the alternative organization to become like the bureaucracy in order to deal with it effectively. Finally, bureaucracies inhibit the ability to conceptualize and pursue alternatives simply because they are able to offer tremendous inducements—frequently high or at least stable salaries, security, status, and a sense of order. For example, Richard Edwards's case study of bureaucratic inducements offered to the workers at the Polaroid Company concluded that

> the positive incentives, the relief from capricious supervision, the right to appeal grievances and bid for better jobs, the additional job security of seniority—all these make the day-to-day worklife of Polaroid's employees more pleasant. They function as an elaborate system of bribes, and like all successful bribes, they are attractive. But they are also corrupting. They push workers to pursue their self-interests in a narrow way as individuals, and they stifle the impulse to struggle collectively for those same self-interests. [92]

Bureaucratic domination, for those who are employees and not clients, usually "does not terrorize; nor does it persuade on rational grounds. It erects a structure that obliterates alternative styles of life and lures the mind by what it offers."[93]

In blue-collar situations the possibilities for opposition are, on the surface, greater, since the relation between workers and management, especially in union shops, is recognized as an adversary relation. Plants with a strong union local can often get better enforcement of the provisions of the contract and thus make a significant difference in the work situation of the individual employees.[94] The practice of opposing the management by calling in the union is a recognized role that some workers consciously decide to take on themselves. It has its own language and rituals. The worker who declares war on the company, at least among those factory workers I interviewed, is known as a "mad dog." Such a person is usually a rebel or misfit in other ways as well—a heavy drinker or pot smoker, a fighter, a "wild" person, or perhaps an intellectual. Mad dogs frequently have outside sources of income such as a working spouse, a farm, a private shop, or a construction job, thus minimizing the financial risk of their opposition. When a mad dog spots a problem that is "strong enough to do paper on" (a serious violation of the union agreement, such as a speed-up of the line or a violation of seniority), she/he calls the foreman. If the foreman's answer is unsatisfactory, she/he asks for the shop committeeman ("call the man"). The worker and the union representative confer about the problem. If the committee representative sees a good case, the foreman is called in and bargaining proceeds. Conflicts unresolved at this level are reported to higher levels of the company and the union as a stalemate, through an elaborate and time-consuming ritual of paperwork. A real mad dog will "put in a call" every day, but is otherwise a model worker to avoid being vulnerable to retribution from management. Several of the workers I interviewed either saw themselves as mad dogs or identified with those who were. The husband/wife team quoted above, who, while in their mid-thirties to late thirties in age, between them have thirty years of assembly line experience, both recounted their experiences as mad dogs. Cindy Carson learned the details of the union contract so effectively that she could often outmaneuver the foreman and outargue her committeeman. Reflecting on management's efforts to coopt resistant workers, she commented that the bosses had learned from their experience with labor rebels in the 1930s: "You don't go out and hit them in the head anymore. You just absorb them." Her husband Phil pursues his mad dog role by using the organization against itself, appealing to the espoused standards of quality and safety to protest the poor parts and inadequate planning that he sees behind the low quality of the cars he helps to make: "If I'm gonna buy that son-of-a-bitch, I want what I'm paying for." Both scorn what they call the "bullshit conferences" where management calls in the workers to "talk out problems" in an encounter group setting. When the ventilation at his station broke down and the company ceased to make even the pretension of trying to remove the fiberglass particles from the air, Phil Carson confronted the organization directly by going to the front office of his plant and asking for the phone number of the Occupational Safety and Health Administration (OSHA). Speaking of her husband's confrontations with management, and his appeal to the official ideology of productivity and safety, Cindy described his tactics as confrontation from within: "He's learned the rules of *their* game."

The relatively strong unions in their shops enable workers such as Cindy and Phil Carson to utilize these tactics. In some shops the committee person is weak, either because he/she fears retribution from management (the foreman can fire the committee representative, so the person whose job is to defend the workers from management abuses is himself/herself vulnerable to those abuses) or because the workers in the shop don't put in enough calls and allow contract violations to become standard procedures. The mad dogs are sometimes resented by other workers, particularly older workers, who see them as "troublemakers" who endanger the good will of the company and earn the opprobrium of the foreman. One worker, who has invoked the union against the company only twice in his eight years in the factory, complained that the activists used the union contract to avoid doing their work: "That's just their main lawyer." Commenting on this attitude, most of the mad dog workers agreed that, while they were viewed with suspicion and distrust by the more conservative or fearful employees, still the camaraderie with others in the factory was its only redeeming feature: "The best part of the factory is the other people."

In white-collar work there is usually no exact equivalent to the mad dog role, although the increasing routinization of low- and middle-level white-collar work and the corresponding rise in unionization may alter this. In particular, clerical and office work is simultaneously becoming more fragmented and alienating, and also more important in the aggregate, since communications is the key to organizational operations.[95] But for the most part the bureaucrat is prone to avoid conflict, to "withdraw from open disagreements, hostility and aggressiveness in his associations with his colleagues; internal confrontations threaten both the system and its individual members."[96] Like women in their relations with men, bureaucrats tend to avoid open confrontation with superiors, to fragment their demands into less objectionable pieces, to "rate diversion and envelopment more highly than direct frontal assault."[97] When genuine opposition does emerge, it generally takes one of two forms: either disputes over individuals, involving opposition to deviation from the bureaucratic ideal (for example, bureaucratic malfeasance of some sort, such as discrimination, corruption, incompetence due to alcoholism, mental illness, or overt disrespect and dishonorable behavior toward subordinates), or disputes over policy, involving opposition to policies that contradict either the norms of bureaucratic efficiency or the general organizational goals or some moral principle held by the employee.[98] Strategies of enactment in bureaucratic opposition are similar in most respects to those undertaken by dissidents in authoritarian political systems, pointing again to the authoritarian nature of bureaucracy: the formation of clandestine informal groups, the use of symbolic protests, appeals to outside or higher authority (for example, whistle-blowing), manipulation of the rules (for example, work to rule), and so forth.

The similarity between the strategies of the mad dog in the unionized factory and those of bureaucratic opponents in general indicates that, even in the most overtly and openly politicized organizational environment, resistance within the organization is a very limited activity. Mad dogs are usually reacting to abuses by particular foremen, and their attack is generally on that individual rather than on the organization as a whole. Bureaucratic opposition of necessity is aimed at limited personnel or policy reforms, not at the transformation of the social setting within which the bureaucracy is situated. Successful bureaucratic oppositions may succeed in removing the abusive individual or altering the objectionable policy, and may also arouse in other employees a spirit of defiance that makes future oppositions more likely. These are not negligible gains, but they leave the bureaucratic order intact.

In light of this conclusion, liberal feminist hopes that organizations will be rendered humane, less oppressive, and more conducive to genuine personal growth by the inclusion of women are revealed to be naive and pious hopes. Advocates of this view scrupulously avoid any critique of organizations as power structures and center instead on the harm that the exclusion of women has allegedly inflicted on everyone and the corresponding benefits to all when women are included: men will be more well-rounded; managers will be more effective; organizations will be more humane; capitalism will be both more compassionate and more successful.[99] Their claims echo those of the personnel managers, asserting that the interests and values of all individuals and groups in the organization are either identical or compatible, and that the interests and values of women (and of feminists) are either identical to or compatible with the interests of bureaucratic capitalism.

I am suggesting the opposite conclusion. By viewing feminization as a political rather than a biological process, one then sees feminization, in the sense used here, as the structural complement of domination. As long as one group of people is primarily concerned with maintaining and exercising power, others will of necessity be primarily concerned with coping with that power held over them. They will need the skills of femininity to accomplish this. Thus as long as people's lives are constrained by radically unequal power relations, whether they are racial, sexual, economic, administrative, or some other, there will be femininity in the sense described here. It both protects the powerless from the worst aspects of subordination and simultaneously perpetuates that subordination.

This being the case, the possibilities for human liberation rest on the elimination of *all* institutionalized dominance/subordinance relations. The constellations of instrumental and expressive traits, allocated in our society by gender, ought to be seen as complementary dimensions of all individuals, male and female. The tensions between them are tensions rightfully placed within individuals, not between groups. The capacities for compassion and for self-assertion, for solidarity as well as confrontation, need to be seen as possible dimensions of *human* behavior, not as male or female traits. But as long as there are groups of people who hold institutionalized undemocratic power over others, femininity will continue to be a trait that characterizes the subordinate populations, and the vision of a liberated community of autonomous individuals is denied. This, if nothing else, should show the importance of linking the feminist critique of male dominance to a larger set of criticisms of all power relations, including those manifested in administrative hierarchies. Feminism must be radical or it ceases to be feminism, and instead becomes only a procedure for recruiting new support for the status quo. To "liberate" women so that they may take an "equal" place in staffing other oppressive institutions and share an "equal" role in perpetuating other kinds of subordination would be a pyrrhic victory indeed.

Four   *The Client as*
          the Second Sex

Despotism . . . sees the separation among men the
surest guarantee of its continuance and it usually
makes every effort to keep them separate.
—de Tocqueville

For those bureaucracies whose "products" are
people or services rendered to people, the
lowest rung of the organization's internal
class structure is occupied by the clients. While
analyses of the organizational hierarchy fre-
quently omit clients, they occupy a crucial role both within the
organization and in the larger class structure of which the organization is a part. One of the main characteristics of bureaucratic capitalism is the growing role of organizations whose
sole ostensible purpose is to process, regulate, license, certify,
hide, or otherwise control individuals. These organizations employ large numbers of people and thus have an enormous impact on the labor market; they serve as resources for other organizations and thus affect the structural relations among
organizations at the macro level; and they exercise greater or
lesser degrees of control over the lives of the individuals who
are recipients of the goods and/or services produced.

The category of recipients can be divided into three distinct
groups, differentiated by the nature of their relationship to
their respective organizations. Clients are those who must interact actively with bureaucracies upon which they are dependent but over which they exercise little or no control; for example, the relationship between the poor and the state welfare
bureaucracies is a client relationship. Constituents are organized groups who are interdependent with a bureaucracy, and
who are able to exercise significant control over it; for example,
the relation between the Farm Bureau and the Department of

Agriculture is a constituent relationship.[1] Consumers are those who purchase goods and services through the market. Close analysis of the similarities and differences among these groups sheds considerable light on the class structure of bureaucratic capitalism.

The liberal distinction between public (governmental) and private (business) activities rests in part on the distinction between clients and consumers. Because consumers render payment in money rather than in some less tangible form such as time, dignity, or autonomy, their dependency on the organization supplying the good or service is less acute. The consumer is a more passive recipient than is the client, who must interact actively with the organization, demonstrating deservedness and proof of eligibility, while the consumer simply pays. Going to the grocery store may be a difficult activity if one has no transportation or money to buy food, but it is still very different from going to the social services or unemployment offices to receive "benefits." However, despite these differences, the two categories are becoming increasingly similar in other respects. Clients and consumers, as distinct from constituents, are seldom organized or able to act in concert, and have little effect on the activities of the organizations on which they depend. Businesses devote increasingly larger amounts of resources to activities that have nothing to do with the actual production of goods or services but rather with an analysis of those who will consume them. Advertising, marketing, sales, and so forth are concerned with controlling the behavior and attitudes of consumers in ways not dissimilar to those used by welfare bureaucracies over poor people or schools over students.

While the distinction between clients and consumers is a familiar one, and the similarities frequently overlooked, the distinction between clients and constituents is a less common one and the difference between them is often disguised. For instance, one can read the greater part of the public administration literature without finding any recognition of the differences; organizational flow charts place agribusiness in the same relation to the Department of Agriculture as the poor occupy in relation to Health and Human Services. But constituents are highly organized, frequently powerful groups that are able to have significant, often decisive, effects on the policies and personnel of their respective agencies: the relation of the American Medical Association to state licensing agencies or the pharmaceutical lobby to the Food and Drug Administration has little parallel to the relation of unemployed single mothers to the welfare bureaucracy. Human service organizations, as welfare agencies are referred to in the social work literature, are not normally compelled to recognize and negotiate with their clients, nor do they draw personnel from client groups; their constituencies are more properly identified as professional social work associations, just as the constituencies of schools are organized teachers and administrators, not students. Human service agencies are embedded within a larger organizational context in which organizations survive and prosper by becoming resources for other organizations, and their relations with their clients are in large part determined by the requirements of their organizational linkages, not by the needs or demands of the clients.

While there are many examples of large recipient populations—for example, students in relation to universities or citizens in relation to government licensing bureaus—by far the most striking and most obviously victimized of recipient populations is the urban underclass. During the last two decades a number of factors—the long-term consequences of the demographic shift of blacks from the rural South to the central cities of the North, a sluggish domestic economy, the decrease in entry-level jobs due to the technological streamlining of production and the increased reliance on foreign labor, the expansion of the public welfare and manpower programs, and others—have contributed to the creation of a "government subsidized and politically inert underclass": the ghetto poor.[2] The impact of social and economic barriers in overlapping networks of urban resource allocation—the housing market, the job structure, the political system, the educational system, and the law—has been to create a "web" of institutional controls that serve to isolate the poor from the surrounding society, to contain them, and ultimately to render them politically passive.[3]

The relation of the underclass to the national labor market is complex. Most of the poor in America, defined as the bottom one-fifth of the population, are working poor; but nearly half of their aggregate income is derived from the social welfare bureaucracies.[4] The working poor move in and out of the secondary labor market, occupying those "casual jobs" that are characterized by low pay, short tenure, few skills or opportunities to learn skills, little chance of advancement, and constant instability or the threat of instability. In the secondary labor market wages do not rise with the age or experience of the worker, and there is little return on education for the worker.[5] The populations who hold these jobs in nonunionized shops and offices, in restaurants and fast food chains, in small businesses, on custodial staffs, and the like are heavily skewed in the direction of minority men and women, all women over twenty-five, teenagers, and some white men in the traditional working class. The poor lack the connections to those established and respected institutions such as unions, the civil service, professional or civic agencies, schools, banking and crediting institutions, or private industry that serve as "feeder systems" into the primary labor market.[6] Despite their labor, they are "as much dependent on the government for their subsistence as they are on the labor market."[7]

Because of this dependence, the urban ghetto is coming increasingly to resemble a total institution as described by Erving Goffman in his classic study *Asylums*: "A place of residence and work where a large number of like-situated individuals, cut off from the wider society for an appreciable period of time, together lead an enclosed, formally administered round of life." While all institutions have "encompassing tendencies," total institutions are qualitatively more extensive in their enclosure of their residents in that they erect a "barrier to social intercourse with the outside" that is often physical in nature. For example, concentration camps, prisons, mental hospitals, and nursing homes are surrounded by barbed wire, armed guards, locked doors, high walls. The occupants of the ghetto are "like-situated" in their economic, and usually their racial, status, and they are only slightly less literally surrounded—by the police and national guard in times of unrest, and all the time by political, economic, and social barriers that contain the population, restrict departure, and enforce control. Goffman further

notes that "the handling of many human needs by the bureaucratic organization of whole blocks of people . . . is the key fact
of total institutions."[8] The urban underclass, increasingly dependent on public subsidies, nutritional programs, and similar
support sources, is more and more dependent on the service bureaucracies that administer these programs. The ghetto as an
internal colony, supplying workers to do the least desirable jobs
under the worst conditions, is now supplemented by the ghetto
as a total institution, one that contains and controls its population by rendering it dependent for basic needs on bureaucracies
that are controlled from the outside.

The ghetto as a total institution combines two strategies for
dealing with those who are deviant and threatening: segregation and administrative control. Foucault traces these two
strategies to their sources in the leper colony, which separated
lepers from nonlepers but otherwise did not interfere in the
lives of the afflicted, and in the plague villages, which applied a
set of disciplinary mechanisms to plague victims and potential
plague victims designed to measure, supervise, and correct the
abnormality. The two strategies converged in the nineteenth
century, creating a double mode of control:

> that of binary division and branding (mad/sane, dangerous/
> harmless, normal/abnormal); and that of coercive assign-
> ment, of differential distribution (who he is; where he must
> be; how he is to be characterized; how he is to be recog-
> nized; how a constant surveillance is to be exercised over
> him in an individual way, etc.).[9]

The urban ghetto is the contemporary version of the merger of
the leper colony and the plague city: it segregates the black- or
brown-skinned and the poor from the white and the nonpoor;
and it defines, monitors, categorizes, produces, and supervises
the behavior of the segregated group, seeing deviance or potential deviance (as in the labeling of poor children as "potential juvenile offenders" prior to the commission of any crime)
throughout the population.

The relations of the urban poor to the various human service
organizations, and to the street-level bureaucrats who administer human service programs at the client level, provide a

stark and unmediated example of the dependency relation of clients to bureaucracies. Clients occupy a radically subordinate place in relation to human service organizations, and to negotiate their role successfully they are in need of the same set of strategies and patterns of behavior that characterize other subordinate groups, traits that, when found among the female members of the population, are identified as aspects of femininity. Like the administrators who staff bureaucracies, clients who receive the goods and services issuing from bureaucracies are required to attend constantly to the image which they present to the organization, to engage in successful impression management, to anticipate the demands that the organization or its representatives will make, and to modify their own behavior accordingly, or be denied crucial services. Thus clients, like bureaucrats, are victims of the "feminization" process that expanding bureaucratization entails. Efforts to organize the urban poor for political action, while sometimes successful, must find ways to deal with the depoliticizing effects of perpetual client status.

Human Service Organizations within Bureaucratic Capitalism

The institutions of the welfare state are inextricably bound up in the contradictions of late capitalism, and they embody those contradictory tendencies within themselves. Welfare programs were introduced to save capitalism from itself, to control its "endemic systemic problems and large-scale unmet needs."[10] The system tries to compensate for the problems it creates; for example, federal and state housing authorities build low-income housing after the inner cities have been destroyed by the destruction of jobs and neighborhoods to make way for government and business headquarters or highway networks; meager financial and medical services are provided to the elderly to compensate for the demise of the extended family following the creation of a mobile labor force. The most substantial benefits offered by bureaucratic capitalism go to corporate and business interests and to the state that dispenses the benefits. This happens in two ways: directly, in that defense and space industries, energy conglomerates, agribusiness, industrial recipients of government-guaranteed loans, private research and development interests, and other groups are directly subsidized by public money; and indirectly, in that the state has socialized many of the risks of capital investment through favorable tax codes and through its unwillingness to hold businesses responsible for the social consequences of their actions, such as pollution, unemployment caused by runaway shops, and so forth. More importantly for understanding the role of human service organizations in bureaucratic capitalism, corporate and government organizations benefit from the stabilization of the underclass that welfare policies entail. Francis Fox Piven, Richard Cloward, and others have convincingly demonstrated that "expansive relief policies are designed to mute civil disorder," to siphon off the political and economic dangers that expanding poverty and hardship entail.[11] Expansion in the ranks of the poor can come about either through a decrease in the demand for labor, arising from some crisis in the market, or from a change in the production process, such as the mechanization of southern agriculture that brought blacks to the North in the post–World War II era or the current substitution of robots for assembly line workers in the automotive industry. Either way, the expansion of the relief rolls follows, as the state tries to absorb the real and/or potential threat to political and economic stability that increasing economic hardship and insecurity pose.

But the expansion of the relief rolls does not solve the problems; it merely reveals a different aspect of the underlying contradictions of bureaucratic capitalism. The expansion of the relief rolls increases the bargaining power of workers by making them more resistant to pressure to take any job at any wage: "The income-maintenance programs have weakened capital's ability to depress wages by means of economic insecurity. . . . These programs have altered the terms of struggle between business and labor."[12] The expansion of relief also increases the number of people who are dependent on public service programs for employment, the vast legions of managers and street-level bureaucrats who become advocates for the continuing expansion of the services that employ them. Since the public social services budget goes about equally to functionaries and to clients, one might well ask who exactly is "on welfare."[13] Efforts to constrict the availability of public services, and thus to reinforce work norms, are then met with resistance from organized and local constituencies located in the bureaucracies that administer the programs. A substantial reduction in social programs has an enormous impact on the entire labor market: the primary labor market is flooded with unemployed managers, supervisors, technical workers, and professionals; the secondary labor market is flooded with former clients, a population disproportionately composed of women with few saleable skills, who then compete for jobs with the women who cook, clean, and serve in restaurants, bars, medical facilities, offices, and so forth.[14] In sum, the contradictions of bureaucratic capitalism cannot be healed by restricting welfare any more than they can be healed by expanding it; consequently, the system vacillates back and forth between classical liberal attacks on "big government" in the name of seventeenth-century laissez-faire mythology, and reformed liberal appeals to humanitarian impulses, or to the requirements of political stability, or both.

The contradictions of the system are institutionalized in the various human service organizations, which stand as "organizational embodiments of contradictory tendencies in American society as a whole."[15] In the mainstream social science literature on organizations, contradictions are usually recognized as "conflicting goals," as problems of poor motivation, inadequate coordination of resources, faulty communications, incompetent management, or other sorts of errors to be overcome so that the organization's rational pursuit of its announced goals can proceed.[16] While all of these problems may well exist, to look to them to explain the organization's conflicting goals is to mistake the symptom for the cause. The "precarious domain consensus" of human service organizations reflects their simultaneous efforts to both reinforce and alleviate the consequences of systemic contradictions: to help the poor and to remove them from the relief rolls; to rehabilitate criminals and to punish them; to reintegrate deviants and to hide them from public view.

One approach that service organizations have historically taken to their internal conflicting goals has been to distinguish between the deserving and the undeserving poor. Throughout the modern age, but most noticeably in the nineteenth and twentieth centuries, the poor have been linked more or less directly with criminals and deviants, and poor relief has always been connected institutionally with enforced labor and imprisonment. But the "truly needy" (the quiet, unthreatening, familiar poor) have been distinguished rhetorically from "freeloaders" (the unruly, the immigrant, and the adult poor) as less morally culpable and therefore deserving of pity rather than punishment.[17] Another approach has been to make the conditions under which people receive aid "so abhorrent and so shameful that even the harshest work was preferable."[18] Both are strategies to simultaneously legitimate and disguise the contradictory mission of the welfare establishment—to stabilize the poor by offering relief and to reinforce the work norms by curtailing relief.

Human service organizations are assisted in their endeavors by the police and military; the former stabilize the economically displaced in times of relative peace, while the latter "stabilize" the ghetto in times of "war." As Alvin Gouldner notes in his discussion of internal colonialism, "Terror and bureaucracy are each ways of reaching down into and dominating a group from some point outside its own ranks, by those who do not belong to it."[19] Increasingly the social services and the police and military bureaucracies are merging, so that the two functions become inseparable; the poor are referred to the military for job "training" and experience; students are referred to ROTC scholarships, with the accompanying commitment to military duty, in lieu of civilian funding for higher education; the police are used to investigate welfare applicants to determine eligibility, prior to the commission of any crime.[20] The increasing overlap and interpenetration of these bureaucracies is indicative of a general tightening of disciplinary controls over clients in particular and citizens in general.

Because human service organizations are located in the organizational context of bureaucratic capitalism, they must become resources for other organizations in order to survive. The relationship between social service agencies and other organizations is not a peripheral aspect of their internal functioning, but is rather a determinant of it.[21] By stabilizing the poor, these agencies benefit other organizational elites: politicians can claim to have "quelled urban unrest," and economic elites are guaranteed a stable investment climate, some subsidized demand for consumer goods, and a dependable—that is, pacified—reserve labor force.[22] Piven and Cloward provide a good summary of the interlocking organizational network surrounding the service delivery bureaucracies:

> This apparatus includes public agencies that administer retirement benefits, unemployment insurance, public welfare, food stamp benefits, Medicaid, Medicare, and housing subsidies. It includes the organizations that operate the job programs and job-training programs, provide counseling or rehabilitation services of one kind or another, and enforce environmental or affirmative action regulations; and it includes the programs that reach into older and larger institutions, such as the enormous public education system, the voluntary social agencies, the hospitals, nursing homes, and other parts of the health system, and even into sectors of private enterprise such as construction, real estate, and the retail food industry. In other words, this apparatus is lodged in all levels of government, and in nongovernmental institutions as well. It is staffed by millions of people who are civil servants and social workers and construction workers and teachers and doctors and mental health workers.[23]

Examples of "helping relationships" among human service agencies are legion. Medicaid clinics serve as guaranteed sources of demand for hospitals and drug companies. Methadone maintenance clinics for heroin addicts provide a guaranteed market for the drug companies, and in fact such clinics frequently have representatives from the drug companies on their policy-making boards. Prisoners working in the prison factories or fields provide both labor and materials to local businesses. Real estate firms lease buildings to New York City's poverty programs and daycare centers at rents many times higher than the market value.[24] Public housing authorities and welfare agencies are mutually supportive; often the rents that welfare clients pay in housing projects are higher than rents paid by nonclients in identical apartments, and the rent goes up automatically when the welfare payments go up.[25] Pursuing the "tactics of organizational consolidation and coalition," agencies use their own experts to forge ties with other agencies in order to facilitate the exchange of both clients and staff. In the jargon of the human services fields this is called a "multifaceted approach to the problem," but in organizational terms it is a process of mutual accommodation among elites. Concentration on interagency planning and multisystem involvement in service delivery results in greater and greater focus on the bureaucracy itself and less and less on the actual delivery of frontline services, but such goal displacement is useful in the organization's pursuit of its own maintenance and expansion.

It would be misleading to suppose that these relationships stem from corruption within particular organizations, or from the ill will of particular administrators. While both corruption and ill will may be present, in fact it is the structural relationships among organizations that account for these connections. Most administrators of service organizations, familiar with the politics of the budgetary process, the importance of maintaining a supportive climate in the organizational environment, and the low status of clients in the larger society, are aware that the actual delivery of services to clients is secondary to two more crucial functions: to adequately regulate and control the behavior of clients, and to maintain secure links with other organizations. With regard to the regulatory function, experienced managers know that their announced service goals are widely recognized as difficult to achieve, and that the organization will be judged more on its ability to monitor, regulate, and hide clients than on its record of helping them. As Charles Perrow argues:

> Wardens are not fired for not rehabilitating prisoners; psychiatric administrators or therapists for not curing the insane; welfare administrators for not getting people to work or mending broken homes or raising their allotments. The criterion is more likely to be "how many people did you regulate at what cost per person?" The effective administrator knows that failure to meet announced goals will not mean his or her demise, and certainly not the demise of the organization. But failure to control, buy off, or regulate his or her charges will bring trouble.[26]

With regard to securing the place of the agency in the organizational environment, adept administrators usually know that both their own careers and the future of their bureaus rest largely on their ability to serve as a resource to other organizations and groups, particularly those with more powerful members, constituents, or organizational linkages. Pursuit of this goal usually results in the fragmentation of services, lack of coordination among staff, zealous defense of territory and domain, and rejection of undesirable clients (that is, those who are physically or psychologically unattractive or seriously troubled or unruly).[27] Since clients are not constituents (except for those few times when clients organize themselves into constituencies), they do not enter into the bargaining process. They are not a primary reference group even for the street-level bureaucrats who administer directly to them, much less for the managers who control the resource allocation for the program.[28] Because clients do not count among the groups who define the operation of the agencies, service workers usually have very little to lose by failing to satisfy clients, and may in fact be rewarded for reducing the services available to clients or the number of clients.[29] The urban poor constitute, in Claus Offe's phrase, a "neglected institutional grouping," in that they lack the resources necessary to bargain effectively with elites and their needs are such that, if articulated, they would endanger the system itself.[30] The institutionalized pattern of priorities of the technocratic political process is such that the underclass, if it plays by the rules, gets nowhere, because the rules are set up to admit only those players who have bargaining clout. The urban poor get results only when, by circumventing the rules, they "present a credible case for the dangerous consequences that ensue (or that they would precipitate) if their claims were ignored."[31] In Cloward and Piven's succinct words: "A placid poor get nothing, but a turbulent poor sometimes get something."[32]

It would also be misleading to imply that no clients are ever assisted by service organizations. The dispossessed and the deviant often receive crucial, if minimal, assistance in their struggle to survive. However, the approach taken to providing services is quite strictly defined in terms that are acceptable to other organizational elites. The programs of the welfare system reflect "a distinctly managerial kind of politics" intended primarily to contain the political dangers of expanding economic hardship without addressing the sources of that hardship.[33] Problems involving the distribution of wealth and of jobs can never be couched in class terms, but only in the language of individual deviance. Again Perrow makes this clear:

> It would not do for the executive of an agency that purportedly is helping the poor to seek a massive redistribution of wealth in the community by taxing the rich heavily and giving it to the poor, or cutting the salaries of highly paid officials and using the money to create jobs for the poor, in, say, renovating slum housing; to investigate inefficiency and corruption in other agencies so that they might give more help; or organize the poor into an effective political force that would remove elected officials or even restructure the government.[34]

The "solution" proposed by one organization must not disturb the established field of activity in other, usually more powerful, organizations. If the poor are discovered to lack equal access to the courts, the bureaucratic solution is to provide them with lawyers; if the poor have inadequate medical care, build clinics; if they are denied educational opportunity, establish preschool development programs and special education classes. The answer always seems to be "Let them eat bureaucracy." More agencies are created, and more employment opportunities for managers and street-level bureaucrats appear, without significantly disrupting the system that produces the income inequities underlying the denial of services to the poor.[35] To actually address the source of deeply rooted economic/political/ social problems would both challenge the interests of interlocking elites and also destabilize the very population upon whom welfare bureaucracies depend to justify their existence—the poor.

Bureaucratic Discourse and the Production of Clients

Like the panopticon that Foucault analyzes, service bureaucracies give rise to knowledge about clients through their power over them. Bureaucratic discourse does not, of course, produce poor people, but it does produce *clients*; that is, it produces individuals whose subjectivity is molded and shaped by the parameters of the discourse, whose attitudes and behavior are created within a field of interaction that is bounded by the institutions and the language of the service organizations. The panopticon, Foucault tells us, "functions as a kind of laboratory of power. Thanks to its mechanisms of observation, it gains in efficiency and in the ability to penetrate into men's behavior; knowledge follows the advances of power, discovering new objects of knowledge over all the surfaces on which power is exercised."[36]

Knowledge about clients is produced in service bureaucracies (and in their academic support institutions, the social work programs), where the poor are officially diagnosed and treated, where the roles that they must play and the scripts that they must follow are laid out. The street-level bureaucrats who interact with clients, including social workers, judges, police, mental health workers, parole officers, counselors, and so forth, and the managers of these bureaucrats, are the recognized experts on the poor. They are entitled to enter the realm of serious speech acts, to offer diagnosis and treatment supported by institutionalized justifications; the poor, the mentally ill, and the criminal, simply by virtue of their deviance, are not entitled to claim the status of serious speech acts for their own self-knowledge, but must redefine themselves in the terms of the bureaucratic discourse if they wish to be heard. Service bureaucracies claim to operate on the basis of rules, which are neutral, objective, and scientific, while clients are seen as operating on the basis of values, which are personal, subjective, and biased.[37]

The language of treatment offers a limited number of roles and events to clients, and these roles and events are defined in terms of therapy, reinforcement, and individual rehabilitation. The client must become a case, and to do so must pass through an examination process and demonstrate both eligibility and deservedness. As Foucault makes clear, it is not one's circumstances but one's subjectivity that is being measured:

> The examination, surrounded by all its documentary techniques, makes each individual a "case": a case which at one and the same time constitutes an object for a branch of knowledge and a hold for a branch of power. The case is no longer, as in casuistry or jurisprudence, a set of circumstances defining an act and capable of modifying the application of a rule; it is the individual as he may be described, judged, measured, compared with others, in his very individuality; and it is also the individual who has to be trained or corrected, classified, normalized, excluded, etc.[38]

Compared to the more diverse and flexible roles available to people in the society at large, the roles available to the client are defined negatively, by reference to nonroles or to unfulfilled roles—one becomes a dropout, an unwed mother, a culturally deprived child, a nonemployable person.[39] Nursing home residents, for example, are called patients and defined by reference to their diseases, the "stroke" in room 204 or the "broken hip" in 121. Through the medicalization of their status the elderly are viewed as incurable and therefore hopeless, and are usually overdiagnosed and overtreated, as nursing homes seek to justify their medical status, to keep their residents docile, and to maintain the requisite occupancy rate.[40] For mental patients, the activities of ordinary life are redefined in the language of treatment and recovery: they do not hold dances, they have dance therapy; they do not play volleyball or card games, they have recreation therapy; they do not have discussions, they do group therapy; they do not read, they engage in "bibliotherapy."[41] To protest the diagnosis of the experts is to engage in "denial" or to "escape to health" by pretending to be healthy in order to avoid having one's problems discovered. To resist therapy, even therapy that strongly resembles torture, such as deprivation of food, sleep, or human contact, severe confinement, public humiliation, hard labor, or extreme sedation, is to be labeled as "incorrigible," an "escapee," or "socially disorganized."[42] The desperation of those who are completely without resources is translated into an inability to delay gratification; the desire to be treated as a whole person and to interact on a personal rather than a bureaucratic basis is seen as "childlike."

The disciplinary context of the service organizations is well illustrated by comparing it to the juridico-discursive context of Social Security programs. Social Security recipients are called "beneficiaries" and benefits are seen as "rights." The image of "social insurance" is stressed, and personnel are called "claims representatives," suggesting a commercial sales transaction. The recipients of Social Security are seen more as consumers than as clients, and the representative's desk is the scene of a calm, white-collar transaction in which citizens receive that which is due them. In comparison, welfare offices are characterized by the assumption of the superior status, apparent in both demeanor and dress, of the workers over the clients. Personnel are called "caseworkers" or "eligibility workers," and the client must prove his or her qualifications in order to become a case. The small interview cubicles lack both egalitarianism and privacy, and bear less resemblance to a commercial transaction site than to a confessional, "with physical survival being traded for a kind of penitence in which the state of desperation is revealed."[43] The welfare inquisition recreates the disciplinary inquiry into sexuality that Foucault attributes to the Victorian era; the client is expected to reveal personal details about sexual behavior, child-bearing and child-rearing practices, and living arrangements, and this knowledge is then used to control other behavior. This inquisitorial process, Foucault observes, "demanded constant, attentive, and curious

presences for its exercise; it presupposed proximities; it pro-
ceeded through examination and insistent observation; it required an exchange of discourses, through questions that
extorted admissions, and confidences that went beyond the
questions that were asked."[44] Just as the Victorians' inquiry
into sexuality produced the perversions which so preoccupied
them through the encroachment of disciplinary power on the
body, so the service organization's obsession with illegitimate
categories such as "welfare cheaters" produces these categories
by the exercise of the powers of bureaucratic capitalism on the
poor.

The attitudes of street-level bureaucrats toward clients are
inevitably structured by the discursive and institutional practices of the service organizations. While some street-level bureaucrats have considerable discretion over their interactions
with clients, most do not; police and homecare delivery personnel, for example, interact with clients "on the street" where
close supervision is impossible, and thus exercise substantial
personal control over who gets arrested or who receives services; but caseworkers and examiners work under tight control
by supervisors and exercise little discretion over the process.[45]
When they do attempt to assert individual control over decision-making, organizational controls are quickly reimposed;
for example, when some welfare rights workers, under pressure from militant welfare rights activists in the late 1960s, began to allocate discretionary and little-known special awards
grants, the agency simply eliminated those grants.[46] The structural environment of the caseworker is such that, no matter
what the individual's feelings are toward recipients, she/he is
institutionally constrained in terms of actions. For example, a
study of the Chicago welfare bureaucracy done by Street, Martin, and Gordon grouped caseworkers into four types, based on
their attitudes toward the agency and toward the clients. The
two most straightforward categories were "persons positive toward the clients and negative toward the agency, thought to be
advocates for client benefits, and persons positive toward the
agency and negative toward clients, called *bureaucrats*." Those
who were positive toward both and who "expected to work ad-
vantageously between both worlds" were labeled "mediators";

the residual category of those negative toward both were called "apathetics."[47] However, the authors found that these differences in attitude did not translate into differences in behavior; the actions of the caseworkers, whether they were advocates, bureaucrats, mediators, or apathetics, were constrained by "the exigencies of the role, the fragmentation of the decision-making power, and the necessity to translate most issues into the convention of bureaucratic forms," leading to "a randomization of inputs and ultimately a homogenization of behavior."[48] Further, over time, the differences in attitudes also tended to disappear, since there was no institutional space or language available for their expression. Such differences were literally written out of the discourse. Workers learned to adopt a "strategy of withdrawal" and to "exercise their discretion by not getting involved."[49]

The welfare worker is faced with clients whose problems— lack of employment, education, medical care, housing, food— are complex and interconnected, but each worker can deal only with the specific problem assigned to her or him. Thus the worker is prohibited from interacting with the client as a whole person, and in any case the client's problems are so mammoth that the worker is in no position to solve them. One of my interviewees, a young white man in his late twenties who works as a claims examiner for a public assistance unit in a county social services office, spoke extensively about the attitudes of workers toward clients: "Everyone starts out, 'How can I help people?' . . . but then you're overwhelmed with work." The really needy clients, those clearly in immediate trouble, usually arouse some compassion: "It's glaring; it shouts at you"; but most applicants are "a nuisance." "If you did feel sorry for them, you'd feel like it's your responsibility to get them something. But you can't. . . . What can I do—it's beyond me—it's the system." Most welfare personnel are overworked and underpaid, some of them earning even less than their clients. The complex and massive array of forms to be filled out and computer work to be done to process each client lead welfare workers to discourage applicants: "They're not gonna be eligible; I've got to get them in and out of here so I can get some work done." "Get some work done" in this context means paperwork,

not interaction with clients; the clients are an interference
with the worker's ability to complete the forms. Street-level bureaucrats are rewarded for their speed in processing cases and
their ability to control clients, not for their service to clients.
For example, in this man's office those workers who are not
tardy in completing their paperwork are rewarded with "down
time," during which they do not have to see clients and they
can catch up still further on their record-keeping. Those who
spend more time with clients and fall behind in their paperwork are penalized for it in that they do not receive down time
and thus fall still further behind. Thus those most in need of
the break are the least likely to get it.

Considerable paperwork is generated by the organization's
need to keep track of other paperwork. The enormous record-
keeping burden affects the delivery of services in complex ways:
one social worker complained that she must exaggerate the
problems of her clients in order to justify their requests for aid;
but these exaggerated reports then go into the client's files,
creating a bad record for the client to which many people have
access. Further, the constraints of the record-keeping system
force workers to ration their services, to hoard information
about programs, to keep clients waiting for long periods, and so
forth. Michael Lipsky cites an official policy statement of the
New York City Budget Bureau that suggests ways to inconvenience clients, to increase the backlog and waiting time, and to
cut the welfare population by forcing eligible clients off the
rolls.[50] The young claims examiner quoted above commented
that "an examiner never calls someone in as soon as they get
there" because the paperwork from the prior case takes precedence. Proud of his own ability to process clients relatively
quickly, he stated that "the most I've ever kept anyone waiting is an hour and a half. Normally, I don't go past an hour."
Referring to the workings of his agency as "bureaucracy in
non-motion," he told of one client who came to collect a much-
needed clothing allotment and was denied access to the building because she had no shoes, violating the "no shoes, no service" rule. He left his desk to go outside and hand her the check
personally, an act of charity that he was under no obligation to
perform. Officially, the woman, while needing the money in or-

der to buy shoes, was supposed to have the shoes before she could receive the money. "It seems so obviously stupid," he commented, "but it just cranks on."

Service workers typically respond to the systemic constraints on their work by distancing themselves from their clients, lowering their opinions of and their hopes for the clients. Service workers attempt to raise their own status by appeals to professionalism, and thus become more preoccupied with attaining the language, code of behavior, and style of analysis of professionalism than with delivering service to clients. The more "professionalized" the workers become, the more likely they are to see the problems of their clients as stemming from defects of socialization or individual motivation, to be remedied by exposure to expert guidance.[51] As the language of social work is increasingly invaded by techniques culled from business management, social workers are further removed from any intimate linguistic or institutional contact with clients that might serve as the base of a common identity.

The consequences of dependency with regard to the clients of bureaucracies are parallel in many respects to those for administrators themselves, although the dependency is more obvious in the case of clients because the situation is not complicated by a parallel reward structure. There are few rewards involved in being a welfare recipient; for the poor, it is a way of surviving acute hardship when other options have been removed. The degrading process of collecting welfare and the humiliating status of being "on the dole" have been amply recorded by both participants and observers.[52] Thus the powerful and inhibiting controls that welfare bureaucracies exercise over and through their clients are less well disguised than those affecting bureaucrats; there are no "carrots" to disguise the "stick."

Welfare clients tend to be isolated from other institutional contexts that might provide support for an independent posture. They are not likely to have stable occupational roles or political status, are unlikely to be able to link their status as clients to any other established set of rights and obligations (for example, those of union members or voters), and are effectively isolated from the mainstream of economic and social life. There are powerful social ties within the ghetto, especially within families, kinship networks, religious communities, and fraternal and sororal associations, but these are not the kinds of organizational links that give the client population any secure connection with the established mainstream political and economic structures. Paradoxically, the very nature of the social ties in the ghetto, while they provide essential material and social resources to the poor, further discredit the poor in the eyes of the service agencies and fix the label of "deviant" even more firmly in place. For example, Carol Stack traces the "organized, tenacious, active lifelong network" of reciprocal kinship rights and responsibilities by which desperately poor ghetto blacks share their resources and their needs.[53] Bettylou Valentine documents the intricate combination of work, welfare, and hustling that poor black families use to secure a minimum level of income and to maintain stable family ties in the face of the massive pressure toward disintegration and defeat that poverty entails.[54] But the welfare, housing, and educational bureaucracies see many of these strategies as manifestations of instability, irrationality, and carelessness: the practice of passing children back and forth among friends and relatives as different people find or lose jobs, or of freely giving, borrowing, and lending money and goods, or of moving frequently from one crowded apartment to another as buildings are condemned, leases lost, rents raised, serve as crucial survival strategies for the poor. But the bureaucracies that dispense services are concerned that the poor have "carefully budgeted and accountable incomes, stable residences, and unambiguous and intact family memberships."[55] The inability of the poor to live by middle-class norms on a lower-class budget is then taken as further evidence that poverty results from inadequate socialization, to be righted by individual rehabilitation.

In their encounters with bureaucracies, clients are disadvantaged by the one-way flow of information. The bureaucracy controls the information that is needed to mount an attack upon it; the information is frequently complex, written in a secret language, and passed through channels not visible to the public. Clients must learn a new language in order to comprehend the maze of bureaucratic regulations confronting them, and this language is one that the administrators are officially taught while the clients must learn it on their own. Only when the client has learned the official jargon and comprehended both the formal rules and the informal norms governing appropriate conduct can she/he convince the bureaucrat that she/he is indeed a "case." Street, Martin, and Gordon found that clients with some "bureaucratic experience and competence" had greater success in obtaining benefits; their single strongest predictor of success in becoming a recipient was experience with filing income taxes.[56]

In other words, the client must learn to please: to present the appropriate image, to give the required recognition to administrative authority, to "bow properly to immense institutional power, understand and flatter the bureaucratic personality," and otherwise legitimate himself/herself before the officials of the organization.[57] Successful impression management for the poor often requires that they be able to bridge many gaps: administrative (client addressing official), economic (lower-class person addressing middle-class person), racial (black or brown person addressing white person), and/or linguistic (person speaking Spanish or street language addressing one skilled in middle-class professionalese). In their efforts to master the bureaucratic rules of the game, clients must interact with those officials who, because they are at the bottom of the organizational hierarchy, are the most constrained by the formal rules and have the least latitude or incentive to bend the rules, to make exceptions, or to assist the clients in negotiating the bureaucracy successfully. Since agencies are judged by their ability to control clients and to complete paperwork, it is in the interest of the agency to select from among those clients who have some mastery of bureaucratic norms and rules; for example, programs such as the Job Corps recruit more from youth with some middle-class socialization than from the "problem kids" who most need the help, because they want clients who will succeed in the program, thus demonstrating the program's efficacy and supporting the search for expanded funding.[58]

The arbitrariness of bureaucratic procedures from the point of view of clients further increases their dependency on the bureaucracy. As Piven and Cloward make clear, "Recipients of benefits are not apprised of procedures but are continually confronted with apparently arbitrary action."[59] Rules such as those requiring a thirty-day waiting period after application, regardless of the urgency of the need, or the repeated trips to the welfare office to show the same papers to the same clerks in order to be "recertified," represent constant harassment to the client. The frequently high level of surveillance over the recipient's conduct—also a trait of total institutions—breaks down arenas of privacy and further cements control.

The strains of successful impression management are immense. At the very least, "there is a fundamental disidentification between the individual and the manipulative role he is playing. Therefore in encountering bureaucracy there is always a potential emotional strain. Put differently, bureaucracy has a strong propensity to make people nervous."[60] More fundamentally, clients are required to internalize and act upon the bureaucratic definition of themselves, to "learn to treat themselves as if they were categorical entities."[61] Clients are required to control themselves in their relation to officials, to learn to read the cues emanating from the officials and from the bureaucratic milieu, to anticipate the demands that will be made, calculate the most acceptable response, and offer it to the officials as a sign of deservedness. Bureaucrats are more likely to approve of the attitudes and behavior of clients who actively work to present the appropriate image than of those who must be constantly reminded of it. The client is rewarded for his/her success in becoming what Foucault calls the obedient disciplinary subject, "the individual subjected to habits, rules, orders, an authority that is exercised continually around him and upon him, and which he must allow to function automatically in him."[62]

Clients, in other words, are required to adopt the strategies of femininity to ensure survival, just as women have traditionally done and just as administrators themselves also must do in the bureaucratic climate. The feminization of the client follows from the structural requirements of the client role, because the only posture permissible toward the bureaucracy is one of dependency. There is only one sort of "demand" that a poor person can ordinarily make upon a welfare agency, and that is more adequately conceived of as a request, a plea for help. One cannot demand to participate in decision-making, to see a policy changed, or to redirect resources. In other words, one cannot demand to be included as a participant in the political process itself; to be a recipient is also to be a spectator.

The process by which clients are rendered dependent and passive is self-perpetuating on two related levels. First, it is self-perpetuating on an organizational level, in that different agencies provide each other with clientele through referrals. Sometimes such referrals aim at (and occasionally accomplish) the goal of removing individuals from client status and from dependency on the service network, as when, for example, a heroin addict is given welfare benefits on the provision that he/she enroll in a drug treatment program that will free him/her from the addiction, a high school equivalency program that will give access to educational credentials, and a job training program that will make the person employable. However, since none of these efforts to change the individual can do anything about the shortage of jobs in the ghetto, such programs do little to affect the structural problems that created the dependency in the first place. Further, the more likely scenario for our hypothetical heroin addict is that he/she will be enrolled in a methadone maintenance program and no effort will be made to free him/her from the addiction or graduate him/her from the program. Since the methadone addict is still drug dependent, and must report frequently to the hospital or clinic for treatment, she/he is still virtually unemployable at any but the most unskilled tasks and is thus condemned to continued dependence on both welfare and methadone. One of my interviewees, a middle-aged black woman who had lived for three years as a heroin addict and seven years as a methadone client, stated, "I became a political prisoner on a methadone program." Methadone clinics, according to another interviewee who left one such clinic after failing to receive any encouragement in his efforts to become drug-free, hold onto their more progressive and motivated clients because they look good on the agencies' financial reports and because they are more readily controlled. Agencies such as these all too frequently become recycling channels for a permanent clientele, whose population is shuffled back and forth to fill the quotas of a variety of inter-connected programs.

Second, the process is self-perpetuating on an individual level, since bureaucratic procedures tend to create in their clients the very traits that are then held to be responsible for the client's situation. Welfare recipients are defined as social "failures," as people who have not made it due to some individual failing of their own. Welfare procedures often reflect "the premise that the poor are unworthy and the constant fear that the client will lapse into sloth and chicanery."[63] Continued dependence on welfare lowers an individual's self-esteem; in the words of the black woman quoted above, who after many years of client status had become a welfare rights organizer, "They take a human soul and destroy it, take a person's dignity and bend it down to nothing." Welfare programs thus demoralize and debilitate their clients, creating conditions under which people become what they are already said to be. When the environment is capricious and arbitrary, it is not suprising that its inhabitants learn to evade the restrictions that are avoidable, acquiesce to those that are not, and generally "live by their wits." This is not the same as saying, as do many conservative critics of welfare, that client status is self-perpetuating because recipients live so well on public assistance that they have no incentive to seek work. Even the maximum level of available benefits falls far short of the cost of living, and in any case, the poor generally have the same attitudes toward the importance of work as does the middle class.[64] Nor am I arguing that client status is self-perpetuating because the poor teach their children that being "on the dole" is an acceptable way of life. More often the opposite is true, in that parents' aspirations for their children far exceed any hopes they hold for themselves. The point is that perpetual client status creates a field of interaction in which individuals must develop certain abilities in order to survive. The skills that allow a poor person to succeed in obtaining benefits are the skills of impression management, plus patience, perseverance, a low profile, and a high tolerance for ambiguity and for insult; these have very little to do with developing abilities to assert oneself, to organize around com-

mon interests, or to marshal the personal and collective resources necessary to oppose the powerful. Since benefits are
distributed to individuals, not to groups, any perception by the
clients of common interests is blurred and the existence of a
shared situation is disguised. Clients are discouraged from
forming groups and acting collectively both because the service
organizations actively oppose such organization and because
"to do so is to collectively acknowledge and label themselves by
the role failure which the client status represents." [65] To protect
themselves from the psychological consequences of being labeled as failures, welfare recipients frequently disassociate
themselves from other clients, viewing themselves as atypical
and speaking of other recipients as "they," not as "we." [66] Like
the bureaucrat, the client needs the skills of impression management to survive his/her organizational role; yet the more
successful the individual is in developing them, the more dependent he/she becomes on the bureaucracy. Like women and
other oppressed groups, clients need to hold onto their anger, to
sustain it and direct it into active confrontation with the powerful; but anger is difficult to maintain through the veils of impression management.

Bureaucratic Solutions and Client Resistance

There is no bureaucratic solution to the problems of
the underclass. As clients, they occupy the bottom rung of the
organizational class structure, and any meaningful change requires change in that class structure and in the society in which
it is embedded. Administrators and street-level bureaucrats,
no matter how well intentioned, are located within an institutional setting in which they are systematically discouraged
from identifying with clients and in which the maintenance of
the existing class structure is the grounding for the delivery of
services to clients. There may sometimes be exceptions, some
heroic individuals or groups who put aside their organizationally defined interests in favor of some ideological or personal
commitment, but on the whole Donald Arnstein is correct in
his observation that

the appearance of an occasional change-agent among administrators no more justifies our *expecting* changes to originate in this group than the appearance of an occasional Marcus Aurelius justifies our expecting emperors to be benevolent or democratic. Just as the concept of emperor implies ruling an empire, the concept of administrator implies administering an institution—not changing it.[67]

The mainstream literature on service organizations and the underclass occasionally recognizes that there is no bureaucratic answer to client problems, but this insight is once again relegated to the fringes of analysis. A good example is the otherwise excellent book by Michael Lipsky, *Street-Level Bureaucracy*. After demonstrating that it is not in either the agency's or the caseworker's interest to provide full information on the programs to clients, he recommends that agencies conduct "routine reviews to determine whether clients were receiving all benefits to which they were entitled." Thus the problems of bureaucracy are "solved" by the creation of still more bureaucracy. Lipsky demonstrates that the organizational interests of service agencies lead them to oppose client organizations, that street-level bureaucrats usually resist efforts by welfare recipients, prison inmates, ex-offenders, students, and other clients to act collectively for two reasons: because the clients are expected to be grateful, and because the bureaucrats "regard client organizations as unnecessary, frivolous, likely to be irresponsible, or not representative of clients' true interests." He then recommends that officials support client organizing efforts and that coalitions of administrators, unions, and clients unite to seek reforms. He speaks approvingly of the Denver Plan in education, where children are given numbers to indicate "the presumed difficulty of teaching them" so that teachers can be rewarded for "having challenging pupils in their class." He sees this as a good way to distribute case loads, when one would expect, given his astute analysis of labeling, that he would be the first to see the self-fulfilling effect this would have on students. Lipsky recognizes at one point that "issues of client control over service bureaucracies are not separable from consideration of large-scale social changes or changes in the organization of public service," but then disregards this insight in order to draw conclusions directly at odds with his own persuasive arguments concerning the systemic limitations of the service delivery system.[68]

The conclusions that one can draw from my analysis have to do with the possibilities for meaningful political action by the underclass. I am not arguing for the elimination of welfare under current circumstances: I fully agree with Piven and Cloward that, in the absence of genuine economic change (for example, a guaranteed livable minimum income and real job opportunity) welfare subsidies are necessary and their expansion is defensible.[69] Nor do I mean to say that the poor are incapable of resisting their oppression; rather I want to explain why such efforts are usually short-lived and without impact on the larger class structure. In some cases resistance takes place openly and directly; for example, Jack Abbott's account of his prison career in *The Belly of the Beast* chronicles the tragic story of one who would rather be a hero than a client. A study of young black men in Watts who have been identified as "hardcore" problems by schools and welfare agencies reveals that "a veritable state of war exists between poor recipients and distributors of services."[70] These young men did not adopt the strategies of impression management. Instead, they did the opposite; they rejected an institutional world that they experienced as one of "tricks, games, and deceit" and formed their own community action organization, the Sons of Watts.[71] The victories of this organization for its members were concrete and real: they formed neighborhood cleanup crews, neighborhood patrols, youth counseling services, a job training center, and a prison release program. They became a political voice for blacks in Los Angeles, and their members developed substantial negotiating skills as well as greater self-respect. These were not insubstantial changes for the individuals involved, but they certainly did not alter the economic facts of life for the residents of Watts.

Other examples of client resistance can be found in militant welfare rights organizations. These groups can claim substantial successes in two major areas: they encourage the development of greater self-esteem in their members, and they attain greater access to welfare benefits for their members. Welfare rights activists have an explicit political orientation and cultivate an adversarial relation with officials. Activists have a much higher feeling of efficacy in relation to the welfare system than do nonactivists, and the activists show little of the dependency, passivity, and alienation that characterize the more traditional clients.[72] Activists have rejected the strategies of impression management in favor of a confrontational posture, often with considerable success. Two of my interviewees are black women who are activists in the New York City Unemployed and Welfare Council, which at the time of the interviews was New York City's only union of welfare recipients. Both women saw the union as the only vehicle for the psychological and material survival of the poor. From one: "They're either gonna fight, gonna be rebellious, or they're gonna lay down and die." From the other: "The system whips people. . . . People join the union because they can clearly see they have no representation." Many welfare rights activists, like my interviewees, are black or Hispanic women who are able to wrest substantial concessions from welfare administrators because the activists have mastered the complex welfare codes and can make a credible case for their own expertise. They often know the rules better than the officials do, and use their knowledge to serve as legal representatives in getting other clients fair hearings, and to gain access to backstage information from caseworkers, supervisors, and sometimes directly from the agencies' files.

These accomplishments are not insubstantial for the individuals involved, but they in no way present a challenge to the hegemony of bureaucratic discourse. Welfare rights organizations struggle for a fairer treatment of clients, not for an end to client status; their strategies require them to immerse themselves in the welfare bureaucracy, to master its language and adopt its categories. Welfare activists, then, are the flip side of the traditional, more obedient client. Both are deeply embedded in the client role, both need to master the norms and rules of the organization, but the activists use their knowledge to pursue a confrontational strategy, while the traditional client applies it to successful image management. If most clients did

not maintain the latter role, the activists would not be so successful in their opposition; it is because they make up such a
small percentage of an agency's total caseload that administrators find it easier to capitulate than to fight.[73] If welfare rights
organizations expand from a local to a regional or national
base, their insurgency is short-lived; they either fade away as
organizations, or else they abandon their oppositional politics
in order to survive. Once organizers look to political and economic elites to provide resources to sustain their organization,
their fate is set: elites will only confer resources on organizations that they know are not a substantial challenge. Historically, it is spontaneous and uncontrolled political disruption
by the poor that most seriously challenges the interests of
elites and that wins the most substantial concessions, not the
creation of mass organizations.[74] When welfare bureaucracies
provide the financial support for client organizations, mili-
tancy is soon abandoned in favor of strategies of organizational
accommodation. Such organizations usually evolve into social
and political resources for their controlling members, rather
than instruments for political action by the poor. For example,
the New York State Legal Services provides public funding for
Clients' Councils, organizations that seek to train poor people
to be advocates for each other in fair hearings and other legal
situations. The goal of the Clients' Council is, in essence, to
make poor people into a constituency, to give them minimal organizational resources with which to bargain with agencies for
better services. One of my interviewees, a young white single
father, discussed his experiences as a founding member of a
Clients' Council: "It turned into a group of people who are paid
to go out and eat and drain legal resources funds. They've done
some very, very small things, but they haven't sought new
membership. When there was new membership out there they
turned away from it." The demise of their organization echoes
the fate of countless other similar groups; efforts to oppose bureaucracies from within bureaucracies, using bureaucratic resources and bureaucratic language, are eventually absorbed
and rendered harmless. The terms of bureaucratic discourse allow for no other outcome.

A second example, this time on a national level, is the National Welfare Rights Organization. This group had its greatest effect when members of local offices acted collectively to disrupt agency routines and to demand action on the grievances of the whole group. The nonrecipient staff and organizers favored greater centralization and expansion of the national office, and pushed the organization to form links with other bureaucracies. The NWRO eventually signed a substantial ($450,000) contract with the Department of Labor, leading to the need to hire more professionals (bookkeepers, lawyers, and so forth) at relatively high salaries. The organization "faltered on the problems of bureaucratization, of inequality and professionalization of reform."[75] As the NWRO received money, support, and legitimacy from outside groups, it became more and more dependent on that flow of resources and turned its energies toward sustaining it rather than toward further organizing. Organizers and leaders became absorbed in negotiating the grievances of individual members, rather than in seeking to create opportunities for members and potential members to participate in collective action; thus "the sense of participation in something larger than oneself, the sense of belonging to a movement, was gradually lost."[76]

It is difficult to put the often heroic activities of welfare rights organizers into systematic perspective without seeming to denigrate their efforts. This I do not mean to do; for those who are economically and socially marginal in America, action that results in greater self-esteem and in some gains in access to welfare benefits is often crucially important to those individuals who are directly involved. But such actions leave the discourse and the institutions of bureaucratic capitalism intact, and thus cannot address the structural source of marginality. Further, these actions do little to affect the lives of most of the underclass, who are still radically dependent on bureaucracies in ways that discourage individual independence, collective organization, and public action. In their dependency the poor have much in common with the powerless in other areas of life, including those bureaucrats who administer their dependency; they too are the victims of the increasing feminization of the polity.

Five   Elements of a Feminist Discourse

Men denigrate our talk at their peril
but that's because they're in ignorance
of its power
our power.
—Astra

Women's experience constitutes a submerged voice within the overall discourse of bureaucratic capitalism. Discourses of opposition are made possible by the reaction of the oppressed and the excluded to the dominant discourse of power. The powerful and the powerless both use the dominant language, but stand in very different relations to it. By unearthing/creating the specific language of women, and comprehending women's experience in terms of that linguistic framework rather than in terms of the dominant discourse, feminist discourse is articulated as a voice of resistance. Ultimately, we can speak no more than our language allows us to speak, and can see and know no more than our social context allows us to experience. Just as our experience is defined by the intuitive and reflective awareness that our language makes available, our language in turn is circumscribed by our experience; to alter the terms of public discourse one must change the experiences people have, and to restructure experiences one must change the language available for making sense of those experiences. To articulate a substantially different voice for women is to break into the dialectic of speech and social structure, changing the relation between them, and thus altering the process by which the identity of individuals is formed:

> I can identify, reflect and decide on feelings, desires, and ways of being only to the extent that I can articulate those feelings, etc. They can become the object of reflection and choice only if they find a place in my language. My possibil-

ities for reflective self-identity are thus circumscribed by
the language available to me.[1]

In other words, both our institutions and our speech must be
transformed because it is the relation between them that defines them.

The aim of this chapter is to look for an alternative to the
discursive and institutional practices of bureaucracy in the
submerged and devalued experience of women. A specifically
feminist discourse can suggest a reformulation of some of the
most central terms of political life: reason, power, community,
freedom. Some questions, especially those concerning the relation between reason and emotion, and between freedom and
community, lend themselves readily to reformulation from a
feminist perspective. Other questions, such as those surrounding the problem of false consciousness and the overall relation
between the individual and the collective, seem to have no stable resolution in either theory or practice; the most one can do
with such perennial questions is to seek to cast them in a fresh,
if tentative, light. Still other issues, those concerning the specific organization of an alternative social order and the means
for achieving it, are never really answered on paper or all at
once; they emerge over time as people begin to think and live
differently. A beginning can be made by showing the inadequacies of the dominant discursive and institutional arrangements; by pointing toward a different set of values, an alternative mode of personal identity and social interaction, out of
which a fresh form of understanding and action might emerge;
and by suggesting critical points of action from which resistance can proceed.

The emergence of a specifically feminist discourse is part
of what Foucault calls "*an insurrection of subjugated knowledges.*"[2] Opposition voices are a vehicle for bringing power to
light as well as for altering that power. They are able to reveal
the politics embedded in the dominant discourse by their an-
tagonism toward that discourse, but are not simply a passive
reaction to it. Foucault makes this point clear:

Where there is power, there is resistance, and yet, or rather
consequently, this resistance is never in a position of exteri-

ority in relation to power. These points of resistance are present everywhere in the power network. Hence there is no single focus of great Refusal, no soul of revolt, source of all rebellions, or pure law of the revolutionary. Instead there is a plurality of resistances, each of them a special case: resistances that are possible, necessary, improbable; others that are spontaneous, savage, solitary, concerted, rampant or violent; still others that are quick to compromise, interested or sacrificial; by definition, they can only exist in the strategic field of power relations. But this does not mean that they are only a reaction or a rebound, forming with respect to the basic domination an underside that is in the end always passive, doomed to perpetual defeat. Resistances do not derive from a few heterogeneous principles; but neither are they a lure or a promise that is of necessity betrayed. They are the odd term in relations of power; they are inscribed in the latter as an irreducible opposite.[3]

Subjugated knowledges, like the powerful knowledge against which they struggle, are distributed irregularly through discursive and institutional fields. Whereas the dominant regimes of thought and action are based on universalistic claims to knowledge, such as the claims of scientific objectivity underpinning the technical civilization, discourses of opposition are based on particular claims, on what Foucault calls localized resistance, specific to the experience of the subjugated group but connected to one another through a serial network of points of struggle.[4] The goal of such localized resistance is not to take over and replace the dominant discourse of bureaucratic capitalism but rather to render that discourse obsolete, to reveal the partiality of its universal claims and the inadequacy of its institutional practices. These points of resistance, Foucault tells us, are often mobile and transitory,

> producing cleavages in a society that shifts about, fracturing unities and effecting regroupings, furrowing across individuals themselves, cutting them up and remolding them, marking off irreducible regions in them, in their bodies and minds. Just as the network of power relations ends by forming a dense web that passes through apparatuses and in-

> stitutions, without being exactly localized in them, so too
> the swarm of points of resistance traverses social stratifica-
> tions and individual unities.[5]

The discourses of opposition, in other words, will not be discovered fullblown and whole, to be laid down in place of the established regimes of thought; rather, they will be articulated
through an ongoing process of self-discovery and self-creation,
an emergent process involving the crafting and recrafting of
particular insights into unfolding and ever-shifting unities of
explanation and action.

The struggle of the subjugated discourse of women is a struggle against the official definition of identity and action imposed
by the dominant field of speech and practice. The simultaneous
denial of autonomy and of community in bureaucratic capitalism is what Foucault calls the "political double bind" of modern
society, "the simultaneous individualization and totalization of
modern power structures."[6] Bureaucratic capitalism separates
us from others without freeing us, resulting in isolation rather
than autonomy; it ties us to roles and rules rather than to
people, weighting us with connections that deny community.
Feminist discourse and practice entail a struggle for individual
autonomy that is *with others* and for community that *embraces
diversity*—that is, for an integration of the individual and the
collective in an ongoing process of authentic individuation and
genuine connectedness.

Like the other subjugated knowledges of which Foucault
speaks—for example, that of the mentally ill against the regime
of psychiatry, of children against parents, of patients against
medicine, and of citizens against administration—feminist discourse contains two related dimensions.[7] The first is the buried
historical knowledge about women, about what women have
done and been, spoken and dreamed, sought and found. These
blocks of historical knowledge are present to a degree in the
dominant domain of discourse, but they are disguised and distorted; the task of feminist scholarship is and has been to un-
earth this buried knowledge. The second is women's invisible
and disqualified knowledge about themselves and their world,
knowledge that has been inadequately elaborated because it is
dismissed by the powerful as "naive knowledge, located low

down on the hierarchy, beneath the required level of cognition or scientificity."[8] These low-ranking knowledges, while lacking unanimity in that they are reflective of the particular experiences of the excluded, nonetheless find a common base in that exclusion and thus constitute a collective voice in protest against it. While the first dimension of women's subjugated knowledge refers to the meticulous, erudite, exact reconstruction of discarded history by careful scholars, and the second refers to the diffuse and specific elements of day-to-day female experience that make up that history over time, these two dimensions are related in that they are both "concerned with a *historical knowledge of struggles*."[9] In both its erudite and its popular forms, feminist discourse resurrects "the memory of hostile encounters which even up to this day have been confined to the margins of knowledge."[10] Feminist discourse thus seeks historical, structural, and linguistic grounding for an emanicipated self-understanding that provides a base for political opposition and struggle. By locating and giving voice to the continuing creation and expression of women's subjugated knowledge, feminist discourse calls upon the newly disinterred past and the newly revealed present to move toward a freshly imagined future.

Sources of Feminist Discourse

The source of feminist discourse is in the characteristic experiences of women as caretakers, nurturers, and providers for the needs of others. Not all women have these experiences equally, of course, but most women have some access to them and nearly all women have far greater access to them than do nearly all men. Out of the lie that women are all the same—"isn't that just like a woman?"; "woman's place is in the home"; "what do women want?"—there has been a truth created about women: in many ways we *are* the same, we have come to be the same, we have been produced at least partially within the patterns of femininity and femaleness that bureaucratic capitalism requires. Divided by lines of class, race, ethnicity, and so on, most of us nonetheless encounter a characteristic set of linguistic and institutional practices constitutive of the life experiences of the second sex.

The world of women, thus qualified, is distinguished from the world of men by different notions of individual identity, by different standards of morality, and ultimately by different approaches to the problems of politics. Women's identity is forthrightly and consistently defined in terms of the contexts of social relationships. The connectedness with others that is at the heart of the survival and development of human infants is retained in female self-identity as a recognition of the continued and fundamental interdependence of self and other. For most women, connection with others is a primary given of their lives, not a secondary option to be contracted at will. Women tend to judge themselves by standards of responsibility and care toward others, with whom affiliation is recognized and treasured. Women's moral judgments are closely tied to feelings of empathy and compassion for others, and more directed toward the resolution of particular "real life" problems than toward abstract or hypothetical dilemmas.[11] Arising out of their experience of connection, women's conception of moral problems is concerned with the inclusion of diverse needs rather than with the balancing of opposing claims.[12]

In contrast, male self-identity is largely formed through the denial of relation and connection with others. In a culture that defines manhood in terms of separation and self-sufficiency, boys become men by breaking affiliative bonds, pursuing individual achievement, and avoiding attachment to others. Male self-identity is founded largely on the repression of affect, the denial of relational needs, and the rupture of connection.[13] Men tend to judge themselves and others by standards of achievement and competency, and to draw moral judgments on the basis of the application of abstract and universal notions of individual rights.[14]

The differences between the two worlds can be summarized, as Carol Gilligan states, in terms of an identity of connection and an ethic of responsibility versus an identity of separation and an ethic of rights.[15] The patterns of belief about the world dominant in male experience perceive a world made up of essentially physically and socially disembodied "things," governed by ultimately predictable laws or rules that can be rationally perceived and controlled by human beings. Knowledge is seen as "impersonal, abstract, universal and absolute." In such a world ethics becomes a "concern for elaborating rules for adjudicating competing and absolute rights between disembodied autonomous others."[16] The standards of knowledge and virtue in the male world, in other words, are based on the constitutive ideas of classical liberalism, in which justice is the equal application of rules, rights are individual and absolute, while responsibilities are derivative from the more primary abstract rights of individuals declared to be formally equal. One suspects that not all men are equally loyal to these notions, since the disadvantaged stand to lose a great deal on these terms, but these rules nonetheless capture the central value commitments embedded in the most dominant and public version of male rationality. The contrasting patterns of belief characteristic of the female world are those that are compatible with an identity of relatedness and an ethic of care. The world is viewed as constituted of essentially physically and socially embodied "things," which are concrete, particularistic, and continuous with one another. These "things" are governed by wants and needs and are thus resistant to rational control. Knowledge is "created through personal and concrete interactions, by following examples," and is "personal, concrete, particularistic, contextual."[17] It is, again, unlikely that all women are equally loyal to these ideas; in particular, women of the privileged economic strata are more likely to be attracted by the male standards that have worked so well in pursuing the class interests of the bourgeoisie. Nonetheless, most women are produced *qua* women through linguistic and institutional experiences that reconceptualize identity in terms of connection, morality in terms of responsibility and care, and knowledge in terms of particularity and process. Gilligan sums up these differences well in terms of the contrasting symbols of hierarchy and web:

> The image of hierarchy and web, drawn from the texts of men's and women's fantasies and thoughts, convey different ways of structuring relationships and are associated with

different views of morality and self. But these images create a problem in understanding because each distorts the
other's representation. As the top of the hierarchy becomes
the edge of the web and as the center of a network of connection becomes the middle of a hierarchical progression,
each image marks as dangerous the place which the other
defines as safe. Thus the images of hierarchy and web inform different modes of assertion and response: the wish to
be alone at the top and the consequent fear that others will
get too close; and the wish to be at the center of connection
and the consequent fear of being too far out on the edge.
These disparate fears of being stranded and being caught
give rise to different portrayals of achievement and affiliation, leading to different modes of action and different ways
of assessing the consequences of choice.[18]

The gender-defined worlds of women and men are created in
part by the developmental consequences of our culture's parenting practices. Woman-raised girls and woman-raised boys
experience a profoundly different relation to the primary parent, a difference that, as Nancy Chodorow shows, creates distinct subjective grounds for later relationships with others.
Mothers tend to experience their daughters as more like, and
more continuous with, themselves, while experiencing their
sons as opposites whose continuity with the mother must be
ended to achieve adulthood. Correspondingly, girls tend to remain more embedded in the early intensity of the mother-
child relation than do boys, and to define themselves more in
terms of participation in that relation than of separation from
it. Chodorow names the consequences of these patterns:

Children first experience the social and cognitive world as
continuous with themselves; they do not differentiate objects. Their mother, as first caretaking figure, is not a separate person and has no separate interests, and one of their
first developmental tasks is the establishment of a self with
boundaries, requiring the experience of self and other as
separate. In addition, this lack of separateness is in the context of the infant's total dependence upon the mother for

physical and psychological survival. . . . The experience of the self in the original mother-relation remains both seductive and frightening: unity was bliss, yet means the loss of self and absolute dependence. The father, by contrast has always been differentiated and known as a separate person with separate interests, and the child has never been totally dependent upon him. He has not posed the original narcissistic threat (the threat to basic ego integrity and boundaries) nor provided the original narcissistic unity (the original experience of oneness) to the girl. Oedipal love for the mother, then, contains a threat to selfhood which love for the father never does.[19]

Our earliest experiences, then, of dependency on a mother toward whom we feel both love/gratitude and rage/frustration leave different marks on male children than they do on female. Each child's love for the more distant father is less affected by the threats and promises of total dependency, and in particular the boy's identification with the father is more abstract and more distant from intense affective ties. Again, in Chodorow's words:

> Girls' identification processes, then, are more continuously embedded in and mediated by their ongoing relationship with their mother. They develop through and stress particularistic and affective relationships to others. A boy's identification patterns are not likely to be so embedded in or mediated by a real affective relation to his father. At the same time, he tends to deny identification with and relationship to his mother, and rejects what he takes to be the feminine world: masculinity is defined as much negatively as positively. Masculine identification processes stress differentiation from others, the denial of affective relation, and categorical universalistic components of the masculine role. Feminine identification processes are relational, whereas masculine identification processes tend to deny relationship.[20]

Women's mothering thus produces daughters who are prepared to mother, and prepared in general to be both capable of and in need of relations of intimacy and care. On the other hand, it produces sons who are not prepared to "mother," and who in general are less capable of and less in need of such relations.

The gender-defined patterns of identity begun in infancy are reinforced in many ways throughout adulthood in both public and private life. Men's notions of their own self-worth are tied to perceptions of success and failure in the rule-governed, achievement-oriented public world, while women's are more tied to their evaluation of their affectional and domestic lives. Men's labor is usually involved only minimally in the direct physical and psychological maintenance of themselves and others that occupies so much of women's time. Women's less visible and prestigious domestic and familial labor is more rooted in the maintenance of processes than in the production of products.[21] For these and many other reasons, the web of social relations that stands at the heart of female self-identity occupies the fringes of the male world, and is as often seen as a barrier to autonomy and adulthood as an avenue toward it.

Evidence of the differences between the two gender-defined worlds is present in the speech and the actions of both children and adults. Developmental psychologists have observed significant differences between the types of games that boys and girls typically play: boys are more likely to play competitive games that involve extensive elaboration of rules and procedures for adjudicating conflicts, while girls tend to play turn-taking or noncompetitive games in which conflict is resolved by ending the game so as to retain the affectional ties.[22] Boys' games teach skills that entail organizing and coordinating the efforts of relatively large numbers of people, dealing directly with conflict and competition, and declaring winners and losers. Girls' games continue the intimate and dyadic patterns of interaction characteristic of the earlier infant-mother relation, and encourage the learning of cooperative skills and the empathetic ability to take the experience of others as one's own.

Experiments, games, and observations of small-group interactions among adults continue these themes. Women talking with women are likely to use "cooperative verbal strategies" involving rotation of speakers and turn-taking, while men talking with men utilize competitive strategies in which a hierarchy of speakers is established and challenged through verbal dueling.[23] Women tend to talk to other women about relationships, while men talk to other men about themselves and tell stories that emphasize aggressiveness and a combative stance. Women's cooperative strategies seem to be based in "a respect for, and competence in, listening."[24] Women's discussions reveal more interest in achieving a "fair outcome" than in determining winners and losers, while the reverse is usually the case for men.[25] One set of researchers found unexpected (to them) differences between an "exploitative" masculine strategy and an "accommodative" feminine strategy in an experimental game:

> The men had gratifyingly manifested the sort of behavior that the (male) experimenters had expected. Thus they seemed to enter with gusto into the game, bargaining competitively, making the best "deals" they could, and, in short, striving to win. The behavior of the females was puzzlingly different. For them, the situation seemed to provide an opportunity for social interaction. It resembled more nearly a discussion than a competitive-bargaining situation. At first, we wondered whether they actually understood the purpose of the game at all.[!] Later, we came to the conclusion that, at least in many instances, the women did not see the objective to be a matter of winning, so much as a problem of arranging a "fair" outcome, one that would be satisfying to all three players.[26]

Concluding that women players "arrived at significantly better outcomes" than did men players, these researchers also noted cultural variation in their results, in that men from Micronesian cultures showed a more accommodative interactional style than did the Western men.[27] Studies in which college students are asked to project meaning into stories show that men "projected more violence into situations of personal affiliation than they did into impersonal situations of achievement," while "women saw more violence in impersonal situations of achievement than in situations of affiliation."[28] Men in our culture, in other words, having come to repress their own needs for connectedness, often become intolerant of those needs in others;

men see danger in connection and the threat of absorption, while women see it in separation and the threat of loss.

The greater attention that women pay to context and field is well documented in the psychological literature on information processing. Males tend to concentrate on one stimulus at a time, while females "tend to process information more globally, responding to a number of stimuli simultaneously." [29] Females tend to merge stimuli with their settings, while males separate the stimuli from the field. Tests of three-dimensional skills show that "males, using more vergence eye movements, search the environment with a narrower field but greater depth, while females, using more peripheral vision, search the environment with a broader field and less depth." [30] In general, men tend to excel at those perceptual activities that involve looking at objects, while women excel at those which entail scanning for order.

Carol Gilligan and others have pointed out that the distinct psychological and moral language that men and women speak pose systemic barriers to communication between the sexes. [31] While this is true, it is important to see that the differences in the worlds of men and women entail far more than simple problems in communication and intention: such differences are *political*, in that they are bound up in relations of dominance and subordination and also in that they provide different approaches to the political problems of conflict and order. Language is far more than simply a system for the transmission of messages; it is a process by which individuals constitute themselves over time by expressing to others and to themselves a set of self-defining and society-defining symbols. In a male-dominant society, the language that men use about women helps to constitute the meaning of womanhood in that society; it is clear that in the English language womanhood has been constituted to be a rather undesirable and dangerous state of being. Our language largely describes women in terms of sexuality (for example, there are approximately two hundred words to describe a sexually permissive female and only twenty to describe the same conduct in a man), and unreliability and danger (for example, pejorative adjectives are used to describe the dangerous talk of women that would seldom be applied to men

—chatter, natter, prattle, nag, bitch, whine, gossip).[32] To resist the meanings that deny or devalue women through the creation of an alternative discourse is a political activity: "It is about a redistribution of power, a reclaiming of the right to name, an end of silence."[33]

Feminist discourse not only provides the means for such resistance; it also provides the grounds for it—that is, it offers a table of values, those surrounding the activities of caring and connection, upon which a politics of democratic community can be built. Feminist discourse can provide for a reconceptualization of some of the most basic terms of political life. In the last section of this chapter I will elaborate what I see as the reconstituted meanings of some of these concepts, but first I want to examine the relationship among feminist discourse, femaleness in our society, and femininity in the sense in which I have defined it.

The source of the values of feminist discourse is in the traditional and characteristic experiences of women in our society, but not simply in womanhood as it has been traditionally defined, because women's traditional experience, by itself, is both distorted and partial. It is distorted in that the commitment to caretaking is bent to the service of power. The deep and intimate links that women characteristically experience to others, when located within a patriarchal political order, are misshapen in the interests of survival. There is a complex relation between the strong, positive, creative aspects of women's experience as caretakers, and the negative, manipulated, coerced aspects of women's experience as subordinates. "Femininity" in the sense used here—that is, femininity as a response to dominance—is not simply a separate, added-on aspect of womanhood; it is, rather, an integral aspect of womanhood, produced by the relations of power that turn caring to the service of male supremacy. While women have been the victims of this process, we have not simply been passive victims, because we have participated in the construction of the dominant discourse in that we have raised sons and daughters to be men and women— men who usually devalue women, women who often devalue themselves. We have also been more than victims, but separating that aspect of our experience that has its own integrity and offers its own achievements from our victimization is no simple task. Women's experience of femininity reveals helping put to the service of pleasing; this results both in a too-great vulnerability to interpersonal loss and in a fear of risk and conflict.

Women's greater vulnerability supports the imbalance of need that frequently characterizes heterosexual love relations. The common patterns of depression in women reveal a pervasive and often debilitating concern over the disruption of emotional bonds, and the corresponding lack of autonomous emotional resources.[34] Taught from childhood to idealize the distant and powerful male and to view other females as competitors for that special male attention, women are often willing to deny men's limitations as long as they feel loved. Dorothy Dinnerstein attributes this unguardedness in love to the patterns of independence and need that characterize early male and female development under conditions of exclusively female parenting:

> Early rage at the first parent, in other words, is typically used by the "masculine" boy during the Oedipal period to *consolidate* his tie with his own sex by establishing a principled independence, a more or less derogatory distance, from women. And it is typically used by the "feminine" girl in this same period to *loosen* her tie with her own sex by establishing a worshipful, dependent stance toward men. Just when that boy is learning to keep his feelings for the mother under control, that girl (precisely because her first emotional problems also centered on the mother) is learning to overidealize the father. This contrast, of course, heavily supports asymmetry of sexual privilege. For without comparably strong, well-defined ways of counterbalancing feelings for the opposite sex with a sense of human identity based on solidarity with each other, women are far less free than men to set their own terms in love.[35]

But since the inequality between the sexes is more than psychic, simply urging women to be less fearful is a lame response. Women's deference to men is rooted in a realistic recognition of the superior political, economic, and social power of males and is not likely to be systematically changed until those power

relations are altered. To emphasize only psychological development, as Carol Gilligan does in her otherwise excellent analysis of women's voice, leads to a view of androgyny that is politically naive. Describing the "conventional female voice,"
Gilligan writes: "The strength of this position lies in its capacity for caring; the limitation of this position lies in the restric-
tion it imposes on direct expression." [36] Prior to women's discov-
ery/acknowledgment of the validity of the male view of equal
rights, she states, women's commitment to care leads both to
deference and to duplicity—that is, to a fear that comes from
being too easily hurt by others and a consequent unwillingness
to be completely honest with others. "The logic of this position
is confused in that the morality of mutual care is embedded
in the psychology of dependence." But this changes, Gilligan
argues, when women recognize "the justice of the rights approach" and see that they themselves have a right to the same
care extended to others:

> The concept of rights changes women's conception of them-
> selves, allowing them to see themselves as stronger and to
> consider their own needs. When assertion no longer seems
> dangerous, the concept of relationships changes from a bond
> of continuing dependence to a dynamic of interdependence.
> Then the notion of care expands from the paralyzing injunc-
> tion not to hurt others to an injunction to act responsibly
> toward self and others and thus to sustain connection. [37]

What is lacking here is an explicit recognition of the political
context within which the male and female voices develop. Since
women's psychology of dependence is tied to the reality of male
power, women are not likely to view self-assertion as safe; as-
sertiveness is always risky for the powerless. The impulse toward helping and caring is held hostage to the need to please;
under conditions of unequal power, the need for approval is a
politically rational need, not a psychologically weak one. As
long as women are subordinate to men, the virtues of female
experience will be turned to the requirements of surviving subordination: the capacity to listen, to empathize, to hear and appreciate the voice of the other, and so forth, will be used as
strategies for successful impression management. Gilligan's

discussion of moral development gives no explicit recognition to the social and political barriers to her vision of androgyny. She writes:

> In women's development, the absolute of care, defined initially as not hurting others, becomes complicated through a recognition of the need for personal integrity. This recognition gives rise to the claim for equality embodied in the concept of rights, which changes the understanding of relationships and transforms the definition of care. For men, the absolutes of truth and fairness, defined by the concepts of equality and reciprocity, are called into question by experiences that demonstrate the existence of differences between other and self. Then the awareness of multiple truths leads to a relativizing of equality in the direction of equity and gives rise to an ethic of generosity and care. For both sexes the existence of two contexts for moral decision makes judgment by definition contextually relative and leads to a new discovery of responsibility and choice.[38]

But this happy ending is mainly hypothetical unless the public context of male power is radically altered. To learn the skills of self-assertion, women must learn to *risk*, to seek adventure and achievement untainted by the pernicious need to please, to act without the debilitating fear that comes from being overinvested in others at the expense of oneself. If society does not recognize the worth of women, then the achievement of the insight that characterizes movement into Gilligan's third stage of development, when women wed care to equality, is a too-rare political victory. Similarly, most men are not likely to call their own perspective into question simply because an alternative perspective, that of women, is available. When men fail to hear women's voice, it is not only because they are not listening but because they do not have to listen. Men are insulated from women's voice by the dominant linguistic and institutional practices that enshrine male experience as absolute and fail to call attention to, or even allow recognition of, its limits. Men, as Simone de Beauvoir stated so well in *The Second Sex*, define the world "from their own point of view, which they confuse with absolute truth."[39] Traditionally women have in many ways conspired to keep men from facing the relativizing experiences that Gilligan describes by mothering men in such a way that the illusion of the autonomous and achieving ego is maintained. As Gilligan points out, when men do embrace the validity of the female voice it is often at or past midlife, when the limitations of the male ethic are coming home to roost and when, conveniently, the hard work of raising children is finished.[40] Since each of us can only decipher that which we are in some sense capable of speaking ourselves, to truly hear a different way of speaking is to begin to reconstitute ourselves in relation to the other—but this is a fairly radical task and relatively few men volunteer for it. Real androgyny, defined not as simply adding together the misshapen halves of male and female, but rather as a complex process of calling out that which is valuable in each gender and carefully disentangling it from that which is riddled with the effects of power, is a *political struggle*.

If women's experience is distorted by oppression in the ways described above, does it then follow that the caretaking experience, rescued from degradation and restored to integrity, provides by itself an adequate base for constructing feminist discourse? The answer, I think, has to be no. Women's experience is not simply distorted; it is also partial and incomplete. It has to be supplemented by an explicit commitment to a public discourse and practice of freedom and equality. To unwind the complex strands of women's experience is to be continually reminded of Foucault's insistence that our subjectivity is produced by the forces of power that operate on us and within us. This tells us both that the process of separating that which has integrity and authenticity of its own from that which does not is a complicated and treacherous task, and that the historical forces of bureaucratic capitalism have rendered us so disindividualized and isolated that even the wholest of personal wholes is merely a part.

Understanding the partiality of women's traditional experience is partly a matter of careful attention to the nuances of description. Caretaking is all too easily romanticized and sentimentalized, reduced to terminal cheerfulness or to a masochistic need for self-sacrifice. Particularly when the core of

female experience is equated with mothering, it is easily mystified through the use of quasi-biological metaphors claiming a
special "organic" way of relating to others for women, one that
is "not contaminated by male systems."[41] At their most extreme, recent feminist celebrations of mothering begin to sound
like academic versions of a Hallmark card. But even when this
sentimentality is avoided, mothering and its related domestic
tasks are still a partial aspect of female experience, not the
whole of it. The ties of mothers to children reveal a particular
aspect of characteristically female experience, one that Sara
Ruddick, Jean Elshtain, and others convincingly applaud for
its devotion to the preservation and protection of children, the
fostering of children's intellectual, spiritual, and emotional
growth, and so forth. Mothering, as Ruddick presents it, is a
special kind of social practice based upon the virtues of "attentive love," of humility and good humor (a recognition of limits
and a concomitant willingness to continue), of a special form of
regard for the fragility of the other that Ruddick calls "holding."[42] In their authentic rather than degenerative forms, maternal thinking and acting offer a crucial pedagogic experience—that of temporary inequality, in which the power of the
mother is used to foster development in the child that rights
the initial disparity and ends the need for the power.[43] But the
fact that the mother-child relation is one of inequality, even
though it is a necessary and temporary mode of inequality,
makes it a poor model for larger relations of citizenship, which
require equality among individuals and which are rooted in respect, not in love.

   Further, mothering only partially captures that which is
unique to the experience of women as caretakers. The women
in Carol Gilligan's development studies are often not mothers,
and are in fact often involved in making the choice *not* to be
mothers, but they nonetheless display the characteristic modes
of thinking and judging here described as the female voice.
Women are produced as caretakers and nurturers more through
their experiences as *daughters* than as mothers.[44] Even when
traditional womanhood is recast in more inclusive terms, as
Roslyn Bologh does in her notion of "female rationality," its
limitations are still apparent. Bologh defines female rational-

ity in terms of three interrelated capacities: that of the mother, defined largely as Ruddick defines it, that of the wife/lover/intimate friend, and that of the homemaker. Like Elshtain's "social feminism," Bologh calls for a rescue of the private realm that places the virtues of private life at the center of a reconstituted public sphere. She defines homemaking as

> the desire to remake or recreate a piece of the world as one's own. Such re-creation transforms nature from an alien and disturbing, unknown and unpredictable, disordered and threatening, unsettling and distressing experience to one that is known and familiar, settled and secure, ordered and harmonious, comfortable and pleasurable. To make oneself at home in the world by making a home out of the world may be thought of as self-consciously and intentionally non-alienating activity.[45]

The partiality of this appeal to the domestic is perhaps best seen by considering two different nuances of meaning attached to the term: domestic can mean, as Bologh claims, that which is comfortable and safe, as in a "quiet, domestic scene"; but it can also mean that which is tame and without wildness of spirit, as in the "domestication of animals." A vision of public life modeled solely upon the domestic suggests a kind of over-confinement, an avoidance of chance and hazard. It puts too great a burden on the private virtues of attentive love and holding to expect them to constitute the entire basis of public life; to do so is to end up advocating a warm, mushy, and wholly impossible politics of universal love, one in which the very meaning of intimacy loses its integrity as it is diluted and applied to all.[46]

What, then, might be the relationship between the newly uncovered voice of women and the revision of public life? Mary Dietz points out that the endorsement of familial caretaking and connectedness "is insufficient as a basis for feminist political consciousness because it has nothing to do with politics."[47] That is, caretaking alone offers no standards by which to judge and/or construct a democratic public order: the connections among people could as easily be nurtured by a benevolent despotism, in which the rulers do what is best for us, as they could be by participatory democracy. When our models of caretaking and nurturance are derived exclusively from family life, we meet with two problems. First, we abstract family life out of its concrete political context. Many families, after all, are scenes of physical and psychological abuse, and most are laden with the consequences of patriarchal power relations. Second, we overlook other sources of intense, reciprocal, face-to-face ties, such as friendships.[48] Martha Ackelsberg points out that the theory and practice of both waves of the women's movement have drawn more heavily on friendship ties than on families, and that feminist activities such as consciousness-raising groups, housekeeping "pools," collective/communal living arrangements, and co-parenting have drawn on support networks based upon the ties of friendship. Friendship is distinguished by its "voluntary and egalitarian quality."[49] Friendships can, of course, become abusive or insidious, but then they cease to be real friendships. Their equality is based on respect for the other, on acknowledgment of the concrete needs and qualities of the other, expressed through a reciprocity of generosity and trust. Friendship challenges the dichotomy between public and private life; while friendships are intensely personal, they can also form the base of radical political association.[50] Friendship does not erase the distinction between the public and private realms, since one could not be and probably would not want to be friends with everyone; but acknowledging the civic as well as the personal importance of friendship can help one rethink the connections between personal life and politics. When caretaking and responsibility are connected to the more equal and reciprocal relations of friendship, rather than to the inequality of the parent-child relation, the connection of the caretaking values to a reconstituted public life become more clear.

One aspect of feminist discourse is the embracing of the values of care and connection; another must be the opposition to femininity as it is here defined, entailing an opposition to all forms of institutionalized dominance and subordination because it is through such relations that femininity is created. Since femininity refers to a series of traits that accompany powerlessness, and that confine femininized people to the depoliticized status of reactive spectators, an opposition to femininity entails a commitment to equality and active participation in public life. Active, participatory citizenship is a process through which individuals create themselves with others through the shared processes of speaking, deliberating, and judging, ordering their collective lives through institutions they have designed and in a language they have made their own. Feminist discourse, then, stands at the intersection of femininity and femaleness, opposing the strategies of the former while endorsing the values of the latter. The commitment to participatory democracy in feminist discourse is not a random and unexplainable choice but is rooted in the convergence of the values that the discourse defends and the linguistic and institutional practices that it opposes. The language of care is united with the language of freedom.

To claim that the values of feminist discourse are rooted in the traditional experiences of women as caretakers is immediately to raise the difficult question of false consciousness: what, exactly, is the relation between feminist discourse and those women who interpret their experience in other than feminist terms? This question is in turn part of a larger epistemological question: what constitutes a feminist theory of knowledge? Foucault's insights into the relations between power, language, and knowledge are again central. There is no pure and neutral language, no pure and neutral knowledge; the point of view of the powerful forces itself upon the world, claiming a privileged status for its particular way of apprehending. "All knowledge is political not because it may have political consequences or be politically useful, but because knowledge has its conditions of possibility in power relations."[51] Those who own the "means of enunciation" are in a position to appropriate the dominant truth claims for their own purposes.[52] There is no ungendered perspective, and the claim to have access to such a perspective is itself a denial of the power relations underlying knowledge. As Catherine MacKinnon points out in her discussion of consciousness, "objectivity—the nonsituated, universal standpoint, whether claimed or aspired to—is a denial of the existence or potency of sex inequality that tacitly participates in constructing reality from the dominant point of view."[53] Recognizing that "what counts as truth is produced in the interest of those with the power to shape reality," feminist discourse commences with the acknowledgment of its own rootedness: "Feminism does not begin with the premise that it is unpremised. It does not aspire to persuade an unpremised audience because there is no such audience. Its project is to uncover and claim as valid the experience of women, the major content of which is the devalidation of women's experience."[54]

This still leaves us with the problem of interpretation: how does one evaluate and/or account for the claims made about female experience by women who are not feminists? The feminist project is to represent and give voice to the experiences of women, and at the same time to criticize anti-feminism and misogyny, including instances of their appearance among women. How can we generate a criticism of patriarchy from the experience of women when not all women experience patriarchy the same way?

There are many angles to be considered on the perennial question of consciousness in radical politics. First of all, it needs to be clearly stated that the claims to have articulated a set of experiences, a perspective on identity and morality, that is typically female is not the same as saying that all women have the same experiences and perspective, or that no men have those experiences or embrace that perspective. Certain experiences are characteristic of women as a group because of the position women have occupied in the social order, not because of some universal or organic trait of the female; there are bound to be both individual exceptions, women who are privileged or unique in some way, and divergences among women who are divided by other factors as well, such as class, race, or ethnicity. Caretaking constitutes a social practice in which women engage much more than men; it carries its own distinct perspective, its own skills and integrity, its own particular way of relating to the world. Women's characteristic experiences as fosterers of care and commitment can serve as a model out of which to construct feminist discourse without being universally applicable to all women or exclusive of all men.

Unfortunately, this observation, while true, does not solve

the problem of judgment. The three most common approaches
to the problem in the history of political thought are all dead-
ends for feminist discourse. The first is the argument, usually
associated with traditional Marxism, that nonfeminist women
are simply manifesting false consciousness; regardless of the
claims they might make to reflexive self-understanding, these
women's views are an "unconscious and conditional reflection of
their oppression, complicitous in it."[55] The initial seductiveness
of this argument is quickly exploded when one sees that it is
based on a self-refuting claim to transcendence. Larry Spence
makes this point beautifully:

> For if he [sic] contends or demonstrates that human beings
> cannot be trusted to learn the truth about themselves and
> the world, the social investigator must invoke some special
> dispensations or ecstatic maneuvers to free himself from
> the defect common to the species. These maneuvers of pu-
> rification, transcendence, or polygonal vision always in-
> volve authority claims that cannot be evaluated, even in
> theory. Thus accounts of social ignorance make social
> knowledge impossible and we are left only with the medici-
> nal lies of those who know what is best for us.[56]

Applied to feminism, the false consciousness argument as-
serts that, while feminist discourse is based on the experiences
of women, some women do not rightly know what their experience has been. Stated this baldly, the argument could be used
equally well to refute feminism itself, since if some women do
not know what their experience has been, feminists could well
be among them. Catherine MacKinnon has made this argument well:

> Just as science devalues experience in the process of un-
> covering its roots, this approach criticizes the substance of a
> view because it can be accounted for by its determinants.
> But if both feminism and anti-feminism are responses to
> the same condition of women, how is feminism exempt from
> devalidation by the same account? That feminism is criti-
> cal, and anti-feminism is not, is not enough, because the

question is the basis on which we know something is one or the other when women, all of whom share the condition of women, disagree. The false consciousness approach begs this question by taking women's self-reflections as evidence of their stake in their own oppression, when the women whose self-reflections are at issue question whether their position is oppressed at all.[57]

The second standard argument is the flip side of the false consciousness position. Usually associated with traditional liberalism, this position claims that whatever version of women's experience a particular female claims for herself is true for her. This view dispenses with the need to judge some perspective to be true and others false, but does so at the expense of a deluded self-understanding and a diluted politics. It is deluded because it proceeds as if women were already free and self-constituting beings, when the entire force of the feminist critique is to show precisely the opposite. Part of the perniciousness of femininity in our society is that it produces people who claim to choose what they are supposed to want, and claim to want what they have. Once acknowledging the ways in which knowledge and power are dialectically bound together, it becomes an act of viciously acquired naivete to equate all expressed preferences with self-defined interests. The political position that follows from this view is diluted in that it reduces to a wishy-washy tolerance, unable to identify or oppose the enemy in any guise.

The third standard position reiterates the first two in a disguised form. The third common argument appeals to the insights of those who have been exposed to a broader and more diverse range of experiences, on the grounds that they have seen more than the rest of us and thus can judge more accurately. On these grounds John Stuart Mill made his plea for the superiority of the intellectual's judgment; Sandra Harding uses the same grounds to claim more complete knowledge for the marginal person, one whose experience transcends the socially stratified division of class, race, and gender.[58] There is some truth here: those who are marginal in the dominant society, who experience life in more than one "world," have access to more than one point of view. Thus those who stand on the fringes of established roles can offer insights less available to individuals more thoroughly and consistently integrated into the established categories. But this does not answer the question of truth: if those who are marginal do not uniformly agree, how does one distinguish among their competing claims? Thus we are brought back either to appeals to false consciousness or to total relativism.

There is, it seems to me, no answer to the question when it is framed in these terms. Perhaps the inability to think past the dilemma suggests an inadequacy in the very concepts of false and true consciousness. Feminist consciousness is neither a perspective that some women have privileged access to, nor is it whatever all individual women happen to believe. Consciousness is not an object that can be divided up into subjective (whatever one believes is right because one believes it) and objective (whatever one believes is wrong unless it matches that privileged knowledge of those with the authority to judge) without doing violence to its wholeness. Consciousness is not an object, but a *process*, an ongoing interaction with others, with nature, and with the world in which the individual both creates herself and is created through these connections. Once this is understood, attempts to judge the contents of consciousness to be true or false must necessarily result in stand-offs between liberalism and Marxism. The question simply cannot be answered this way; so perhaps it is the wrong question. There seem to be many different forms of "false" consciousness, but no one form of "true" consciousness. That is, there are many ways in which one's perceptions and self-perceptions can be distorted to serve the interests of others, but no simple grounds for "pure" consciousness, consciousness unconfined by the needs of others and/or the pull of power. Since consciousness is by definition an ongoing process of interactions with others, produced by, and producing itself within, the prevailing discourse and structures, all consciousness is social; but not all social situations are the same. Instead of judging the content of consciousness, feminist discourse looks to judge its *context*, distinguishing between situations that are relatively autonomous and those that are relatively manipulative. Consciousness as a temporal process is judged by its authenticity, its integrity: is it developed in a context of freedom and community, where connections with others are rooted in equality, not domination; or is it shaped by institutionalized links with others that express and enforce the values/interests/knowledge of the powerful? This reformulation does not eliminate the problem of judgment, since the standards of authenticity and integrity have to come from somewhere, and be evaluated by someone, but it does recast the question and redirect the inquiry. Each person, finally, judges her own consciousness, her own relations with herself and the world that create her consciousness over time; yet each person's judgment can be limited by those relations as well. In shaping the question as one primarily of process rather than substance, feminist discourse seeks to allow for the presence of differing perspectives without accepting patriarchal claims when they are made by women. Carol Gilligan conceptualizes the shift from substance to process as a shift from classical to Biblical metaphors: "The underlying epistemology correspondingly shifts from the Greek ideal of knowledge as a correspondence between mind and form to the Biblical conception of knowing as a process of human relationship."[59]

Feminist discourse, like all knowledge, is intentional and purposive. Its goal is to reveal the meaning of acts and events from the point of view of women, acknowledging that this point of view contains inconsistencies and is continuously emergent over time. Individuals never fully coincide with their roles. We wear a series of disguises, some socially assigned and some self-created, that reveal our fragility and tenuousness; we constantly struggle both to survive and to grow. Avoiding the cognitive fallacy of claiming that moral problems can be solved through adequate cognition, and simultaneously avoiding the degradation of moral and political action to the level of casual preference, feminist discourse seeks a view of identity and morality as open-ended, ongoing, social processes. Judgments about whether this process is relatively autonomous or relatively manipulated are neither made from some privileged outside standpoint nor are they completely arbitrary; rather, they are made and remade by each individual from the precarious and changing point of view of her/his own experience.

What Is (and Is Not) to Be Done?

In order for the feminist movement to move toward the radical promise inherent in feminist discourse, it cannot go the way of other opposition groups such as the mainstream trade unions and welfare rights organizations. Feminism is not compatible with bureaucracy, and like all forms of opposition it is endangered by too-close contact with bureaucratic linguistic and institutional forms. If opposition can be rendered bureaucratic by the powerful, it can be absorbed, integrated, and eventually rendered harmless. Bureaucracy can be resisted, but not on its own terms, since they are terms that render opposition invisible.

But there is also a dilemma here, in that entry into the public realm, now increasingly a bureaucratic realm, is necessary for any voice of opposition that wishes to be heard. Often conceptualized as the tension between reform and revolution, or means and ends, it comes down to the tension between living/surviving in the world as it is and making the world into what it should be. Nancy Hartsock articulates the problem clearly:

> Creating political change requires that we set up organizations based on power defined as energy and strength, groups that are structured, not tied to the personality of a single individual, and whose structures do not permit the use of power to dominate others in the group. At the same time, our organizations must be effective in a society in which power is a means of making others do what they do not wish to do.[60]

Feminism cannot simply turn its back on the existing public world because that world does not oblige by leaving us alone: the state makes laws about women's bodies and women's lives; conglomerates control most employment opportunity and most resources; bureaucratic channels are sometimes the only ones available for individuals to press grievances or even to live at all. My point is not that no one should ever turn to such channels, but that those avenues are inherently and severely limited in what they can accomplish. Feminists, as individuals and as groups, will often have to confront bureaucracies and to work within them, but if the feminist movement allows its own organizations or ideology to become bureaucratic, it ceases to carry any critical edge.

In thinking through the relation between reform and revolution, between living in the world and changing it, the fate of the First Wave of the women's movement is instructive. By the 1920s the liberal voices that had become dominant in the movement, faced with a large and well-funded right wing opposition and hampered by internal conflict and "burn out," were increasingly coopted into the burgeoning consumer culture. Much of what passed for feminism was concerned solely with individual choices and opportunities, abandoning the collective identity of a social movement to define female independence in terms of personal fulfillment.[61] In the obscure and complex way of discourse, the first feminist movement capitulated to the development of the cult of rationality. The movement articulated the claims for equal legal status for women, and appealed to the theory of state sovereignty, legal rights, and contract to make its case. But the judicial discourse of rights is subverted by the cult of rationality; the procedures of normalization colonize those of law. In some ways still a voice of opposition, as in the more militant struggle for reproductive freedom in the legislatures and courts, the liberal voice of contemporary feminism has in other ways become subservient to the dominant political discourse of technical society. As Foucault points out, discourses that are in opposition on one level are wound together on another; they are "tactical elements or blocks operating in the field of power relations."[62] If advertising and the consumer culture were early capitalism's answer to the first feminist movement, bureaucracy and the cult of rationality is late capitalism's answer to the second. Feminism cannot pursue its own goals through disciplinary strategies, since these, I have argued, are fundamentally at odds with the feminist project; nor can feminists turn back to the discourse of sovereignty and the state in search of grounds for opposition to disciplinary power, because the juridical discourse of rights has been married to the discourse of administration. In Foucault's words:

> If one wants to look for a non-disciplinary form of power,
> or rather, to struggle against disciplines and disciplinary
> power, it is not towards the ancient right of sovereignty
> that one should turn, but towards the possibility of a new
> form of right, one which must indeed be anti-discipli-
> narian, but at the same time liberated from the principle
> of sovereignty.[63]

Contemporary liberal feminism, which is the face of feminism
most evident in the popular media, has largely embraced the
two related discourses of administration and of juridico-legal
rights: the first is evident in the ubiquitous array of books,
magazines, seminars, workshops, et cetera, et cetera for the
upwardly mobile career woman; the second appears in the
large-scale lobbying efforts and the focus on legal change and
organizational accommodation dominant in the large national
women's organizations. The first of these is a deadend for feminism and the second offers only very limited opportunities for
change.[64] By looking at these two aspects of liberal feminism, I
seek to sort through the difficult problem of reform versus revolution, separating those avenues of activity within the dominant discourse of bureaucratic capitalism that are destructive
of feminist goals from those that offer some promise of change.

Individual Upward Mobility: The Illusion of the Epoch

Popular culture in America has always evinced a
fondness for literature that proclaims the power of positive
thinking as a cure for socioeconomic disadvantage. In the late
nineteenth and early twentieth centuries books with titles such
as *Your Forces and How to Use Them*, *Thought Force in Business*, *Acres of Diamonds*, *Pushing to the Front*, and *Success Under Difficulties* enjoyed great popularity.[65] Another great burst
of books and articles touting the power of positive thinking and
the importance of image management emerged in the 1950s. So
the current spate of "how to succeed in the organization" books

are simply variations on a long-standing theme. Belief in an "individual solution," ironically pursued *en masse* by legions of ambitious candidates, is the great American illusion.

The important difference now is that substantial numbers of these books are directed at women. They are, by their own definition, survival manuals for women in bureaucracies. They are also, again by their own definition, feminist—at least of a sort. They exemplify the logical consequences of liberal feminism's search for entry into the established institutions of bureaucratic capitalism. For example, Betty Lehan Harragan, author of the popular book *Games Mother Never Taught You*, and Margaret Hennig and Anne Jardin, authors of the more academically respectable *The Managerial Woman*, refer to themselves as feminists and refer approvingly to standard feminist arguments. Marilyn Moats Kennedy's *Office Politics*, while not self-avowedly feminist, is directed at the same audience—upwardly mobile, "aware" women.[66] They take the existing institutional arrangements for granted and seek strategies to integrate women into these arrangements. This search for entry requires them to analyze bureaucracy in terms of the obstacles it poses to women, obstacles that they acknowledge to be barriers to women as a group and not simply as individuals. Thus, like other feminists, they argue that women are oppressed collectively simply because they are women; but they tie this insight to a set of values and assumptions that leads to virtually total acceptance of the *status quo*. The ability of these authors to avoid confronting this mammoth contradiction in their own argument is indicative of the conservative political consequences of this brand of feminism.[67]

Each of these books focuses on the language of bureaucratic interactions, explaining it as a particularly male form of communications that rests upon metaphors and analogies drawn from sports, the military, and pornography. The objects and events named in bureaucratic discourse are rendered inaccessible to most women because they refer to a set of experiences that women are not likely to have had: Harragan argues that "male business terminology is almost foreign speech to women, replete as it is with secret codes, double meanings, and colloquial slang."[68] Hennig and Jardin maintain that "organizations in general are dominated by a male culture" and that access to the informal network of communications in this culture is the key to organizational success:

> The ability to take advantage of equal opportunity is the critical starting point and it has less to do with technical knowledge and much more to do with fundamental differences in perception which stand in the way of acquiring new and necessarily very different skills—differences which have left women trapped in supervisory positions and too often branded as lacking in management potential.[69]

All three books attack the "Horatio Alger" myths equating hard work with success and point to acceptance into the informal network of norms and rules as the crucial point of entry into the discursive relations of the organization. In fact, the naivete of many women in believing that ability and achievement are the bases for reward is one of the important objects of attack. Kennedy points out that not only women, but blacks and Hispanics as well, are excluded from the informal network and thus from participation in the flow of information through which alliances are created and important bureaucratic resources are exchanged. Harragan is perhaps the most articulate of all the authors in demonstrating that the barriers to women's entry into the central arenas of organizational power are structural, not personal. Thus she points out that much of the career advice to women that emphasizes self-scrutiny and self-improvement is irrelevant: the ability to participate in bureaucratic discourse must be acquired within the bureaucratic environment itself.

The various recommendations that each of these authors makes for gaining access to the discourse of the organization consist of several different versions of the same message: *conform*. Women are urged to learn to look at themselves from the point of view of the organizational hierarchy, to be "well mannered participants in the organization" (don't rock the boat), and to remember that they, like blacks and Hispanics, must work doubly hard at fitting into the system in order to overcome the initial disadvantage of gender and/or color:

Remember that the more you differ from the norm, for example, if you're a black male in a predominantly white male group, the more you'll have to show that you accept the group values. It's not just winning acceptance that's important but also showing that you're not opposed to group values—that you can live with the things the group believes.[70]

Any display of individualism, whether in dress, mannerism, thought, or speech, is discouraged. Harragan frequently admonishes the reader to remember the new rules of the game ("You didn't forget you're in the army, did you?"), and Kennedy forthrightly advises her reader to "keep individualism to a minimum when it doesn't count anyway."[71] This advice squares with that given by the legions of "dress for success" advocates who advise women and men to avoid expressing their personality in their clothing for fear of compromising their professional image.[72]

Great emphasis is placed on learning an uncritical deference to authority; Rule No. 1 for Harragan is "absolute deference to the authority invested in your immediate boss," and Hennig and Jardin advise women to avoid confrontations with men at all costs.[73] This means that women should ignore any and all forms of insults, sexual advances, or challenges; in other words, never acknowledge that the organization is a political arena and never rebel against oppressive attitudes or actions. Women are further advised that "*lawful deception is admirable*" and that the skills they learned for manipulating men in their traditional feminine role can be pressed into service:

Women who look over the field with clear-headed realism and learn all the rules can counter-attack with delicate refinements of the same techniques. Women are naturals at playing this artful dodger game because their powerless, subservient position in society has taught them to cultivate an unlimited repertoire of manipulative, two-faced, guileful tricks to survive economically.[74]

Women are advised to learn to "love money" and to put aside any other table of values; after all, "money is synonymous with 'life' as we know it." [75] Some enthusiasts of socioeconomic climbing offer prosperity training seminars so that women can overcome their ambivalence about money and cultivate a single-minded preoccupation with material success. [76] Women's failings in this regard are said to stem from their unwillingness or inability to view their activity as a means to an end rather than an end in itself:

> Women see a career as personal growth, as self-fulfillment, as satisfaction, as making a contribution to others, as doing what one wants to do. While men indubitably want these things too, when they visualize a career they see it as a series of jobs, a progression of jobs, as a path leading upward with recognition and reward implied. [77]

Women must learn to view their careers in terms of movement up through the hierarchy, not in terms of the intrinsic value of their actions; they must develop a personal strategy that always asks, "What's in it for me?" [78] The cultivation of these organizational values and skills—conformity, deception, deference, instrumentalism, and greed—should enable women to overcome the obstacles to success posed by their traditional feminine socialization, so that they can present the appropriate image to male colleagues and superiors, emulate the appropriate conduct, and gain access to the field of bureaucratic discourse.

Guidance for women bureaucrats seeking the right image is readily available. Organizations like Career Track Seminars, Inc., offer "Image and Self Projection" workshops for "Today's Woman in Business, Government, and the Professions." These workshops teach women an "image investment strategy" designed to achieve "The Power Look." Women are advised to "launch their personal publicity campaigns," to "repackage themselves" according to the rules for successful impression management, and to "program themselves for progress." [79] Outfits like Career Track Seminars teach women to abandon their orientation toward process and toward connectedness with others in order to offer themselves as commodities on the bureaucratic exchange.

Beneath the crass materialism and slick instrumentalism of these recommendations are two very interesting themes: one is that, despite the glib and breezy manner in which organizational values are taken for granted, these books contain some genuinely useful observations concerning organizational survival; the other is the persistent and unacknowledged ambivalence about those very values. Some of the authors' concrete insights into sexism in the office ring true to any woman who has ever worked in an organizational setting, regardless of her politics. For instance, the authors point out the ease with which many women are trapped into doing other people's (men's) work by appeals to "need" or to loyalty, and the ways in which organizations try to substitute interpersonal for material rewards for women. Many of the concrete recommendations in these books are aimed at getting men to take women seriously as colleagues, a perennial problem for women in most work situations. They see clearly into the burden imposed by the "two jobs" syndrome facing most women, and they recommend ways in which women can integrate their work lives and their domestic lives more easily. Hennig and Jardin are particularly insightful in articulating the sexual dilemma facing women in bureaucracies: if women develop the necessary relationships with authority (that is, men) that allow them to get sponsors within the organization, to learn the rules of the game, and so forth, they are likely to be perceived as a sexual risk, to elicit a sexual response from men or else to be totally "desexed" as "one of the boys"; but if they don't develop these relationships, they don't get access to the bureaucratic discourse. Since most of us will spend most of our lives working in bureaucratic organizations simply because there are relatively few opportunities to earn a living elsewhere, bureaucratic survival is a necessary skill in the contemporary sociopolitical environment. These books articulate the disadvantages that women face in such a setting in a straightforward manner.

The other central, though unintended, message of these bureaucratic survival manuals for women is their own ambiguity concerning their project. Each of these books repeatedly characterizes the "games" women must play to enter the bureau-

cratic arena as silly, childish, and irrational, then each goes on
to give specific advice on how to play these games effectively.
For example, Harragan elaborates on the struggles for status
that go on among competing bureaucrats (over size of desk, lo-
cation of office, number of windows, style and source of food
eaten at lunch, handling of mail), makes clear how infantile
such concerns are, then advises the reader that "as an ambitious woman you have to care."[80] They make clear that the
bias against women in organizations is a form of *institutional*
sexism, not an accidental consequence of male prejudice, but
they refuse to see this insight as an indictment of the bureaucratic system. For example, Hennig and Jardin follow their
sensitive and insightful discussion of the "two jobs" problem by
saying that "it is beside the point to say that men don't have to
deal with this issue. The point is that women do."[81] Their own
analysis shows that it is the clash between women's traditional
domestic role, which has largely remained unchanged, and her
new public role that is the source of this contradiction, but this
insight leads them to criticize neither the institutional arrangements of the family nor of the organization. Nor do they
acknowledge that if men *did* have to deal with this issue by
taking equal responsibility for domestic work and child care,
then the problem would not be so severe for women, both because the burden would be shared and because, once the problem became a problem for men, organizations would be more
willing to try to solve it.

Above all, these books are ambivalent about the worth of
women themselves, and this ambivalence is expressed in many
ways. The authors all urge aspiring female bureaucrats to see
other women as allies; yet they insist over and over that other
people (of both sexes) should be seen primarily as competitors
for scarce organizational resources. Since the main goal is always "winning," alliances would of necessity be viewed instrumentally and "mutual aid" would be at best temporary and
self-interested. The authors reject the idea that they are urging
women to become like men—"*The key is not to 'join them' but
to surpass them*"—when in fact that is precisely what they are
doing.[82] Hennig and Jardin claim to "put no value judgment
whatsoever on the aim to win" but then say that "if men need

to lessen the drive to win, women as certainly need to develop it."[83] While they want to avoid the conclusion that women should be more like men, all of their examples and recommendations indicate that the typical point of view that women bring to the bureaucratic arena is inferior:

> Corporate manners tend to be the manners of a society whose members are bent on winning at one extreme and on sheer survival at the other, and one's position in relation to either extreme tends to define the status of one's membership. . . . The manners women bring with them are those of another society, a society whose members are bent on the maintenance of relationships for they are the most immediate definition of who one is.[84]

Women are advised to drop their inclinations to view their jobs in terms of the value of the process, to concentrate solely on outcome, to adopt a "different style for reasons of self-interest," and to learn to treat others as objects.[85] By doing so women will succeed in achieving "a better fit between the management environment and themselves."[86]

The typically female values and experiences that the liberal feminists urge women to leave behind are precisely the ones that radical feminists seek to preserve within their own organizations. Most nonliberal feminists, regardless of ideological differences among themselves, view the acceptance of bureaucratic values as synonymous with the abandonment of feminist values. They see their organizations as ends in themselves, not simply as means to an end; thus one of the purposes of radical feminist groups is to encourage individual autonomy and self-development. These feminists have tended, on the whole, to eschew any contact with bureaucratic structures. Many of the most visible and active radical feminist projects—book stores, health collectives, newsletters and periodicals, battered women's shelters, rape crisis centers, and so forth—are economically self-sufficient (if precarious) and minimize their ties with bureaucratic organizations. As the early manifestos of the radical feminists make clear, they are committed to an internal style of organization that is deliberately anti-bureaucratic: the groups are decentralized; they rely on personal, face-to-face relations rather than formal rules; they are egalitarian rather than hierarchical; and they see skills and information as resources to be shared, not hoarded.[87] They are frequently more concerned with process than with outcome, operating with a view of power that stresses the ability to empower the members to do collectively that which they could not do alone. Debates among radical feminists over the role of leadership and formal structure, while often heated, take place within a context in which all assume that hierarchy should be minimized in favor of equality.[88]

Thus the discourse generated by radical feminism offers a deliberately anti-bureaucratic vision. However, this mode of acting is usually not available within bureaucracies. Some bureaucrats may successfully maintain a commitment to radical feminist ideals, and this may be of considerable importance to their immediate co-workers, since the personal style of a manager can be important in creating a humane office environment. Similarly, some women (and a few men) may carry feminist ideals into professions such as medicine, law, teaching, counseling, or law enforcement in a way that provides a valuable service to their clients. For example, women doctors typically spend more time with their patients than do male doctors, are sued less often for malpractice, and are generally preferred by women for obstetrical and gynecological treatment. But the presence of women in medicine (currently 30 percent of first-year medical students are women) has not, and is not likely to, alter the structure of the medical profession. Medicine remains an authoritarian and hierarchical profession; the training process scars and desensitizes its recruits, emphasizing the privileged image and financial standing of doctors over their service to patients. The American Medical Women's Association, the biggest organization of women doctors, is oriented toward career advancement for its members, not toward structural change in the profession such as, for example, lowering the cost of health care or opposing overspecialization.[89] In the area of law enforcement, women police officers tend to have a more positive attitude toward the public and to have more sympathy for the victims than do their male colleagues; this is no doubt welcomed by those individuals who come into contact with the women officers, but it does little to alter the hierarchical and authoritarian organization of the police force or the role of the police in the larger society.[90] Feminists in academia probably have considerable control over their interactions with their students, and may provide students with a nonbureaucratic refuge or with a valuable role model, but this is not going to alter the university's role vis-à-vis the state or the corporations. Feminists may survive in bureaucracies with their personal integrity and commitment intact, but they will probably not succeed within the organization, on the terms of the organization, and they certainly will not be able to alter the organization's power structure in a radical feminist direction. Many people resist organizational demands for conformity; if done with skill, one can resist and survive, but one seldom both resists and prospers.

The difference between this version of liberal feminism and the radical feminist approach to organization can be summed up as a dispute over the value of women's cultural experiences. The authors of the bureaucratic success manuals view the value of traditional femininity in light of its utility in developing "winning strategies" within the bureaucracy. They share the central feminist insight that much of traditional feminine socialization presents obstacles to women's ability to exercise any power over their lives, and that the "'typically feminine virtues' of being sweet, helpful, helpless, agreeable, sentimental, loyal, obedient, and self-effacing" lead more readily to subordination than to autonomy.[91] But the conclusions they draw are the exact opposite of those drawn by radical feminists; the liberals wish to reject those aspects of the traditional feminine role that lead women to be more cooperative, more nurturant, or more sensitive to the needs of others, and utilize those aspects of the traditional role that teach women how to manipulate men: "Women are experts at playing roles; as they learn this game, they should be great at outwitting the pros."[92] A noted female biologist gives the following advice to women in organizations: "If you're going to go through life competing with aggressive bastards, it helps to be an aggressive bitch. . . . She's going to have to do two things which men have always done: (1) she's going to have to manipulate the person at the top, and women are pretty good at that kind of thing, and (2) she's going to have to be aggressive."[93] In contrast, the radicals' conclusions are that, while women's powerless position in society has often led them to develop interpersonal survival strategies that are manipulative of others, the central values of the expressive role are more humane and more livable than those embodied in the masculine ethic. Both groups see that the male-dominated organizational ethic devalues people, while the traditional values of women do not; but the advocates of upward mobility accept this devaluation as the inevitable and acceptable price of entry into the bureaucratic world.

These "how to succeed in the organization" books are reflective of a version of feminism that poses absolutely no threat to the dominance of bureaucracies over both private and public life. These success manuals for women show that bureaucracies can be made to accept as recruits individuals who have the right middle-class communications skills, the money to look and act the organizational role, and the willingness to "play the game"—even if these individuals happen to be female.

The meticulous account that these authors give of the requirements of conformity in bureaucratic life shows clearly that the price of success within the system is that one abandon any thought of changing that system. Yet, they hold out the hope that once women have made their way to the top, they will then change the rules: "When they get to be dealer—they can exercise their prerogative to change the rules to 'dealer's choice.'"[94] Jardin and Hennig state that women who make themselves "more effective in the managerial environment" will change men's prejudices about women as well as changing general social beliefs about the family.[95] Acknowledging that "the quality of life in most American corporations has disintegrated into a way of life which is almost wholly instrumental," they then see women as the hope for humanizing the work world and convincing men of the need for change.[96] By their own analysis, this hope is absurd. After internalizing and acting on the rules of bureaucratic discourse for most of their adult lives, how many women (or men) will be *able* to change? After succeeding in the system by using those rules, how many would be *willing* to change? The conformity that bureaucratic participation requires is, by their own account, much more than skin deep; it affects the way one thinks, feels, responds to others, and conceives of and presents oneself. To enter the bureaucratic realm successfully one must subject oneself to what Foucault calls "the universal reign of the normative," which requires that "each individual, wherever he [sic] may find himself, subjects to it his body, his gestures, his behavior, his aptitudes, his achievements." [97] The requirements of public conformity infiltrate private life as well. It is hard to be a "closet radical" when an inspection of the closets is part of the organization's daily routine.

Juridico-Legal Discourse and Liberal Feminism

Liberalism, applied to women, has generally advocated state intervention on behalf of women as abstract citizens with formal rights in order to guarantee them access to the institutions and legal protections of the larger system. Liberal feminism was often a voice for change in the past because it made claims for women's right to participate in established public life—that is, to vote, to own property, to work outside the home—that challenged the society's entrenched definition of woman as domestic being and as property of the male. Now, however, when most of the legal barriers to women's public activity have been successfully challenged, and when entry into public life has come to mean acceptance of the rules of the game of bureaucratic discourse, this is no longer true. Liberal feminism used to be, in Foucault's terms, a voice raised against the dominant discourse; it has now largely become a voice subservient to that discourse.

The requirements of living/surviving in the world at hand prohibit feminists from simply ignoring the juridico-legal realm, however, despite its inherent limitations. The utility of various liberal reforms should be evaluated on the basis of their ability to challenge, not simply extend, the language and the practice of bureaucratic capitalism. [98] Reform efforts such as the battles for reproductive freedom in the legislatures and the courts are crucial for feminism because they make other struggles possible. Efforts to unionize women or to achieve comparable pay for jobs of comparable worth may also be means to further change. By providing for real material improvement in the lives of substantial numbers of women, these reforms may alleviate the pressure of immediate needs; they also allow women to develop important political skills and to use the economic "breathing space" to plan and work toward further change. Reforms that create feminist counseling services or feminist studies programs may build in individual women the capacity to translate personal problems into public issues, thus encouraging further, collective, struggle.

There is no simple formula for distinguishing reforms that make further change possible from those that do not, but some broad and general distinctions can be made. Sometimes the problems at hand are so immediate that recourse to the juridico-legal realm of reform is urgent, even if inherently limited. Catherine MacKinnon makes this argument succinctly with regard to rape and battery laws: on the one hand, individual women need strong legal protection from these threats; on the other, tightening the laws concerning rape and battery does not address the conditions that produce men who beat and rape women. Rape law reform proceeds from "the model of the deviant perpetrator and the violent act, as if the fact that rape is a crime means that the society is against it, so law enforcement would reduce or delegitimize it." [99] But rape is a particularly violent expression of the violence-laden imagery of masculinity and heterosexuality prevalent in our culture. Law enforcement in these areas penalizes men for seeking the control over others that, in other contexts, they have been taught to need and paid to exercise. Of course rapists must be stopped. But can rape and battery ever be effectively stopped without addressing in a radical way—that is, getting to the roots of—the conditions that produce men who beat and rape women?

Laws concerning equal opportunity and affirmative action are examples of reforms that often benefit individual women, but that do little to challenge the larger system or to make further change likely. Without those laws, many women would have no access to the relatively higher pay, pleasanter working conditions, and greater security of the primary labor market. Of course access to better jobs at better pay is important to women. But the fact is that most women do not have much access to these jobs despite these laws, and that the price of entry is often high. Poverty, unemployment, and underemployment, among women as well as men, are conditions generated by the class structure of bureaucratic capitalism; they won't be changed by recruiting more women into the upper and middle levels of that class structure.[100] Equal opportunity and affirmative action offices all too frequently become a kind of bureaucratic safety valve for organizations, a place where the outsiders—women of all colors, blacks and Hispanics of both genders, and others—fight over the crumbs.

Efforts to recruit women into the military have very little relevance to the goals of feminist discourse. Most of the arguments against women in active military duty are echoes of old sexist prejudices: women will break down and cry in battle; they will not be reliable soldiers; their menstrual cycles will interfere with their military performance; they will distract the men. None of these alleged problems have seemed to have any serious effects on the guerilla armies of the Vietnamese or the Nicaraguans, both of which contained a substantial number of women soldiers and officers.[101] But to counter these insults by advocating the entry of women into the military, or the drafting of women along with men, is to capitulate to the constricted terms of argument that liberalism offers and to abandon the values and goals of feminist discourse. Militarism is a threat to feminism, not an opportunity. The military establishment is one of the most powerful organizational constellations in bureaucratic capitalism; recruiting women into it will not keep it from undermining Third World experiments in socialism, or fueling a wasteful, war-based economy, or escalating the arms race. The liberal argument that "equal rights entail equal responsibilities" for all citizens is grounded in the abstract conceptual categories of juridico-legal discourse. But the actual public domain within which these rights and responsibilities take their meaning is a barren bureaucratic realm, where there are few genuine opportunities for the collective, public activity that is properly called citizenship. Feminism should try to debunk and demystify the claims of the dominant discourse, not perpetuate them by collaborating in their pretensions.

Directions for Feminist Discourse

Feminist discourse offers the potential for reconstituting the basic terms of political life, of altering the discursive field in which knowledge and power are appropriated and expressed. The forms of speaking and acting dominant in bureaucratic discourse offer no legitimized place for feminist discourse; so the creation of this discourse by calling out the suppressed knowledge of women is itself a political act. Feminist discourse, while connected to bureaucratic discourse as all voices of resistance are connected to the power they resist, is a radical project that fundamentally subverts the bureaucratic capitalist definition of the subject and of politics. Because the relation of theory to practice is not contingent or instrumental but conceptual and constitutive, the act of changing the way we think about the world is a way of changing the world, since it is a world partly constituted by people's beliefs about it and about themselves.[102]
The notion of the subject that is inherent in bureaucratic capitalism views individuals as essentially separate from one another, seeing each self as an independent, coherent unity in much the same way that each body is a unified whole separate from every other body. But women's experience of connectedness, rooted in modes of interaction that bureaucratic capitalism discounts even though these connections cannot be destroyed without destroying the social order itself, gives the lie to the modern, masculine notion of the separate self. The imaginary unification of the subject is revealed as an ideological construction, the projection of "the imaginary wholeness which is identified in the mirror" onto the shifting sociality of individuals-in-relation.[103] The feminist view of the subject leads to a radical reconceptualization of the basic political terms of freedom and community. Freedom in bureaucratic capitalism refers to an arena of privacy surrounding each individual, protected from encroachments by other individuals; community, to the

extent the word can be used at all, is a secondary arrangement among already autonomous beings. Freedom in feminist discourse, on the contrary, is to be found in relations with others; the risk that others pose to one's own projects is balanced by a deep acknowledgment of our essential relatedness, of the extent to which our projects are given meaning through this relatedness. The caretaking values that inform feminist discourse, when not distorted by subordination or rendered partial by a too-great fear of loss, entail caring for others by caring for their freedom. To encourage the development and autonomy of others in a genuine way is to accept the instability and threat of loss that the nurturance of change requires. A community that recognizes the dialectical need for connectedness within freedom and for diversity within solidarity would strive to nurture the capacity for reflexive redefinition of self.

This does not mean that all tension between the individual and the collective is abolished. Recognizing that as temporal beings we never completely coincide with ourselves, and always have other possibilities before us, a certain primary alienation is an irrevocable dimension of human life. The ongoing, emergent quality of personal identity can never be adequately captured within an established organizational role. This means that any group, even one built upon feminist grounds, may try to squelch other possibilities within its members in order to contain them within a definition that is consistent with the needs of the group. But if no individual or subgroup within the collective possesses the permanent institutionalized power to enforce particular definitions of the group and its members, then the group is more open to processes of redefinition that can allow and even encourage change. In light of the ongoing tension between the individual and the collective as well as their intimate and constitutive connection, active participation in public decision-making takes on a two-fold importance: it connects us to one another, offering a political arena in which we can define ourselves publicly through speech and action with equals; it also protects us from one another, providing access for each individual to the decision-making process and thus lessening the danger of a tyranny of the collective.[104] Feminist discourse seeks conceptual and practical grounds for maintenance of the dialectical tension between freedom that does not entail isolation and community that does not enforce uniformity.

Feminist discourse does not envision some underlying unanimity in political life, but it does envision a polity in which modes of conflict and definitions of interests are worked out within a context of general concern for the humanness of others. This vision is not based on some abstract idea of human nature or on pie-in-the-sky hopes for a promised land, but on the concrete experiences of women as caretakers, and on the concrete evidence that women do in fact live in ways that are substantially different from those proclaimed inevitable/universal/natural by the discourse of bureaucratic capitalism. Presumably there would still be conflict in a feminist society, but there would be a public space available for the ongoing process of conflict resolution. All interested individuals would have access to this space; it would be decentralized to the maximum extent feasible; the central decisions of collective life, including decisions about the constitution of public life and its exact relation to private concerns, would be made there. The accommodative strategies of conflict resolution that women typically use would be encouraged and legitimated, calling on the cooperative and respectful processes of talking and listening that express care and maintain connection. Conflict would not be either eliminated or suppressed; rather, individuals and groups would be drawn into an interactional process in which adaptation and reconciliation are encouraged by a feminist understanding of the relation between the individual and the collective. Methods would be sought to adjust to differences among individuals and groups and to build bridges between them. The specific forms that this process could take would have to be created by the women and men engaging in the process, but the structures created by existing feminist groups and other collective experiments could serve as models.[105] Such a society would not necessarily be a nonviolent society, but it would certainly be *less* violent, since the major incentives to violence, those stemming from gross inequalities in power, wealth, and status and from the dominance of masculinity in public life, would be eliminated.

The reconceptualization of self-other relations in feminist terms suggests a mode of human rationality that is distinct from the forms of instrumental or value rationality that are dominant in Western thought. In the dominant way of thinking, rationality is either formal or substantive; it is either directed toward the pursuit of subjectively defined self-interest at the expense of others, or toward altruistic sacrifice of self-interest for the sake of others. From a feminist point of view this very opposition is untenable, since it rests on an unfounded separation of self and other. If people are seen as beings who come to be who they are in their relations with others, rationality becomes a trait characterizing their relations, and their choices within relations. Interests are not defined simply in terms of opposition between individuals and groups, but in terms of the forms of relatedness individuals and groups sustain with one another. Feminist rationality, as Roslyn Bologh has suggested, stems from an "orientation to a general, diffuse, intangible and hence unmeasurable sense of well being" for both self and others.[106]

A feminist perspective on rationality explicitly connects reason to emotion. Arlie Hochschild argues convincingly for a view of emotion as akin to the senses of sight or hearing. Emotions should be viewed actively, like other aspects of perception, as something we *do*. The ways in which we attend to sensations and define situations are not external to feelings but are constitutive of them. Emotion, she argues, "functions as a messenger from the self, an agent that gives us an instant report on the connection between what we are seeing and what we had expected to see, and tells us what we feel ready to do about it."[107] Our emotions are one of the ways in which we know the world, and are thus *not* the opposite of reason. We need the connection to the world that emotion allows in order to reflect on and evaluate that world. The long-standing association of feeling with irrationality reflects masculine illusions of separateness and masculine fears of loss of control more than any universal traits of human reason. While vast unmediated feeling may distort perception and hinder the capacity for reflection, the suppression and denial of emotion does the same. In Hochschild's words:

A person totally without emotion has no warning system, no guidelines to the self-relevance of a sight, a memory, or a fantasy. Like one who cannot feel and touches fire, an emotionless person suffers a sense of arbitrariness, which from the point of view of his or her self-interest is irrational. In fact, emotion is a potential avenue to "the reasonable view." . . . We need feeling in order to reflect on the external and "objective" world. Taking feelings into account as clues and then correcting for them may be our best shot at objectivity. Like hearing or seeing, feeling provides a useful set of clues in figuring out what is real.[108]

Through its recasting of the relation between self and other, and between the individual and the collective, feminist discourse suggests a radically different view of the relation of public to private life from that made available in bureaucratic capitalism.[109] As discussed in Chapter Two, our society imposes a contradictory burden on the family, expecting it to provide both the instrumental and the expressive satisfaction that is denied in a public life rendered barren and sterile by the combined forces of bureaucracy and capitalism. In order to rescue private life from this contradictory burden, public life must be restructured so that it allows opportunity for both autonomy and community. Family life (defined broadly as any small, intimate, and stable grouping of adults and at least potentially of children) could then come to bear a more realistic burden, providing an intimacy that is matched by public community, and an autonomy that parallels public freedom. The boundary between public and private life would not be collapsed, but would now be shown to be shifting, subject to redefinition by the community's members. Public and private life would not be the same, but they would be related, situated at opposing ends of a continuum of proximity and distance. This continuum is not a quantifiable, linear progression of evenly spaced units, but is rather a processual flow with its own durational form not capturable in number. It does not collapse the political and the psychological but shows their essential relatedness.

The relation of public to private in feminist discourse is one of extension of the traits of each into the other, but the act of extension entails transition, making public life both like and not like private life in important ways. They are alike in that the relation of self to others sustained in personal, face-to-face encounters provides the grounds for the experience of community in the larger arena, for the recognition of connection and commonality with those who are strangers but who are still human, like oneself, and thus not easily discarded as enemies. Similarly, the experience of risk and loss that the nurturance of freedom entails can prepare us for the encounter with the unfamiliar, the unknown, and the dangerous that public life requires. The two realms are unlike in that relations in the larger public arena cannot be based on the intimate knowledge that sustains the personal realm, but on a more distant knowledge based on respect and equality. The conflict and confrontation and compromise necessary to any vital political realm are not simple echoes of the private; they are aspects of a specifically public civility and citizenship in a participatory, democratic polity.

This suggests that any radical reconstruction of either private life (as in the feminist argument that men must take an equal role in mothering in order to change traditional patterns of gender) or public life (as in the classic Marxist demands for revolution) entails a reconstruction of the *relationship* between them, since they are in part defined by each other. For example, it has often been pointed out that social change along Marxist or Leninist lines could, and sometimes has, restructured the public realm without fundamentally altering the power relations between women and men in private life. Similarly, one could imagine a society in which men and women took equal part in raising their children within the confines of late capitalism, teaching sons and daughters alike to be upwardly mobile young contenders for bureaucratic advantage. The argument for equally shared parenting, in this light, is shown to be both powerful and partial: its power comes from its potential to alter the primary conditions under which gender identity is created; its partiality stems from its limited impact on public life. Drawing upon arguments made by Chodorow and Dinnerstein, Isaac Balbus makes the case for shared parenting in a way that shows both its weakness and its strength:

Once the father joins the mother as an early caretaker of the male child, this child will now experience a primary identification with a parent of *his* sex; the formation of his masculine identity will therefore no longer demand the complete suppression of his primary identification and the assumption of an exclusively oppositional stance toward his first love-object. Under these conditions, boys can be expected to grow up far more "relationally-oriented" than they are under mother-monopolized child rearing. At the same time, once the mother is no longer the only original love-object of the female child, the girl's fusion with the mother will no longer be nearly so encompassing, and thus her predisposition is likely to give way to an enhanced sense of her own independence. The men and women who emerge from shared parenting, then, will be equally prepared emotionally for both the "public" world of "enterprise" and the "private" world of interpersonal relationships and will therefore be able to establish relationships with each other in which intimacy and autonomy go hand in hand. Shared parenting thus holds the key to the liberation of the relation between the sexes.[110]

But if the public world that these liberated daughters and sons are being readied to enter is a bureaucratic world, then their liberation is soon lost. Genuine enterprise, the active and autonomous pursuit of self-defined and self-defining projects, is not available to most people in a bureaucratic world, and the relational skills and needs of both sexes are soon perverted to serve bureaucratic ends.

Genuinely shared parenting, widely adapted, would alter the relations of children to adults and would probably, over time, encourage greater androgyny and more balanced personal life. But shared parenting would not alter the relations of workers to bosses or clients to functionaries; the dominance/subordinance relations that have traditionally characterized the family would still be recreated in public life. And shared parenting would not stop the invasion of the cult of rationality into personal life; it would not, in short, alter either the organizational class structure or the ethos of bureaucratic capitalism.

Androgynous child-rearing by itself is not an adequate lever of change. The source of change that feminist discourse invokes is women's experience, translated into feminist consciousness and used by feminist women and men to restructure both public and private life. The reshaping of family life has to be linked to the creation of nonbureaucratic organizations outside the family, or at least to alternative "spaces" within existing organizations. Otherwise, the unequal power relations within bureaucracy will recreate "femininity" in subordinates and will block the emergence of an ethic of responsibility and a politics of democratic community.

Conclusion

Women need power in order to change society, but power within bureaucracies is not change-making power. The organizational forms and discourse of bureaucratic capitalism institutionalize modes of domination that recreate the very patterns of oppression that feminism arose to combat. Feminist discourse offers both a critical vantage point from which to comprehend the inadequacies of the dominant language and structures and a fresh direction for both our political speech and our political practice.

The skeptic might well argue at this point that feminist discursive and organizational strategies are irrelevant to modern life because bureaucracy is inevitable. Arguments for the inevitability of bureaucracy are usually either psychological or technological at bottom; that is, they look either to some alleged innate tendencies in human nature or to the requirements of modern technology. For example, Robert Michel's famous claims concerning an "iron law of oligarchy" rest both upon his analysis of the consequences of large-scale organization on internal democracy and upon his belief that "man as individual is by nature predestined to be guided."[111] The first argument rests upon an untenable notion of universal subjectivity. Once it is recognized that, as individuals, we are produced by our circumstances, and that these circumstances are themselves the product of human activity, appeals to some underlying and essential human nature lose much of their force. Bureaucratic discourse both creates and reflects the masculine notion of the subject, then posits that version of subjectivity as universal. But women's experience provides a vision of human relatedness and autonomy in which subjectivity is rooted in but not reduced to social relations. And case studies of cooperative organizations employing nonbureaucratic principles of organization show that they do not inevitably self-destruct due to some alleged need for centralization and control. In her study of egalitarian workers' collectives in the 1960s, Katherine Newman points out that those collectives that became bureaucratic over time did so because of encroachment of bureaucratic forms from the *outside*, not from internal pressures toward hierarchy. Those collectives that were able to finance their own activities, such as health food stores, leather work shops, and printing shops, did not become dependent on outside funding and were able to retain their egalitarian processes for making decisions and allocating tasks, even as the organizations expanded in membership and in scope of activity.[112]

The second argument for the inevitability of hierarchy, that which appeals to the requirements of technology, also loses its force when taken out of the context of bureaucratic discourse. As was pointed out in Chapter Two, hierarchical control of production was initially introduced as a strategy for increasing profits, not for enhancing the production process. The selection among possible technologies in bureaucratic capitalism is based on a complex calculation of profitability involving three main factors: "One is technical efficiency, the ratio of the physical outputs to the physical inputs; another is the cost of the various inputs and the value of outputs; yet a third is the extent to which any technology provides managers with leverage in transforming purchased labor power into labor actually done."[113] In an economy based on genuine workers' control and participatory self-management, the third function, the control function, could be substantially reduced. The first two could be reformulated in accordance with the values and goals of feminist discourse, so that calculations of efficiency and cost take into consideration the human and environmental "costs" of different technical options, their efficiency in developing skills of artisanship or collective decision-making in their workers, and so forth.

In technocratic society the omnipresent technology comes to be judged by rules of its own making—that is, by standards reflecting technical values and assumptions and generated by a concern for technique. But if technology is seen in terms of its ability to meet human needs, to fit to human scale, and to accommodate the natural environment, then technical decisions become judgments of a different sort. Feminist discourse would insist upon judging technology in light of the standards of autonomy and community named in the discourse. Many kinds of modern technologies, such as those of the radio, television, and recording industries, are compatible with decentralized and participatory decision-making; their current manifestation as highly centralized and homogeneous mass media is an indictment of the powerful corporations that control them, not of the technologies themselves.[114] There are usually many different technical alternatives for the performance of particular tasks, many ways, for example, to weave cloth; those that allow for artisanship and craft autonomy could be developed and expanded. Those technologies that are inherently centralized and capital intensive, such as nuclear power, could be rejected in favor of alternatives that are technically sophisticated and productive while still amenable to local control, such as photovoltaic solar cells.[115] Under the value system named in feminist discourse, calculations of efficiency and productivity would include an ongoing concern for the development of the individual, the needs of the community, and the requirements of nature.

A feminist restructuring of work entails rejection of the hierarchical division of labor of bureaucratic capitalism and the reintegration of the planning and performance of tasks. It requires "creating a situation in which we can both develop ourselves and transform the external world."[116] Radical feminist groups frequently pursue these goals by adopting a vertical rather than a horizontal division of labor, dividing the work process into areas within which each individual has responsibility for both the creative and the routine aspects of the task.[117]

The group collectively defines and periodically redefines those decisions that must be made by the entire group versus those decisions that are to be made by each individual within her own task area. The labor is divided in such a way that the members learn skills and develop their own powers within a flexible work situation that allows for change over time.

Just as the bureaucratic division of labor creates incompetence, so a vertical division of labor can create ability. Feminist organizations do not need to dispense with expertise, but can wed it to a different form of power; the expertise possessed by particular individuals, in an environment that supports cooperation, can be shared with others so as to empower both the individual and the group, providing an opportunity both to learn and to teach. Power would be redefined as the ability to act with others to do things that could not be done by individuals alone. Leadership would become a form of empowerment; as Nancy Hartsock has stated, "To lead is to be at the *center* of a group rather than in front of others."[118] Authority based on skill and knowledge would be "compelled persistently to demonstrate its force to those concerned in terms which they can grasp and, by dint of being so compelled, is made in some real measure responsible to them."[119]

A final objection commonly raised against any vision of nonbureaucratic collective life is the assertion that egalitarian and democratic organizations cannot work because they have never really worked. This is simply untrue. Countless examples of genuine member-controlled collectives exist and have existed. Perhaps the most famous example is the worker-owned and operated community at Mondragón, Spain, composed of seventy interlocking cooperatives and a workplace of 14,000 people; it has been in existence for nearly thirty years. Its ratio of highest to lowest paid members is 3:1, compared to the 50:1 or 70:1 ratio in most U.S. firms.[120] In *Beyond Adversary Democracy*, Jane Mansbridge provides two detailed case studies of democratic communities; both the crisis center and the Vermont town meetings that she studied had maintained egalitarian and participatory organizational forms over a considerable period of time, and had developed strategies to deal with the internal problems of the group within a nonbureaucratic framework.[121] That most people know so little about the remarkable successes of cooperatives, particularly in the face of a hostile environment, is an indication of the ability of bureaucratic discourse to suppress knowledge about alternatives.

Genuine egalitarian and participatory organizations face a persistent set of problems: decision-making is usually time-consuming and often frustrating to some members; the intensity of the interaction often advantages the most verbally skilled members at the expense of those less assertive or vocal; inequalities of ability and/or contribution surface among members. Feminist groups have developed strategies for dealing with these problems: rotating the chair; integrating social and organizational activities; electing one delegate to canvass the less active members.[122] The small size necessary for participatory decision-making necessitates structures for coordination among the groups; coordination can be achieved by voluntary cooperation and by election of delegates within a federated structure, rather than through hierarchy and control. We do not have blueprints for large, nonhierarchal organizations, but we have numerous indications that such organizations are possible. The problems of decentralization and participation have been faced and dealt with many times over by participants in democratic communities, and their experiences are readily available to those who would learn.[123] My purpose is not to reproduce in detail their stories, but rather to point to the possibility that such examples offer for the restructuring of society and to ground this possibility in the theoretical and practical terms of feminist discourse.

Recommendations such as these are often dismissed as simplistic and impractical, but they are in fact more cognizant of complexity than bureaucracies can ever be. Most admonitions toward "practicality" translate into an unwillingness to consider any change that is not consistent with existing arrangements, when it is precisely those arrangements that stand in need of change. Kirkpatrick Sale makes this point beautifully:

It is our modern economy that is simple: whole nations given over to a single crop, cities to a single industry, farms to a single culture [sic], factories to a single product, people to a single job, jobs to a single motion, motion to a single purpose. Diversity is the rule of human life, not simplicity: the human animal has succeeded precisely because it has been able to diversify, not specialize: to climb *and* swim, hunt *and* nurture, work alone *and* in packs. The same is true of human organizations: they are healthy and they survive when they are diverse and differentiated, capable of many responses; they become brittle and unadaptable and prey to any changing conditions when they are uniform and specialized. It is when an individual is able to take on many jobs, learn many skills, live many roles, that growth and fullness of character inhabit the soul: it is when a society complexifies and mixes, when it develops the multiplicity of ways of caring for itself, that it becomes textured and enriched.[124]

While the best avenue of resistance to bureaucratic capitalism is the formation of alternative organizations, this is not an option readily available to everyone. People have to resist from where they are, not from where they would like to be; since most people find themselves inside bureaucracies, it is toward their own organizational environment that they can direct their protests. The resistance that *can* go on within a bureaucratic setting is a very limited form of opposition; understanding its limits is an important aspect of estimating its promise, and avoiding the debilitating disappointment that follows when ungrounded and unrealistic hopes are raised and then dashed.

It is, I have argued, impossible to resist bureaucratic domination by recruiting individual women into bureaucracies, or by organizing bureaucratically; in both cases the voices of opposition are engulfed and defused. It is possible to resist bureaucratic domination if a substantial number of people act collectively and in a nonbureaucratic fashion to challenge the discourse. Since the terms of bureaucratic discourse mystify politics by shrouding conflict in the pseudo-neutral language of administration, to explicitly politicize its language is to challenge the dominant discursive framework. As I argued in Chapter One, bureaucracies are essentially authoritarian systems in that they allow no legitimate opposition from below. To challenge bureaucracy in the name of the values and goals of feminist discourse is to undermine the chain of command, equalize the participants, subvert the monopoly of information and secrecy of decision-making, and essentially seek to democratize the organization. This requires reformulating the organization's central issues in a language of power and responsibility, making it possible to name ends for which one might take an ethical stand.

This cannot usually be done by individuals in isolation, because they are too vulnerable to organizational retribution and they lack the base of mutual support that gives energy to sentiments of resistance. But a substantial number of people acting together can help to protect and support one another, forming a group that, at its best, can function as a cross between a consciousness-raising group and a union. A sufficiently large number of voices in opposition can act as a counterforce to bureaucratic power; for example, Robert Denhardt's research on poverty programs in Appalachia shows that, when a large number of the local poor came into the organization, they brought with them the anti-bureaucratic norms of the local culture and modified the bureau's procedures in the direction of greater personalism and equality.[125] Collective opposition within an organization can threaten the terms of bureaucratic discourse by encouraging a critical reading of power, and by helping the members to lose their fear of the authorities and to see as problematic that which the organization considers to be standard operating procedure.

There is always the possibility that these groups will be co-opted and incorporated into the bureaucratic structure; Karen Sacks's research on women's networks found that in managerial and professional contexts networks usually become selective or exclusive in their membership, turning from group improvement or organizational change to individual advancement up the career ladder.[126] These groups carefully refrain from politicizing the managerial language or coming into confrontation with management. But among working-class women networks tend to be inclusive in membership standards, and to use their social ties as a foundation for planning and carrying out successful collective action in the name of the entire group.

If the network becomes internally bureaucratic in its ideology or its structure, it enters the terms of bureaucratic discourse and the sentiment of opposition is lost. But if it operates on feminist terms, and creates a nonbureaucratic space within the organization, then the group can demonstrate the feasibility of an alternative type of organization and provide a refuge within the larger organization for those who cannot or will not fit in elsewhere. For example, Karen Louis and Sam Gieber's study of an experimental education program describes a decentralized, flexible field-based program with little supervision from above and high identification of workers with clients; this dispersed organization was able to provide a nonbureaucratic space within the larger state educational bureaucracy.[127]

Women's studies programs within universities can, at their best, serve as consciousness-raising groups/unions for their members and provide an alternative, nonbureaucratic space within the larger organization. Women's studies programs provide homes for the creation of feminist discourse, in that they support the scholarship necessary to disinter the buried historical knowledge of women and to make this knowledge available without recodifying and encapsulating it into the standard terms of the dominant discourse.[128] Because the members provide support and protection for one another, and because as a group they are providing a valuable resource to the university—that is, they draw students—feminists within women's studies programs can sometimes appeal to the liberal arts rhetoric of the university, as well as to its organizational interests, to protect themselves. This is only a limited success, since organizational survival, particularly during times of tight money, propels women's studies programs into the same search for protected turf, for alliances, and for legitimizing techniques that characterizes the other actors within the bureaucratic setting. The requirements of organizational survival are likely to penetrate into the program and endanger the alternative values and processes that the insurgents seek to maintain. Even if this can somehow be avoided, women's studies programs cannot restructure the university, any more than unions can restructure corporations or welfare rights organizations can restructure social services. To hope otherwise is to place an impossible burden on these programs and then condemn them for failing to do what they could not do instead of using them to do most fully what they are capable of doing, which is publicly and collectively to challenge the dominant discourse in the name of an alternative way of thinking and acting.

In sum, the conclusions that can be drawn from this analysis concern the relation between feminism and bureaucracy. Feminist organizations, even those that routinely encounter and work with bureaucracies, cannot be themselves bureaucratic or they cease to be truly feminist. They can be large organizations, and often must be to take advantage of the power of numbers that is the only advantage the powerless have over the powerful, but they must be decentralized organizations in which the grassroots units are connected and coordinated within a federated structure through the selection of delegates from below. And they must avoid, if possible, dependence on outside bureaucracies for their funding. When alternative organizations become dependent on outside bureaucracies for crucial resources, a dangerous process often ensues. Egalitarian and collective organizations must make themselves acceptable to bureaucrats by constructing the appropriate hierarchy of offices and functions so that banks are willing to lend money or state officials to turn over grants. But the outside money creates internal changes: members salaried through grant money become more and more involved in the grantsmanship necessary to keep the funds flowing; to make their case they need to employ bureaucratic devices for defining their own organizations; they also need more and more staff and/or volunteers to help deliver the output promised in the grant package. Since the paid staff has greater involvement and better information about the daily activities of the organization, they accrue more power than is available to the others, and bureaucratic stratification patterns emerge.[129]

The strength of feminist organizations lies in their ability to demonstrate the potential of feminist discourse to restructure the basic terms of political life. My presentation of this discourse has left many questions unanswered and inadequately formulated; I've offered only the briefest of outlines of alternative institutions, and a few suggestions about how to achieve them. My more modest aim has been to demonstrate the real possibility of an alternative vision of collective life, one based on the concrete life experience of women. By rethinking politics in light of women's experiences as caretakers and as subordinates, the possibilities of collective action can be reconceptualized so as to make feminist principles central to public life. Real social change comes about when people think and live differently. Feminist discourse and feminist practice offer the linguistic and structural space in which it is possible to think, live, work, and love differently, in opposition to the discursive and institutional practices of bureaucratic capitalism. At least it is a start.

Notes

Preface

1 Approximately 7 percent of women employed outside the home are managers and administrators; 17 percent are professional and technical, broadly defined. (Both nurses and grade school teachers are included in the professional category.) The big "gain" in women's work has come among the remainder, in that more women than ever are working in low-paying, deadend jobs. See introduction to Barbara L. Forisha and Barbara H. Goldman, eds., *Outsiders on the Inside: Women and Organizations* (Englewood Cliffs, N.J.: Prentice-Hall, 1981).

2 I am using the term "organizational society" synonymously with "bureaucratic society" because in contemporary American society most organizations are bureaucratic and because the increasing organization of nearly all aspects of our lives is the focus of my concern. I do not mean that all forms of organization are the same, or that a society could exist without organization.

3 This discussion owes much to Richard J. Bernstein's analysis of the task of critique in *The Restructuring of Social and Political Theory* (Philadelphia, Pa.: University of Pennsylvania Press, 1976).

4 Alvin Gouldner, "Metaphysical Pathos and the Theory of Bureaucracy," in Lewis A. Coser and Bernard Rosenburg, eds., *Sociological Theory* (New York: Macmillan, 1964), p. 509.

5 Herbert L. Dreyfus and Paul Rabinow, *Michel Foucault: Beyond Structuralism and Hermeneutics* (Chicago: University of Chicago Press, 1982), p. xxii.

6 Michel Foucault, *Power/Knowledge: Selected Interviews and Other Writings* (New York: Pantheon Books, 1972), p. 220.

7 Foucault specifically takes Lawrence Stone to task for confusing his arguments made about insanity with arguments about education (Michel Foucault, "An Exchange with Michel Foucault," letters to the editor, *The New York Review of Books* 30 [March 31, 1983]: 42–43). Foucault does address education in *Discipline and Punish* (New York: Vintage Books, 1979), especially pp. 140 and 191.

8 In fact Foucault criticizes Bergson in a passing remark in *The*

Birth of the Clinic (New York: Vintage Books, 1975), p. 170, for his reliance on time to conceive of individuality.

9 Dreyfus and Rabinow, *Michel Foucault*, p. 216.

10 By "episteme" Foucault means the underlying set of conditions that give rise to the dominant view of the world in a given historical era.

11 Dreyfus and Rabinow, *Michel Foucault*, p. 57.

12 *Ibid.*, p. viii.

13 Michel Foucault, "The Subject and Power," in *ibid.*, Afterword, p. 210.

14 Alan Sheridan, *Michel Foucault: The Will to Truth* (New York: Tavistock Publications, 1980), p. 221.

15 Roberto M. Unger, *Knowledge and Politics* (New York: Free Press, 1975), p. 17.

16 Foucault, "The Subject and Power," pp. 222–223.

17 Foucault, *Power/Knowledge*, pp. 53–54.

Chapter One

1 See Margery Davis, "Woman's Place Is at the Typewriter: The Feminization of the Clerical Labor Force," *Radical America* 8 (1974): 1–28; and Evelyn Nakano Glenn and Roslyn L. Feldberg, "Clerical Work: The Female Occupation," in Jo Freeman, ed., *Women: A Feminist Perspective* (2nd ed.; Palo Alto, Calif.: Mayfield, 1979), pp. 313–338. While poor women, particularly black women, have always worked outside the home, it was white women of the middle class who were more involved in and affected by feminism and bureaucratization.

2 I am oversimplifying the theoretical complexities here by not distinguishing among Marxist feminism, socialist feminism, anarchist feminism, lesbian feminism, and others, but that has been adequately done elsewhere (see Alison M. Jaggar and Paula Rothenberg Struhl, eds., *Feminist Frameworks* [New York: McGraw-Hill, 1978]). For my purposes the most important distinction is between demands to "let us in" versus those to "set us free." I am also somewhat overstating the opposition between liberal feminism and the various forms of radical feminism, since the two often work together; however, basic differences in both theory and practice are widely recognized. If pressed to label my own argument more specifically, I should call it anarchist feminism because the critique of bureaucracy draws heavily on well-established anarch-

ist arguments concerning hierarchy. However, I am more interested in making the argument than in labeling it.

3   Lynda M. Glennon, *Women and Dualism* (New York: Longman, 1979), p. 18.

4   *Ibid.*, pp. 22–23.

5   Roslyn Wallach Bologh, "Max Weber and the Dilemma of Male Rationality," unpublished manuscript, St. John's University, October 21, 1982.

6   Jean Bethke Elshtain, *Public Man, Private Woman* (Princeton, N.J.: Princeton University Press, 1981); Sara Ruddick, "Maternal Thinking," *Feminist Studies* 6 (Summer, 1980): 342–367.

7   Robert B. Denhardt and Jan Perkins, "The Coming Death of Administrative *Man*," *Women in Public Administration* 36 (July/August, 1976): 382.

8   Marge Piercy, *Woman on the Edge of Time* (New York: Fawcett, 1981); Charlotte P. Gilman, *Herland* (New York: Pantheon Books, 1979); Dorothy Bryant, *The Kin of Ata Are Waiting for You* (New York: Moon Books, 1971).

9   For discussions of radical feminist organizations, see Charlotte Bunch *et al.*, *Building Feminist Theory: Essays from Quest* (New York: Longman, 1981). For brief discussions of the "bureaucracy" debate, see Glennon, *Women and Dualism*, p. 10, and Denhardt and Perkins, "Coming Death," p. 381.

10 Max Weber, *The Theory of Social and Economic Organizations*, trans. A. M. Henderson and Talcott Parsons (New York: Free Press of Glencoe, 1964). I am using the concept of hierarchy to mean horizontally graded authority relations entailing "top-down" supervision and control. One might imagine a radically different form of hierarchy, a representative one in which members at each level are selected and empowered from below; but this is not the kind of hierarchy found in modern bureaucratic organizations.

11 Robert Presthus, *The Organizational Society* (New York: Alfred A. Knopf, 1962), pp. 11, 27, *et passim*.

12 Like others who have written about bureaucracy, I find myself repeatedly using the verb "penetrate" to describe the invasion of society by bureaucracy. Without making too much of a symbol, perhaps this usage is a sign of the "maleness" of bureaucracy as a social form.

13 Claude Lefort, "What Is Bureaucracy?" *Telos* 22 (Winter, 1974–1975): 49. I am confining my analysis to the United States, but feel that it is probably applicable to most Western societies.

14 Hannah Arendt, *The Human Condition* (Chicago: University of Chicago Press, 1958), p. 40.

15 The process by which instrumental values are made into terminal values is analyzed by Robert K. Merton, "Bureaucratic Structure and Personality," in Merton, *Social Theory and Social Structure* (New York: Free Press, 1968), pp. 249–260.

16 Robert N. Kharasch, *The Institutional Imperative* (New York: Charterhouse Books, 1973). Charles Perrow argues that the goal displacement argument needs qualification because "the dominant organizations or institutions of our society have *not* experienced goal displacement and have been able to institutionalize on their own terms, to create the environments they desire, shape the existing ones, and define which sections of it they will deal with" (Charles Perrow, *Complex Organizations: A Critical Essay* [2nd ed.; Glenview, Ill.: Scott Foresman, 1979], p. 196). However, one can accept Perrow's argument that organizations such as the oil companies, the big banks, and the Pentagon, don't simply "drift," that their elites are able deliberately to set policies that maximize power, profit, and control, while still seeing the applicability of goal displacement. In such large and powerful organizations goal displacement takes place but is simply less important or visible because their enormous resources allow them to expand continuously. Many organizational analysts see goal displacement as "pathological" (for example, Steven A. Waldhorn, "Pathological Bureaucracies," in Virginia B. Ermer and John H. Strange, eds., *Blacks and Bureaucracy* [New York: Thomas Y. Crowell, 1972], pp. 184–191), whereas I see it as an inevitable aspect of bureaucracy and simultaneously as an indictment of bureaucratic claims.

17 Ben Agger, "On Science as Domination," in Alkis Kontos, ed., *Domination* (Toronto: University of Toronto Press, 1975), p. 193.

18 Paul Goldman and Donald R. Van Houten, "Managerial Strategies and the Worker: A Marxist Analysis of Bureaucracy," *Sociological Quarterly* 18 (Winter, 1977): 108–125.

19 Stephen A. Marglin, "What Do Bosses Do? The Origins and Functions of Hierarchy in Capitalist Society," *Review of Radical Political Economy* 6 (Summer, 1974): 62. Foucault, in his avoidance of Marxism, overstates the anonymity of disciplinary power. It is true that such power is experienced as "a strategy with no one directing it and everyone increasingly enmeshed in it, whose end is the increase of power and order itself" (Herbert L. Dreyfus and Paul Rabinow, *Michel Foucault: Beyond Structuralism and Hermeneutics* [Chicago: University of Chicago Press, 1982], p. xxii). But its overall impact is to pacify ordinary people and cement the power of those who own and rule.

20 Harry Braverman, *Labor and Monopoly Capital* (New York: Monthly Review Press, 1974), p. 114.
21 Marglin, "What Do Bosses Do?" p. 84. See also Dan Clawson, *Bureaucracy and the Labor Process* (New York: Monthly Review Press, 1980), p. 54.
22 Perrow, *Complex Organizations*, p. 213. Perrow is citing research by Paul M. Hirsch, "Organizational Effectiveness and the Institutional Environment," *Administrative Science Quarterly* 20 (September, 1975): 327–344.
23 Peter Berger, Brigitte Berger, and Hansfried Kellner, *The Homeless Mind: Modernization and Consciousness* (New York: Random House, 1974), p. 31.
24 Merton, "Bureaucratic Structure," p. 259.
25 Ralph P. Hummel, *The Bureaucratic Experience* (New York: St. Martin's Press, 1977), p. 16.
26 Roberto M. Unger, *Knowledge and Politics* (New York: Free Press, 1975), p. 184.
27 Hummel, *Bureaucratic Experience*, p. 30.
28 *Ibid.*, p. 37.
29 *Ibid.*, p. 150.
30 Murray Bookchin, "Beyond Neo-Marxism," *Telos* 36 (Summer, 1978): 18–19.
31 Presthus, *Organizational Society*, p. 53.
32 David Schuman, *The Ideology of Form* (Lexington, Mass.: D.C. Heath, 1978), p. 69.
33 Deena Weinstein, *Bureaucratic Opposition* (New York: Pergamon Press, 1979), p. ix.
34 Theodore Roszak, *The Making of a Counterculture* (New York: Anchor Books, 1969), p. 8.
35 Herbert Marcuse, *One-Dimensional Man* (Boston: Beacon Press, 1964), p. 84.
36 Roszak, *Making of a Counterculture*, p. 9 *et passim*. Voices from within the ranks of middle management also evoke the comparison of bureaucracy to totalitarian political regimes, although they usually do not draw particularly radical conclusions from the insight. See Earl Shorris, *The Oppressed Middle: The Politics of Middle Management* (New York: Anchor/Doubleday, 1981), p. 93 *et passim*.
37 Weinstein, *Bureaucratic Opposition*, p. 107.
38 Alvin W. Gouldner, "Stalinism: A Study of Internal Colonialism," *Telos* 34 (Winter, 1977–1978): 43.
39 Bookchin, "Beyond Neo-Marxism," p. 18.

40 Harold L. Wilensky, *Organizational Intelligence* (New York: Basic Books, 1967), p. 179.

41 Lloyd I. Rudolph and Susanne H. Rudolph, "Authority and Power in Bureaucratic and Patrimonial Administration: A Revisionist Interpretation of Weber on Bureaucracy," *World Politics* 3 (January, 1979): 215–216; Jeffrey Pfeffer, "Who Governs?" in Oscar Grusky and George A. Miller, eds., *The Sociology of Organizations* (2nd ed.; New York: Free Press, 1981), p. 254.

42 Clawson, *Bureaucracy and the Labor Process*, pp. 29–30 *et passim.* Clawson draws heavily on Braverman's arguments and also provides a useful summary of the criticisms of Braverman on pp. 31–33.

43 Thomas Gray and Cynthia Roberts-Gray, "Structuring Bureaucratic Rules to Enhance Compliance," *Psychological Reports* 45 (October, 1979): 587.

44 These insights, and many others as well, were brought home to me in discussions with Wolf Narr and Bruce Berman at the First International Conference on the Comparative, Historical, and Critical Analysis of Bureaucracy at the Gottlieb Duttweiler Institute in Zurich, Switz., October 4–8, 1982.

45 In some ways I am working from, and taking for granted, a particular view of the self and self-other relations. I hope it is not seen as cheating to refer the reader to the place where this view of the self is articulated and defended; otherwise I fear that I will be writing the same book over again. I offer what I consider to be a sound feminist view of the self in my first book, *Self, Society and Womankind: The Dialectic of Liberation* (Westbury, Conn.: Greenwood Press, 1980).

46 Michael A. Weinstein, *Structure of Human Life: A Vitalist Ontology* (New York: New York University Press, 1979), p. 143.

47 José Ortega y Gasset, quoted in Michael A. Weinstein, *Meaning and Appreciation: Time and Modern Political Life* (West Lafayette, Ind.: Purdue University Press, 1978), p. 18.

48 Roslyn Wallach Bologh, "Beyond Weber's Analysis and Critique of Bureaucracy," paper presented at the First International Conference on the Comparative, Historical, and Critical Analysis of Bureaucracy, Gottlieb Duttweiler Institute, Zurich, Switz., October 4–8, 1982.

49 Anthony Downs, *Inside Bureaucracy* (Boston: Little, Brown, 1967), p. 18.

50 *Ibid.*, p. 19.

51 Peter Selznick, "An Approach to the Theory of Bureaucracy," *Amer-*

ican Sociological Review 8 (1943): 47, quoted in Nicos P. Mouzelis, *Organization and Bureaucracy* (Chicago: Aldine, 1968), p. 61.

52 Stanley Aronowitz, *False Promises* (NewYork: McGraw-Hill, 1973), p. 301. Richard Edwards points out that the number of foremen employed per 100 workers during the period 1910–1940 grew by 15 percent; between 1940 and 1970, it expanded by an astonishing 67 percent (Richard C. Edwards, *Contested Terrain* [New York: Basic Books, 1979], p. 135). While the large number of supervisors may provide employers with a form of "strike insurance," it is still costly and inefficient (Aronowitz, *False Promises*, p. 308).

53 Alvin Gouldner, *Patterns of Industrial Democracy* (New York: Free Press, 1954), quoted in Mouzelis, *Organization and Bureaucracy*, pp. 60–61.

54 Michel Foucault, *Power/Knowledge: Selected Interviews and Other Writings* (New York: Pantheon Books, 1972), p. 82.

55 Robert B. Denhardt, "Bureaucratic Socialization and Organizational Accommodation," *Administrative Science Quarterly* 13 (December, 1968): 442.

56 Foucault, *Power/Knowledge*, pp. 81, 82.

57 Jean Bethke Elshtain, "Antigone's Daughters," *Democracy* 2 (April, 1982): 52 *et passim*.

58 For examples of the early writings of the Second Wave, see Shulamith Firestone, *The Dialectic of Sex* (New York: Bantam Books, 1970), and Kate Millet, *Sexual Politics* (New York: Avon Books, 1970). For examples of theorists who have in some ways overcompensated by glorifying traditional family roles, see Elshtain, *Public Man, Private Woman*, and Ruddick, "Maternal Thinking." While I see much that is of value in these accounts, there is real danger in looking too enthusiastically to mothering or to the family for a profile of liberation. Also, Elshtain's dismissal of the early radical feminist writings ignores both the context in which they were written and the important contribution they made to opening up political theory to feminist questions.

59 Jesse Bernard, *The Female World* (New York: Free Press, 1981), p. 28.

60 Carol Gilligan, "Woman's Place in Man's Life Cycle," *Harvard Educational Review* 49 (November, 1979): 440.

61 Maggie Scarf, *Unfinished Business* (New York: Ballantine Books, 1980). Scarf points out that the obsession with interpersonal loss characterizes the stories and advice columns in women's magazines, as well as the common patterns of clinical depression in women's life cycles.

62 Weinstein, *Structure of Human Life*, p. 10 *et passim*. Weinstein's brilliant insight into the dualistic, incomplete quality of our existence is marred only by his tendency to see as universal experiences that are in fact male. His argument is very complex and it is difficult to make a criticism that is both brief and accurate; basically, his account of appreciation leans too far in the direction of "essential solitude." The act of "peering behind the conventional ego's veil" is less likely to be an experience of solitude and aloneness for women, whose ties to others are more firmly rooted in basic psychic structures and processes (p. 119).

63 The connections between the theory and practice of anarchism and the ideas I am exploring here are investigated in my article "Toward a New Anarchism," *Contemporary Crises* 7 (January, 1983): 39–57.

64 Bologh, "Beyond Weber's Analysis," p. 6.

65 Sandra Harding, "Toward a Strong Program for Epistemology: Clues from Feminist Inquiry," paper presented at the American Political Science Association Meetings, New York City, September, 1981, p. 24.

66 Dorothy Sayers, *Are Women Human?* (Grand Rapids, Mich.: Eerdmans, 1971), p. 37.

67 For an excellent discussion of the anthropological conditions under which male dominance develops, see Peggy Reeves Sanday, *Female Power and Male Dominance* (London: Cambridge University Press, 1981). For an explanation of the historical and conceptual evolution of the public/private split, see Linda Nicholson, *Feminism as Political Philosophy*, forthcoming. For a summary of the "difference feminists," see Elaine Marks and Isabelle de Courtivron, eds., *New French Feminisms* (Amherst, Mass.: University of Massachusetts Press, 1980), and Alison M. Jaggar, "Human Biology and Feminist Politics," unpublished paper, University of Cincinnati, 1981. Alice Rossi, "A Biosocial Perspective on Parenting," *Daedalus* 106 (Spring, 1977): 1–31, provides a "feminist" version of sociobiology, a coupling that I see as a contradiction in terms. Phil Green provides an excellent analysis of the truth claims behind the sociobiology arguments in *The Pursuit of Inequality* (New York: Pantheon Books, 1981).

68 Foucault, *Power/Knowledge*, p. 86.

69 Adrienne Rich, "Privilege, Power, and Tokenism," *MS* 8 (September, 1979): 42–44.

70 Elshtain, "Antigone's Daughters," p. 58.

Chapter Two

1 Henry Jacoby, *The Bureaucratization of the World* (Berkeley, Calif.: University of California Press, 1973), p. 50.
2 *Ibid.*, p. 55. The expansion of bureaucracy in so-called socialist nations indicates bureaucracy's ability to penetrate a variety of political and economic climates. The bureaucratization of socialism, while intriguing, is not my subject here; for a discussion of that topic, see Donald C. Hodges, *The Bureaucratization of Socialism* (Amherst, Mass.: University of Massachusetts Press, 1981).
3 For a very useful overview of Weber's view of history, see Steven Seidman and Michael Gruber, "Capitalism and Individuation in the Sociology of Max Weber," *British Journal of Sociology* 28 (December, 1977): 498–508.
4 Isaac Kramnick, "Joseph Priestly—English Philosophe," paper presented to the Columbia University Seminar on Political and Social Thought, December 16, 1982.
5 Michel Foucault, *Discipline and Punish* (New York: Vintage Books, 1979), pp. 220, 219.
6 Michel Foucault, *The Birth of the Clinic* (New York: Vintage Books, 1975), p. xii.
7 Michel Foucault, *Power/Knowledge: Selected Interviews and Other Writings* (New York: Pantheon Books, 1972), p. 133. Foucault's terminology is often confusing, in part because he makes up new terms as he goes along without indicating their relationship to other terms, and in part because his language and his emphasis shift as his position evolves from the early emphasis on autonomous discourse to the more recent concern with power. (For an excellent analysis of this shift, see Herbert L. Dreyfus and Paul Rabinow, *Michel Foucault: Beyond Structuralism and Hermeneutics* [Chicago: University of Chicago Press, 1982].) In light of this confusion, a few definitions of key terms are in order.

"Discursive relations" or "discursive practices" are the characteristic ways of speaking that constitute the situations and objects we study. "Discursive formations" I take to be a more particular term referring to regularities among speech acts (statements) that have been "formed by the same set of rules" (Donald J. McDonell, "On Foucault's Philosophical Method," *Canadian Journal of Philosophy* 7 [September, 1977]: 549). The "underlying set of rules governing the production of discourses in any single period" is the *episteme* (Alan Sheridan, *Michel Foucault: The Will to Truth* [New York: Tavistock Publications, 1980], p. 209). By "episteme" Foucault says he means "*not a sort of grand underlying theory*," but "a space of *dispersion,* . . . an *open field of relationships and no doubt indefinitely describable*" (Foucault, "History, Discourse, and Discontinuity," *Salmagundi* 20 [Summer/Fall, 1972]: 228 [italics in original]). In the notion of the episteme Foucault seems to be seeking a way "to reconcile change with the notion of cultural totality" (Sheridan, *Michel Foucault*, p. 209).

In *The Archaeology of Knowledge* (New York: Pantheon, 1972) Foucault refers to the larger set of relations between discursive (linguistic) and nondiscursive (institutions, physical and social arrangements) practices as "the enunciative modality"; in *Power/Knowledge* as "apparatus" or "strategies of relations of forces, supporting and supported by types of knowledge" (p. 196); and again in *Power/Knowledge* as "*dispositif,*" which is a term for both his method and the structure of cultural arrangements and practices he examines (p. 194). The dispositif includes "discourses, institutions, architectural arrangements, regulations, laws, administrative measures, scientific statements, philosophic propositions, morality, philanthropy, etc." (p. 194).

Foucault's definitions of his method are equally confusing. His "archeological method" analyzes the development of an episteme, or epistemological field, without reference to its rational value or to a knowing subject and without appeal to causal argument (Foucault, *The Order of Things* [New York: Vintage Books, 1973], p. xxii; Foucault, "History, Discourse and Discontinuity," pp. 234–235). As Dreyfus and Rabinow point out, the archeological method has no moral or political theory and renders the influence of social institutions on discourse incomprehensible. It also contains an inherent paradox, since it "works" only if no one believes it, if everyone but the analyst himself shares the "illusion of meaning."

Foucault's shift to the "genealogical method" allows a more explicit turn toward power without turning either to the transcendental subject or to the concepts of ideology or repression, both of which Foucault regards as tainted by their respective Marxist and Freudian usages (*Power/Knowledge*, pp. 117–118). (I do not share Foucault's distaste for the term "ideology" and use it frequently to mean worldview.) Genealogy looks past the dominant discourse to those that have been suppressed: "What it really does is to entertain the claims to attention of local, discontinuous, disqualified, illegitimate knowledges against the claims of a unitary body of theory which would filter, hierarchise and order them in the name of some true knowledge and some arbitrary idea of what constitutes a science and its objects" (*Power/Knowledge*, p. 83).

8 Dreyfus and Rabinow, *Michel Foucault*, p. 153.
9 Andrew J. Polsky, "The Administered Citizen," paper presented at the American Political Science Association meetings, Chicago, Ill., September 1–4, 1983, p. 3. Polsky provides an excellent analysis of the Progressive reformers' writings and the official documents of the era. See also James A. Stever, *Diversity and Order in State and Local Politics* (Columbia, S.C.: University of South Carolina Press, 1980), pp. 137–189.
10 *Ibid.*, p. 7.
11 Jacques Ellul, *The Technological Society* (New York: Alfred A. Knopf, 1964), from the introduction by Robert Merton, p. vi. His critics have argued that Ellul can be faulted for criticizing bureaucracy and technology but not capitalism. Despite this failing, Ellul's eye for the invasion of technique is sharp.
12 Ellul, *Technological Society*, p. 97. This list of traits is culled from a longer list provided by Ellul, and some of his categories have been collapsed. Foucault emphasizes the same set of traits when he says that, in disciplinary society, "the goal desired and the techniques designed to achieve it merge" (quoted in Dreyfus and Rabinow, *Michel Foucault*, p. 154).
13 Foucault, *Discipline and Punish*, p. 223. See also Claus Offe, "Political Authority and Class Structure," *International Journal of Sociology* 2 (Spring, 1972): 73–107.
14 Peter Berger, Brigitte Berger, and Hansfried Kellner, *The Homeless Mind: Modernization and Consciousness* (New York: Random House, 1974), p. 98.
15 Offe, "Political Authority," p. 99.
16 Foucault, *Power/Knowledge*, p. 106.
17 Polsky, "Administered Citizen," pp. 8, 10.
18 The War on Poverty provided legal resources to the poor and encouraged the establishment of academic centers for the study of welfare law, thus bringing the two discourses together (David Street, George T. Martin, Jr., and Laura Kramer Gordon, *The Welfare Industry* [Beverly Hills, Calif.: Sage Publications, 1979], p. 128).
19 Foucault, *Discipline and Punish*, p. 228.
20 Stanley Aronowitz, *False Promises* (New York: McGraw-Hill, 1973), p. 217. Aronowitz's study of the American working class focuses on the historical relationship between working-class culture and working-class institutions, especially trade unions.
21 *Ibid.*, p. 218.
22 Paul M. Hirsch, "Organizational Effectiveness and the Institutional Environment," *Administrative Science Quarterly* 20 (September, 1975): 327–344, quoted in Charles Perrow, *Complex Orga-*

nizations: A Critical Essay (2nd ed.; Glenview, Ill.: Scott Foresman, 1979), pp. 214–215.

23 For general discussion of the interlocking organizational network see Bertrand Gross, *Friendly Fascism* (New York: M. Evans, 1980); Charles Perrow, "Demystifying Organizations," in Rosemary C. Sarri and Yeheskel Hasenfeld, eds., *The Management of Human Services* (New York: Columbia University Press, 1978), pp. 103–120; James Knowles, "The Rockefeller Family Group," in Ralph L. Andreano, ed., *Superconcentration/Supercorporation* (New York: Irvington, 1974), pp. 1–59.

24 See Francis Fox Piven and Richard Cloward, *The Politics of Turmoil* (New York: Random House, 1965).

25 Harry Braverman, *Labor and Monopoly Capital* (New York: Monthly Review Press, 1974), p. 167.

26 *The New York Times*, November 9, 1969, p. 49, quoted in Robert Goodman, *After the Planners* (New York: Simon and Schuster, 1971), pp. 44–45.

27 Edgar Litt, "The Rise of the Public Vocational University," in Philip H. Melanson, ed., *Knowledge, Politics, and Public Policy: Introductory Readings in American Politics* (Cambridge, Mass.: Winthrop, 1973), p. 28.

28 Paul Goldman, "The Organization Caste System and the New Working Class," *Insurgent Socialist* 3 (Winter, 1973): 45.

29 Donald Arnstine, "The Use of Coercion in Changing the Schools," *Educational Theory* 23 (Fall, 1973): 282.

30 Steinar Kvale, "Examinations: From Ritual Through Bureaucracy to Technology," *Social Praxis* 3 (1975): 198.

31 John T. Molloy, *Dress for Success* (New York: Warner Books, 1975); John T. Molloy, *The Woman's Dress for Success Book* (New York: Warner Books, 1977); Kenneth Blanchard and Spencer Johnson, *The One-Minute Manager* (New York: Berkley Books, 1981); John Budd, *The Fast Track: How to Survive in the Corporate Labyrinth* (New York: St. Martin's Press, 1982).

32 William G. Scott and David K. Hart, *Organizational America* (Boston: Houghton Mifflin, 1979), p. 49.

33 This insight, as well as many of the others in this book, I owe to conversations with Mark Bertozzi in which he generously shared his insights into organizational life.

34 William E. Connolly, *Appearance and Reality in Politics* (Cambridge, Eng.: Cambridge University Press, 1981). See also Lillian Breslow Rubin, *Worlds of Pain* (New York: Basic Books, 1976); and Richard Sennett and Jonathan Cobb, *The Hidden Injuries of Class* (New York: Vintage Books, 1972).

35 Herbert G. Wilcox, "The Culture Trait of Hierarchy in Middle Class Children," *Public Administration Review* 28 (May/June, 1968): 229, 231, 232. In his test Wilcox asked participants to interpret the social relationships represented by a hierarchical grid. He administered the test to elementary and high school students, undergraduate and graduate students in public administration, and city managers. The average number of correct responses (i.e., responses that identified "top-down" authority relations, hierarchical chain of command, etc.) in the fourth-grade classes was approximately 55 percent; for the sixth grade, 75 percent; for high school freshmen, 85 percent; for high school seniors 88 percent; for college juniors, 84 percent; for graduate students, 88 percent; for city managers, 90 percent. The biggest difference in mean scores was that between the fourth and the sixth grades. Beyond the level of high school freshmen, the scores were remarkably stable.

36 Aronowitz, *False Promises*, p. 83.

37 Laura A. Handrahan, "Teachers Increasingly Becoming Targets of Violence," *Albany Times Union*, March 29, 1983, p. 1.

38 Francine D. Blau, "Women in the Labor Force: An Overview," in Jo Freeman, ed., *Women: A Feminist Perspective* (2nd ed.; Palo Alto, Calif.: Mayfield, 1979), p. 265.

39 For an excellent presentation of the anthropological evidence behind this argument, see Peggy Reeves Sanday, *Female Power and Male Dominance* (London: Cambridge University Press, 1981). There is some dispute about the level of sexual egalitarianism in colonial America; see, for example, Heidi Hartmann, "Capitalism, Patriarchy, and Job Segregation by Sex," in Zillah R. Eisenstein, ed., *Capitalist Patriarchy and the Case for Socialist Feminism* (New York: Monthly Review Press, 1979), pp. 206–247, and Mary Beth Norton, *Liberty's Daughters* (Boston: Little, Brown, 1980). At any rate, I am not claiming that pre-industrial America was a sexually equal society, only that the relation of public to private life was closer and that the labor of women was more readily acknowledged and highly valued.

40 Blau, "Women in the Labor Force," p. 269.

41 Polsky, "Administered Citizen," p. 6.

42 Barbara Ehrenreich and John Ehrenreich, "The Professional-Managerial Class," in Pat Walker, ed., *Between Labor and Capital* (Boston: South End Press, 1979), p. 16.

43 Mary P. Ryan, "Femininity and Capitalism in Antebellum America," in Eisenstein, ed., *Capitalist Patriarchy*, p. 155 *et passim*.

44 Michel Foucault, *The History of Sexuality*, I (New York: Random House, 1980), 101.

45 See Ann Douglas, *The Femininization of American Culture* (New York: Alfred A. Knopf, 1977).

46 Foucault, *History of Sexuality*, I, 102.

47 For a good discussion of the place of the more radical voices within the First Wave of feminism, see Ellen DuBois, "The Nineteenth-Century Woman Suffrage Movement and the Analysis of Women's Oppression," in Eisenstein, ed., *Capitalist Patriarchy*, pp. 137–150; and Jean Bethke Elshtain, *Public Man, Private Woman* (Princeton, N.J.: Princeton University Press, 1981).

48 Richard Sennett, *The Fall of Public Man* (New York: Vintage Books, 1978).

49 Margaret R. Davis estimates that, in 1972, in two-job couples, husbands averaged 2.5 minutes of housework for every hour their wives worked outside the home; by 1976 husbands' participation had crawled to an average of 5 minutes for every hour their wives worked outside the home. See Davis, *Families in a Working World: The Impact of Organizations on Domestic Life* (New York: Praeger, 1982), p. viii.

50 The importance of the theme of survival in contemporary culture was pointed out by Christopher Lasch in a lecture entitled "American Life in an Age of Diminishing Expectations" presented at Russell Sage College, March 17, 1983.

51 Arlie Russell Hochschild, *The Managed Heart* (Berkeley, Calif.: University of California Press, 1983), pp. 171, 7.

52 *Ibid.*, pp. 96, 97.

53 *Ibid.*, p. 186.

54 *Ibid.*, pp. 19, 7.

55 Foucault, *History of Sexuality*, I, 103.

56 *Ibid.*, pp. 120–121.

57 *Ibid.*, p. 131.

58 There has been substantial controversy concerning various claims, including feminist claims, about the extent and meaning of the witchcraft trials. For an interesting interpretation of the evidence, see Mary Nelson, "Why Witches Were Women," in Freeman, ed., *Women*, pp. 451–468.

59 See James Cook, "The X-Rated Economy," *Forbes* 122 (September 18, 1978): 81–89.

60 The production of discourse about the rules for serial monogamy is a striking example of the standardization of sexuality. I owe this example to a vital (and intoxicated) conversation about Foucault with Steve Leonard and Terry Ball.

61 Andrea Dworkin, *Pornography* (New York: Perigee Books, 1979),

p. 68. Dworkin's account, while powerful, should be read with a careful eye. Her insistence on seeing all exploitation, including that based in economically and racially defined experience, as evidence solely of male power over women is reductionist and incomplete. See especially her discussion of wealth (p. 21) and of race (p. 178). Nonetheless, her explanation of the ubiquity of pornography in our culture is a strong one.

62 Ralph P. Hummel, *The Bureaucratic Experience* (New York: St. Martin's Press, 1977), p. 51.

63 Timothy W. Luke, "Regulating the Haven in a Heartless World: The State and Family Under Advanced Capitalism," *New Political Science* 2 (Fall, 1981): 69–71.

64 Murray Bookchin, "Beyond Neo-Marxism," *Telos* 36 (Summer, 1978): 18.

65 Braverman, *Labor and Monopoly Capital*, p. 27.

66 For a suggestive discussion of the rationalization of desire, see Joel Kovel, "Rationalization and the Family," *Telos* 37 (Fall, 1978): 5–21.

67 Foucault, *Power/Knowledge*, p. 257.

68 Hochschild, *Managed Heart*, p. 21.

69 Michael J. Shapiro, *Language and Political Understanding* (New Haven, Conn.: Yale University Press, 1981), p. 137.

70 *Ibid.*, p. 140.

71 *Ibid.*, p. 218.

72 Foucault, *History of Sexuality*, I, 100.

73 Shapiro, *Language and Political Understanding*, p. 5 *et passim* (italics in original).

74 *Ibid.*, pp. 59, 141 *et passim*.

75 Robert R. Denhardt, *In the Shadow of Organization* (Lawrence, Kan.: Regents Press of Kansas, 1981), p. vii.

76 I intend to present an analysis and critique of this field, not simply a review of it; I am interested in accounting for this literature, not summarizing it, a task done adequately elsewhere. For sound reviews of the organizational literature, see Bengt Abrahamsson, *Bureaucracy or Participation: The Logic of Organization* (London: Sage Publications, 1977): Nicos P. Mouzelis, *Organization and Bureaucracy* (Chicago: Aldine, 1968); Perrow, *Complex Organizations*; Nancy DiTomaso, "The Problem of Organizing: Ends versus Means," unpublished paper, Northwestern University, January, 1981.

77 Thomas Kuhn, *The Structure of Scientific Revolutions* (2nd ed.; Chicago: University of Chicago Press, 1970), p. 182.

78 Robert T. Golembiewski, *Public Administration as a Developing Discipline* (New York: Marcel Dekker, 1977), preface.
79 Berger, Berger, and Kellner, *Homeless Mind*, p. 98.
80 Michel Foucault, *L'ordre du discours*, (Paris: Gallimard, 1971), p. 46, quoted in Sheridan, *Michel Foucault*, p. 127.
81 Alvin Gouldner, "Metaphysical Pathos and the Theory of Bureaucracy," in Lewis A. Coser and Bernard Rosenburg, eds., *Sociological Theory* (New York: Macmillan, 1964), pp. 500–510.
82 Jacques Ellul, *Propaganda* (New York: Alfred A. Knopf, 1965), quoted in Scott and Hart, *Organizational America*, p. 126.
83 Dreyfus and Rabinow, *Michel Foucault*, p. 48.
84 Scott and Hart, *Organizational America*, p. 5.
85 Foucault, *Power/Knowledge*, p. 102.
86 The quote that I am paraphrasing is from Donald J. McDonell's explanation of Foucault's method. The full quote is as follows: "The appearance of psychiatry as a discipline in the nineteenth century was made possible by a shift in the relations between hospitalization, internment, the conditions and the procedures of social exclusion, the rules of jurisprudence, the norms of industrial work and bourgeois morality; in short a set of relations governing a discursive formation. Every discipline, every science that appears does so within a given discursive formation and on the basis of the knowledge therein existing" (McDonell, "On Foucault's Philosophical Method," p. 551). McDonell seems to be using the concept of "discursive formation" to include institutional arrangements, which is contrary to my reading of Foucault; but that does not mitigate the usefulness of his explication of Foucault's method.
87 Golembiewski, *Public Administration*, p. 123.
88 *Ibid.*, p. 117. For a straightforward summary of the "new public administration" and of OD, see Thomas Vocino and Jack Rabin, *Contemporary Public Administration* (New York: Harcourt, Brace, Jovanovich, 1981).
89 Chester Barnard, *The Functions of the Executive* (Cambridge: Harvard University Press, 1938).
90 Perrow, *Complex Organizations*, pp. 87, 89 *et passim*. The institutional school is represented by Philip Selznick, *Leadership in Administration* (New York: Harper and Row, 1967). The decision-making school is represented by Herbert Simon, *Administrative Behavior* (2nd ed.; New York: Macmillan, 1957), and parts of James G. March and Herbert A. Simon, *Organizations* (New York: John Wiley and Sons, 1958). Representatives of the human relations school abound and are well summarized by Perrow in *Complex Organizations*, pp. 90–138.

91 Perrow, *Complex Organizations*, p. 200, and Perrow, "A Framework for the Comparative Analysis of Organizations," *American Sociological Review* 32 (1967): 194–208.

92 Peter M. Blau, Cecelia M. Falbe, William McKinley, and Phelps K. Tracy, "Technology and Organization in Manufacturing," in Oscar Grusky and George A. Miller, eds., *The Sociology of Organizations* (2nd ed.; New York: Free Press, 1981), p. 449.

93 Warren Bennis, *Changing Organizations* (New York: McGraw-Hill, 1966).

94 Gerald E. Caiden and Heinrich Siedentop, eds., *Strategies for Administrative Reform* (Lexington, Mass.: D. C. Heath, 1982), p. xv.

95 David A. Wren, "The Origin of Industrial Psychology and Sociology," in Thomas H. Patten, Jr., ed., *Classics of Personnel Management* (Oak Park, Ill.: Moore, 1979), p. 7.

96 This particular column on "individual style" appeared in *Esquire* 98 (July, 1982): 76–79.

97 Wren, "Origin of Industrial Psychology," p. 7.

98 Patten, ed., *Classics of Personnel Management*, p. 1.

99 *Ibid.*

100 Jay M. Shafritz, Walter L. Balk, Albert C. Hyde, and David H. Rosenbloom, *Personnel Management in Government* (New York: Marcel Dekker, 1978), p. 62.

101 Ordway Tead and Henry T. Metcalf, "The Reasons for a Personnel Department," in Patten, ed., *Classics of Personnel Management*, pp. 12–13.

102 Foucault, *History of Sexuality*, I, 27.

103 Braverman, *Labor and Monopoly Capital*, p. 86.

104 Richard Sennett, *Authority* (New York: Alfred A. Knopf, 1980), p. 115.

105 Betty Friedan, *The Second Stage* (New York: Summit Books, 1981), pp. 245–247; Barbara L. Forisha and Barbara H. Goldman, eds., *Outsiders on the Inside: Women and Organizations* (Englewood Cliffs, N.J.: Prentice-Hall, 1981), p. 5. This theme will be elaborated in Chapter Five.

106 Braverman, *Labor and Monopoly Capital*, p. 87. Braverman points out that the obsession with efficiency in scientific management—the constant counting of steps and actions, the elaborate rituals of repetition, the reduction of wholes to their parts, and so forth—would be seen as neurotic in individuals but is seen as normal in bureaucracy. Taylor, it seems, was seen as a very strange person, something of a crank, by those who knew him (p. 92). If Plato is right that the state is the individual writ large, perhaps

Taylorism represents the collective neurosis of bureaucratic capitalism.

107 For elaboration see Neil Tudiver, "Business Ideology and Management in Social Work: The Limits of Cost Control," *Catalyst* 13 (1982): 24–48, and Neil Tudiver, "Quality of Work Life: The New Shape of Employer Paternalism," paper presented at the First International Conference on the Comparative, Historical, and Critical Analysis of Bureaucracy, Gottlieb Duttweiler Institute, Zurich, Switz., October 4–8, 1982.

108 David Jenkins, *Job Power: Blue and White Collar Democracy* (New York: Doubleday, 1973), pp. 313–315, quoted in Richard C. Edwards, *Contested Terrain* (New York: Basic Books, 1979), p. 156.

109 Thomas Fitzgerald, "Why Motivation Theory Doesn't Work," *Harvard Business Review* 49 (July/August, 1971): 42, quoted in Edwards, *Contested Terrain*, p. 156.

110 See Robert E. Cole, "Work Redesign in Japan: An Evaluation," in Grusky and Miller, eds., *Sociology of Organizations*, pp. 495–529.

111 John W. Meyer and Brian Rowan, "Institutionalized Organizations: Formal Structure as Myth and Ceremony," in Grusky and Miller, eds., *Sociology of Organizations*, pp. 530–554.

112 Patten, ed., *Classics of Personnel Management*, p. xi.

113 George Gordon, *Public Administration in America* (2nd ed.; New York: St. Martin's Press, 1982), p. 30.

114 Shafritz, Balk, Hyde, and Rosenbloom, *Personnel Management*, pp. 293, 296.

115 Martin J. Gannon, *Organizational Behavior* (Boston: Little, Brown, 1979), pp. 107, 108, 109.

116 Stewart Clegg, "Power, Organization Theory, Marx and Critique," in Stewart Clegg and David Dunkerley, *Critical Issues in Organizations* (London: Routledge and Kegan Paul, 1977), p. 22.

117 Peter Allan and Stephen Rosenberg, *Public Personnel and Administrative Behavior* (Monterey, Calif.: Duxbury Press, 1981), p. xiv.

118 Richard M. Steus, *Introduction to Organizational Behavior* (Glenview, Ill.: Scott, Foresman, 1981), p. 431.

119 Patten, ed., *Classics of Personnel Management*, p. 589.

120 For an excellent case study of this process see Katherine Newman, "Incipient Bureaucracy: The Development of Hierarchy in Egalitarian Organizations," in Gerald M. Britan and Ronald Cohen, eds., *Hierarchy and Society* (Philadelphia: Institute for the Study of Human Issues, 1980), pp. 143–164.

121 Patten, ed., *Classics of Personnel Management*, p. 2.

122 Fred Kramer, *The Dynamics of Public Bureaucracy* (2nd ed.; Cambridge, Mass.: Winthrop, 1981), p. 308.

123 Golembiewski, *Public Administration*, pp. 139, 102, 113.

124 Richard E. Boyatzis, *The Competent Manager* (New York: John Wiley and Sons, 1982), p. 21.

125 *Ibid.*, p. 259.

126 Shafritz, Balk, Hyde, and Rosenbloom, *Personnel Management*, p. 62.

127 Don Hellbriegel and John W. Slocum, Jr., *Organizational Behavior* (2nd ed.; St. Paul, Minn.: West, 1979), p. 207.

128 Marvin D. Dunnette and Bernard M. Bass, "Behavioral Scientists and Personnel Management," in Patten, ed., *Classics of Personnel Management*, p. 86.

129 Patten, ed., *Classics of Personnel Management*, p. 58.

130 Aronowitz, *False Promises*, p. 279. An interesting example in this regard is the story of John B. Watson. Dutifully acknowledged in introductory psychology texts as the father of modern behaviorism, Watson made his own contribution to the birth of technical society by advocating the use of behavioral psychology to turn child-rearing practices away from the home and from emphases on loving and touching toward "encouraging a passive fidelity to the unsympathetic character of the workplace" (Stuart Ewen, *Captains of Consciousness: Advertising and the Social Roots of the Consumer Culture* [New York: McGraw-Hill, 1976], p. 82). Pursuing his vision of pleasure through consumption of commodities to its logical conclusion, he left Johns Hopkins in 1922 to become vice president of the J. Walter Thomson advertising agency.

131 Earl Shorris, *The Oppressed Middle: The Politics of Middle Management* (New York: Anchor Doubleday, 1981), p. 98.

132 Frederick C. Mosher, *Democracy and the Public Service* (New York: Oxford University Press, 1968), p. 108. For an interesting case study of the bureaucratization of a field of study, see Bette Denich, "Bureaucratic Scholarship: The New Anthropology," in Britan and Cohen, eds., *Hierarchy and Society*, pp. 165–175.

133 Mosher, *Democracy and the Public Service*, p. 104.

134 Denhardt, *In the Shadow of Organization*, p. 5.

135 Perrow, "Demystifying Organizations," p. 112.

136 Mosher, *Democracy and the Public Service*, p. 153.

137 The phrase "radical deafness" is Foucault's.

138 Golembiewski, *Public Administration*, pp. ix–x.

139 Perrow, *Complex Organizations*, p. 200 *et passim*.

140 See Vincent Ostrum, *The Intellectual Crisis in American Public*

Administration (University, Ala.: University of Alabama Press, 1973).

141   See Michael M. Harmon, *Action Theory for Public Administration* (New York: Longman, 1983).

142   See Graeme Salaman, "Classification of Organizations and Organization Structure: The Main Elements and Interrelationships," in Graeme Salaman and Kenneth Thompson, eds., *Control and Ideology in Organizations* (Cambridge, Mass.: MIT Press, 1980), pp. 56–84; Amitai Etzioni, *A Comparative Analysis of Complex Organizations* (New York: Free Press, 1961).

143   William H. Whyte, Jr., *The Organization Man* (New York: Doubleday, 1957), p. 14; Scott and Hart, *Organizational America*, p. 223; Perrow, *Complex Organizations*, p. 5; Elliott Jacques, *A General Theory of Bureaucracy* (New York: Halsted Press, 1976), p. 141. Guy B. Adams's arguments in "Prolegomenon to a Teachable Theory of Public Administration" (in Thomas Vocino and Richard Himovics, eds., *Public Administration Education in Transition* [New York: Marcel Dekker, 1982], pp. 93–114) vary somewhat from the standard public administration fare. Adams shows a substantial acquaintance with political theory and with the literature in philosophy of knowledge. He acknowledges an ideological dimension to public administration and calls for greater attention to issues of democracy and community. Such concerns are unusual in this field.

Chapter Three

1   Michel Foucault, *Power/Knowledge: Selected Interviews and Other Writings* (New York: Pantheon Books, 1972), p. 156.

2   Richard C. Edwards, *Contested Terrain* (New York: Basic Books, 1979), pp. 163–199. Edwards's excellent history of social relations in the workplace draws on the records of a "panel" of large companies: American Telephone and Telegraph (AT&T), International Business Machines (IBM), Ford Motor Company, General Electric (GE), Polaroid, Pabst Brewing, Pullman, United States Steel, and International Harvester.

3   See Barbara Ehrenreich and John Ehrenreich, "The Professional-Managerial Class," in Pat Walker, ed., *Between Labor and Capital* (Boston: South End Press, 1979), pp. 5–45, for a summary of the contributions of Andre Gorz, Serge Mallet, Pierre Balleville, Nicos Poulantzas, and others to the debates about the new working class. See also Paul Goldman, "The Organization Class System and the

New Working Class," *Insurgent Sociologist* 3 (Winter, 1973): 41–52, and Kenneth W. MacDonald, "A Class Analysis of Perception and Explanations of Opportunity in America: An Empirical Test of William Ryan's *Blaming the Victim* Thesis," Ph.D. dissertation, Northeastern University, 1983. Ehrenreich and Ehrenreich's "professional-managerial class" is roughly equivalent to Goldman's (and others') new working class, and to Stanley Aronowitz's concept of "middle strata" (Stanley Aronowitz, "The Professional-Managerial Class or Middle Strata," in Walker, ed., *Between Labor and Capital*, pp. 213–242).

4   Edwards, *Contested Terrain*, p. 185.

5   Bryce Nelson, "Bosses Face Less Risk than the Bossed," *The New York Times*, April 3, 1983, p. 16E. Citing a study led by Dr. Robert A. Karasek at Columbia University, Nelson states that "the lowest tenth of such workers, measured in ability to control their own jobs, was approximately five times as likely to develop coronary heart disease as the privileged top tenth of workers in job control."

6   Doris Delaney, "Before the Robots," *UAW Solidarity*, December 16–31, 1981, p. 10.

7   Sandy Carter, "Class Conflict: The Human Dimension," in Walker, ed., *Between Labor and Capital*, pp. 97–119. Given the methods that companies have devised to avoid reporting job-related injuries, these figures are probably low.

8   These are the benefits provided by the 1976 Illinois Workmen's Compensation Law, cited in Charles Spencer, *Blue Collar* (Chicago: Lakeside Charter Books, 1977), pp. 232–233.

9   Richard Sennett, *The Fall of Public Man* (New York: Vintage Books, 1978), p. 15. For an excellent account of the policing of workers by both supervisors and peers in the clerical factories, see Barbara Garson, *All the Livelong Day* (New York: Doubleday, 1975).

10   John W. Meyer and Brian Rowan, "The Structure of Educational Organizations," in Marshall W. Meyer and associates, eds., *Environments and Organizations* (San Francisco: Jossey-Bass, 1978), p. 98.

11   *Ibid.*, p. 106.

12   Michel Foucault, *Discipline and Punish* (New York: Vintage Books, 1979), pp. 206–207.

13   *Ibid.*, p. 220.

14   Harry Braverman, *Labor and Monopoly Capital* (New York: Monthly Review Press, 1974), p. 293 *et passim*; Edwards, *Contested Terrain*, p. 132.

15   Stanley Aronowitz, *False Promises* (New York: McGraw-Hill, 1973), pp. 289–290.

16 Garson, *All the Livelong Day*, p. 219.
17 Larry Spence, *The Politics of Social Knowledge* (University Park, Pa.: Pennsylvania State University Press, 1978), p. 7.
18 *Ibid.*
19 Foucault, *Power/Knowledge*, p. 119.
20 Herbert L. Dreyfus and Paul Rabinow, *Michel Foucault: Beyond Structuralism and Hermeneutics* (Chicago: University of Chicago Press, 1982).
21 Roberto M. Unger, *Knowledge and Politics* (New York: Free Press, 1975), p. 62.
22 Peggy Reeves Sanday, *Female Power and Male Dominance* (London: Cambridge University Press, 1981), talks about the particular environmental and cultural contexts of different gender relations. Margaret Mead's classic study *Sex and Temperament in Three Primitive Societies* (New York: William Morrow, 1935) discusses the tremendous variety in gender-based roles and rules, as does Ruby R. Leavitt, "Women in Other Cultures," in Vivian Gornick and Barbara K. Moran, eds., *Women in Sexist Society* (New York: Basic Books, 1971), pp. 383–430. Suzanne J. Hessler and Wendy McKenna argue in their study *Gender: An Ethnomethodological Approach* (New York: John Wiley and Sons, 1978) that culturally defined expectations concerning both gender and sex take precedence over biological traits.
23 Elizabeth Janeway, *Between Myth and Morning: Women Awakening* (New York: William Morrow, 1975), p. 188.
24 Lionel Trilling is cited in Arlie Russell Hochschild, *The Managed Heart* (Berkeley, Calif.: University of California Press, 1983), p. 167. John Killens, *Black Man's Burden* (New York: Trident Press, 1965), and Simone de Beauvoir, *The Second Sex* (New York: Alfred A. Knopf, 1952), have both noted the parallel between race and gender. Jo Freeman cites some interesting evidence from a classic study by Gordon W. Allport, *The Nature of Prejudice* (Reading, Mass.: Addison-Wesley, 1954), pp. 1080–1100, in his chapter entitled "The Traits of Victimization": "Included are such personality traits as sensitivity, submission, fantasies of power, desire for protection, indirectness, ingratiation, petty revenge and sabotage, sympathy, extremes of both self and group hatred and self and group glorification, display of flashy status symbols, compassion for the underprivileged, identification with the dominant group's norms, and passivity. Allport was primarily concerned with Jews and Negroes, but compare his characterization with the very thorough review of the literature on sex differences made by Terman and Tyler. For girls, they listed such traits as sensitivity, confor-

mity to social pressures, response to environment, ease of social control, ingratiation, sympathy, low levels of aspiration, compassion for the underprivileged, and anxiety. They found that girls, compared to boys, were more nervous, unstable, neurotic, socially dependent, submissive, had less self confidence, lower opinions of themselves and of girls in general, and were more timid, emotional, ministrative, fearful and passive" (cited in Jo Freeman, "The Social Construction of the Second Sex," in Michele H. Garskoff, ed., *Roles Women Play* [Belmont, Calif.: Brooks/Cole, 1971], p. 125).

The connection of gender to class, with regard to this argument about impression management, is particularly complex, because working-class people, unlike women, do not usually live with their oppressors. When power is more distant and less personal, the incentive to develop the feminine skills of impression management is missing. I am not arguing that class, racial, and sexual oppression are identical. There are obvious differences in their histories and their contexts. I am arguing that members of subordinate groups, when they are face to face with the powerful, utilize similar strategies to negotiate the dangerous social terrain.

25 Lynda Glennon has given a concise summary of the different motivations and interactional styles that characterize the two roles: "A person who is acting instrumentally in social relations would typically inhibit emotions, act from self-interested motives, rely on standardized or "objective" codes for judgment, evaluate others in terms of performance or achievement, and display involvement with the other that is limited to specific aims. Any instrumental relationship is construed as a means to an end. Expressive behavior, on the other hand, emphasizes such integrative goals as emotional fulfillment, group cohesiveness, and stability. A person who is acting expressively would typically show emotion, be oriented toward the collective interest, rely on personal relational criteria for the evaluation of others, judge others in terms of their personal qualities, and show a wide interest in the other. Here the relationship is an end in itself, to be enjoyed for its own sake and not because of a specific interest" (Lynda M. Glennon, *Women and Dualism* [New York: Longman, 1979], p. 28).

26 Ann Douglas, *The Femininization of American Culture* (New York: Alfred A Knopf, 1977). Two other uses of the term "feminization" should be noted and distinguished from those employed here. The "feminization of poverty" refers simply to the increasing presence of women in the ranks of the poor and/or among those on public assistance. The "feminization" of men is sometimes decried by

anti-feminists, and they seem to mean some alleged emasculation
of men by aggressive women. The first of these, while important, is
not my subject here; the second is uninteresting.

27 The term comes from Erving Goffman, *Presentation of Self in Everyday Life* (New York: Doubleday, 1959).

28 Elizabeth Janeway, *Man's World, Woman's Place* (New York: Delta Books, 1971), p. 112.

29 Nancy Henley, *Body Politics: Power, Sex and Nonverbal Communication* (Englewood Cliffs, N.J.: Prentice-Hall, 1977), p. 78. See also Dale Spender, *Man Made Language* (London: Routledge and Kegan Paul, 1980).

30 Nancy Henley and Jo Freeman, "The Sexual Politics of Interpersonal Behavior," in Jo Freeman, ed., *Women: A Feminist Perspective* (2nd ed.; Palo Alto, Calif.: Mayfield, 1979), p. 478.

31 Henley, *Body Politics*, pp. 74, 104.

32 Henley and Freeman, "Sexual Politics."

33 Henley, *Body Politics*, p. 104.

34 Robin Lakoff, *Language and Woman's Place* (New York: Harper and Row, 1975), pp. 11–12. The exception here is homosexual men, who often explicitly use feminine language.

35 Leonore Weitzman, "Sex-Role Socialization," in Freeman, ed., *Women*, p. 118.

36 Jesse Bernard, *Women and the Public Interest* (Chicago: Aldine, 1971), p. 88.

37 Pamela Fishman, "Interactional Shitwork," *Heresies: A Feminist Publication on Arts and Politics* 2 (May, 1977): 99–101, cited in Spender, *Man Made Language*, p. 49.

38 Janeway, *Man's World, Woman's Place*, p. 114.

39 Joyce Ladner, *Tomorrow's Tomorrow: The Black Woman* (New York: Doubleday, 1971).

40 Lenore Weitzman quotes this young woman in "Sex-Role Socialization," p. 174.

41 For a summary of these findings, see H. Edward Ransford and Jon Miller, "Race, Sex and Feminist Outlooks," *American Sociological Review* 48 (February, 1983): 46–59.

42 Rosabeth Moss Kanter, "Women and the Structure of Organizations," in Marcia Millman and Rosabeth Moss Kanter, eds., *Another Voice* (New York: Doubleday, 1975), p. 54.

43 Grace E. Manson, "Occupational Interests and Personality Requirements of Women in Business and the Professions," *Michigan Business Studies* 3 (April, 1931): 281–409. This study is an interesting one for many reasons. The author collected survey and questionnaire data on 14,000 women. The sample had a median

age of 38 years and a median work experience of 14 years. The "occupational interests" section listed 160 occupations commonly open to women, including companion, tea room proprietor, and YWCA secretary, and asked the respondents to rate their attractiveness on a five-point scale. The "personality requirements" section cited above listed thirty personality traits and asked women to rank in order the most important ten in terms of their necessity for the women's work.

44 See Rosabeth Moss Kanter's discussion of the secretarial staff in *Men and Women of the Corporation* (New York: Basic Books, 1977).

45 Robert Presthus, *The Organizational Society* (New York: Alfred A. Knopf, 1962), p. 15.

46 Anthony Downs, *Inside Bureaucracy* (Boston: Little, Brown, 1967), pp. 88–89.

47 Harold L. Wilensky, "The Professionalization of Everyone?" *American Journal of Sociology* 70 (September, 1965): 151.

48 Kanter, *Men and Women of the Corporation*, p. 5; see also Hugh Heclo, *Government of Strangers* (Washington, D.C.: Brookings Institution, 1977), pp. 143–144.

49 Foucault, *The History of Sexuality*, I (New York: Random House, 1980), 45.

50 Foucault, *Discipline and Punish*, pp. 173, 183 (italics in original).

51 Frederick C. Mosher, *Democracy and the Public Service* (New York: Oxford University Press, 1968), p. 152.

52 Hochschild, *Managed Heart*, p. 96.

53 Presthus, *Organizational Society*, p. 282.

54 Downs, *Inside Bureaucracy*, p. 223.

55 *Ibid.*, p. 230 (italics mine).

56 George Benello, "Wasteland Culture," *Anarchy* 88 (June, 1968): 168–188.

57 William H. Whyte, Jr., *The Organization Man* (New York: Doubleday, 1957).

58 Robert B. Denhardt and Jan Perkins, "The Coming Death of Administrative *Man*," *Women in Public Administration* 36 (July/August, 1976): 382.

59 Roy C. Smith, "How to Be a Good Subordinate," *The New York Times*, November 25, 1979, p. 16F.

60 Dick Bruner, "Why White Collar Workers Can't Be Organized," in Sigmund Nosow and William H. Form, eds., *Man, Work and Society* (New York: Basic Books, 1962), p. 194. As white-collar jobs become more routinized and fragmented, and as the status differences shrink between blue- and white-collar labor, white-collar unionism grows.

61 Hochschild, *Managed Heart*, pp. 25, 116 *et passim*.
62 Downs, *Inside Bureaucracy*, pp. 67–68.
63 Presthus, *Organizational Society*, pp. 171–172.
64 Kanter, *Men and Women of the Corporation*, p. 52.
65 Mosher, *Democracy and the Public Service*, p. 29; Jay M. Shafritz, Walter L. Balk, Albert C. Hyde, and David H. Rosenbloom, *Personnel Management in Government* (New York: Marcel Dekker, 1978), p. 155.
66 Paul W. Vogt, "The Theory of the Credentialed Class," *The Review of Education* 7 (Spring, 1981): 141.
67 Victor Thompson, *Modern Organization* (New York: Alfred A. Knopf, 1965), pp. 170–171, quoted in Orion F. White, Jr., "The Dialectical Organization: An Alternative to Bureaucracy," in Virginia B. Ermer and John H. Strange, eds., *Blacks and Bureaucracy* (New York: Thomas Y. Crowell, 1972), p. 260.
68 Kanter, *Men and Women of the Corporation*, p. 68.
69 *Ibid.*, pp. 211–212 *et passim*. For an empirical confirmation of Kanter's argument, see Eve Spangler, Marsha A. Gordon, and Ronald M. Pipkin, "Token Women: An Empirical Test of Kanter's Hypothesis," *American Journal of Sociology* 84 (1978): 160–170.
70 Robert B. Jansen, *The ABCs of Bureaucracy* (Chicago: Nelson Hall, 1978), p. 2.
71 Smith, "How to Be a Good Subordinate," p. 16F.
72 Deena Weinstein and Michael A. Weinstein, "Self, Society, and Social Control: An Existential Perspective," *Humanity and Society* 1 (Summer, 1977): 104–115.
73 Downs, *Inside Bureaucracy*, p. 223.
74 Jansen, *ABCs of Bureaucracy*, p. 41.
75 Wilbert Moore, *The Conduct of the Corporation* (New York: Random House, 1962), p. 109, quoted in Kanter, *Men and Women of the Corporation*, p. 48.
76 Robert K. Merton, "Bureaucratic Structure and Personality," in Merton, *Social Theory and Social Structure* (New York: Free Press, 1968), p. 254.
77 Kanter, *Men and Women of the Corporation*, p. 192.
78 Presthus, *Organizational Society*, pp. 184–185.
79 Susan Harding, "Women and Words in a Spanish Village," in Zillah R. Eisenstein, ed., *Capitalist Patriarchy and the Case for Socialist Feminism* (New York: Monthly Review Press, 1979), pp. 302–303.
80 I am indebted to a conversation with Larry Spence for this insight into the dual function of rumor in organizational life.

81 J. Patrick Wright, with John DeLorean, *On a Clear Day You Can See General Motors* (New York: Avon Books, 1979), pp. 23, 53.

82 Garson, *All the Livelong Day*, p. 152; Braverman, *Labor and Monopoly Capital*, pp. 293–326.

83 Braverman quotes from this literature in *Labor and Monopoly Capital*, pp. 332–337.

84 Kanter, *Men and Women of the Corporation*, p. 73.

85 *Ibid.*, p. 96 *et passim*.

86 Garson, *All the Livelong Day*, p. xi.

87 Wright, *On a Clear Day*, p. 206.

88 Spence, *Politics of Social Knowledge*, p. 12.

89 Melville Dalton, "The Interlocking of Official and Unofficial Rewards," in Oscar Grusky and George A. Miller, eds., *The Sociology of Organizations* (2nd ed.; New York: Free Press, 1981), pp. 324–350.

90 In an early article on foremen, written for management, Burleigh Gardner and William F. Whyte caution that workers with too good a relation with foremen are seen as company stooges by the other workers ("The Man in the Middle: Position and Problems of the Foreman," *Applied Anthropology (Human Organization)* 2 [1945]: 1–28).

91 Murray Bookchin, "Beyond Neo-Marxism," *Telos* 36 (Summer, 1978): 19.

92 Edwards, *Contested Terrain*, p. 145.

93 Alkis Kontos, "Domination: Metaphor and Political Reality," in Kontos, ed., *Domination* (Toronto: University of Toronto Press, 1975), p. 219.

94 See Garson, *All the Livelong Day*, for a good contrast of strong-union, weak-union, and no-union shops.

95 Evelyn Nakano Glenn and Roslyn L. Feldberg, "Clerical Work: The Female Occupation," in Freeman, ed., *Women*, pp. 323–324.

96 Mosher, *Democracy and the Public Service*, p. 153.

97 Heclo, *Government of Strangers*, pp. 143–144.

98 Deena Weinstein, *Bureaucratic Opposition* (New York: Pergamon Press, 1979), pp. 11–36.

99 Barbara L. Forisha and Barbara H. Goldman, eds., *Outsiders on the Inside: Women and Organizations* (Englewood Cliffs, N.J.: Prentice-Hall, 1981).

Chapter Four

1 Eugene Lewis, *American Politics in a Bureaucratic Age* (Cambridge, Mass.: Winthrop, 1977).

2   Stephen P. Erie, "Two Faces of Ethnic Power: Comparing the Irish and Black Experiences," *Polity* 13 (Winter, 1980): 261–284.

3   See Harold Baron, "The Web of Urban Racism," in Louis Knowles and Kenneth Prewitt, eds., *Institutional Racism in America* (Englewood Cliffs, N.J.: Prentice-Hall, 1969).

4   Richard C. Edwards, *Contested Terrain* (New York: Basic Books, 1979), p. 186; Francis Fox Piven and Richard Cloward, *The New Class War* (New York: Pantheon Books, 1982), p. 15. Slightly over half of the poor are working poor; the rest are predominantly the elderly, the disabled or chronically ill, children, or single mothers with no adequate childcare available. The majority of heads of poor families work at least part time; most single mothers receiving welfare have work experience and often use welfare to supplement low wages. Three-fourths of the poor live either in the rural areas or the central cities. The rural poor, by virtue of their isolation, are less affected by the social service system; the central focus of my discussion is the urban poor, who make up the client population of service agencies.

5   Edwards, *Contested Terrain*, pp. 161–183.

6   Douglas G. Glasgow, *The Black Underclass* (New York: Vintage Books, 1980), p. 7.

7   Piven and Cloward, *New Class War*, p. 15.

8   Erving Goffman, *Asylums* (Garden City, N.Y.: Anchor, 1961), pp. xiii, 4, 6.

9   Michel Foucault, *Discipline and Punish* (New York: Vintage Books, 1979), p. 199.

10   Claus Offe, "Advanced Capitalism and the Welfare State," *Politics and Society* 2 (Summer, 1972): 480.

11   Piven and Cloward, *Regulating the Poor* (New York: Random House, 1971), p. xiii. See Edward T. Jennings, Jr., "Social Amelioration Through Mass Insurgency Revisited: Another Look at the Welfare Consequences of Urban Riots," paper presented at the Midwest Political Science Association meetings, Cincinnati, Ohio, April 16–18, 1981. For a dissenting argument (and response from Piven and Cloward), see Robert B. Albritton, "Social Amelioration Through Mass Insurgency? A Reexamination of the Piven and Cloward Thesis," *The American Political Science Review* 73 (December, 1979): 1003–1023.

12   Piven and Cloward, *New Class War*, p. 31.

13   David Street, George T. Martin, Jr., and Laura Kramer Gordon, *The Welfare Industry* (Beverly Hills, Calif.: Sage Publications, 1979), p. 8.

14   Piven and Cloward, *New Class War*, pp. 36–37.

15 Michael Lipsky, *Street-Level Bureaucracy* (New York: Russell Sage, 1980), p. 183.

16 Charles Perrow, whose excellent article "Demystifying Organizations" is an exception to the overall tendency in the literature, makes this point well. See Perrow, in Rosemary C. Sarri and Yeheskel Hasenfeld, eds., *The Management of Human Services* (New York: Columbia University Press, 1978), pp. 103–120.

17 Dario Melossi and Massimo Parvarini, *The Prison and the Factory* (Totowa, N.J.: Barnes and Noble, 1981), p. 66 *et passim*. For a brief history of welfare programs in the United States, which shows that the deserving/undeserving distinction is at the heart of welfare debates, see Kristen Grønbjerg, David Street, and Gerald D. Suttles, *Poverty and Social Change* (Chicago: University of Chicago Press, 1978); see also Betty Reid Mandell, *Welfare in America: Controlling the Dangerous Classes* (Englewood Cliffs, N.J.: Prentice-Hall, 1975).

18 Piven and Cloward, *New Class War*, p. 61.

19 Alvin W. Gouldner, "Stalinism: A Study of Internal Colonialism," *Telos* 34 (Winter, 1977–1978): 43.

20 Robert Lindsey, "California Weighs Plan to Curb Welfare Fraud," *The New York Times*, February 27, 1983, p. 26.

21 Perrow makes this point well; mainstream organization theory usually recognizes the importance of the "environment," then disregards the point or relegates it to the fringe of the analysis.

22 Piven and Cloward, *The Politics of Turmoil* (New York: Random House, 1965), pp. 7–8 *et passim*.

23 Piven and Cloward, *New Class War*, p. 120.

24 Perrow, "Demystifying Organizations," pp. 113–114, 110.

25 Paul Jacobs, "Prelude to Riot," in Virginia B. Ermer and John H. Strange, eds., *Blacks and Bureaucracy* (New York: Thomas Y. Crowell, 1972), pp. 93–108.

26 Perrow, "Demystifying Organizations," p. 109.

27 Sarri and Hasenfeld, eds., *Management of Human Services*, p. 2.

28 Lipsky, *Street-Level Bureaucracy*, p. 47.

29 *Ibid.*, p. 55.

30 Claus Offe, "Political Authority and Class Structure," *International Journal of Sociology* 2 (Spring, 1972): 83.

31 *Ibid.*, p. 100–101.

32 Piven and Cloward, *Regulating the Poor*, p. 338. In their book *The New Class War* Piven and Cloward suggest that service agencies are "firmly linked to popular constituencies by the benefits and services provided, or by the regulations enforced, linkages that continually expose and connect [them] to broad groups in the popu-

lation" (p. 120). But their estimate of the accessibility of service agencies to clients is, I believe, excessive; the fact that the agencies are mandated to act in the interest of certain groups does not make them accessible to those groups. Welfare agencies are dependent on the underclass for survival, but the only "resource" that the underclass can withdraw or threaten to withdraw is their compliance to the client role, either by organizing effectively against it or by rioting.

33 Piven and Cloward, *Regulating the Poor*, p. 249.
34 Perrow, "Demystifying Organizations," p. 114.
35 Lipsky, *Street-Level Bureaucracy*, p. 7.
36 Foucault, *Discipline and Punish*, p. 204.
37 See Giorgio Inzerilli, "The Organization-Client Relationship as an Aspect of Interorganizational Analysis," *Human Relations* 32 (1979): 419–437, for an example of the discursive attribution of objectivity to the agency and subjectivity to the client. This article is a good example of systems theory run amok. The author is concerned about the "debureaucratization" of organization-client relations, a situation in which the relationship shifts "too far" in favor of the client. His examples, drawn from the famous study by Elihu Katz and S. N. Eisenstadt, "Some Sociological Observations on the Response of Israeli Organizations to New Immigrants," *Administrative Science Quarterly* 5 (1960): 113–133, concern situations in which bureaucrats treat clients as whole people and try to teach them needed information, such as bus drivers teaching immigrants how to be passengers or nurses telling immigrant women their rights vis-à-vis their husbands. Inzerilli's fear is that, in such circumstances, clients get too much power and can disrupt the organization's "equilibrium," making it no longer an "ideal bureaucracy."
38 Foucault, *Discipline and Punish*, p. 191.
39 Piven and Cloward, "The Professional Bureaucracies: Benefit Systems as Influence Systems," in Ermer and Strange, eds., *Blacks and Bureaucracy*, p. 214.
40 Jeffrey Wack and Judith Rodin, "Nursing Homes for the Aged: The Human Consequences of Legislation-Shaped Environments," *Journal of Social Issues* 34 (1978): 7–21.
41 Murray Edelman, "The Political Language of the Helping Professions," *Politics and Society* 4 (1964): 297.
42 Lipsky, *Street-Level Bureaucracy*, p. 56. See also Jack Abbott, *The Belly of the Beast* (New York: Random House, 1982).
43 Charles T. Goodsell, "Client Evaluation of Three Welfare Programs," *Administration and Society* 12 (August, 1980): 126.

44 Michel Foucault, *The History of Sexuality*, I (New York: Random House, 1980), 44.

45 Lipsky, *Street-Level Bureaucracy*, p. 13, emphasizes the relative autonomy of the street-level bureaucrat, but looks to police, judges, and teachers as examples rather than to welfare workers. Sarri and Hasenfeld, eds., *Management of Human Services*, emphasize the lack of discretion (p. 4), as does Grønbjerg, Street, and Suttles, *Poverty and Social Change* (p. 151).

46 Lipsky, *Street-Level Bureaucracy*, p. 149.

47 Street, Martin, and Gordon, *Welfare Industry*, pp. 50–51 (italics in original).

48 *Ibid.*, p. 62.

49 Joel Handler and Ellen J. Hollingsworth, *The "Deserving Poor": A Study of Welfare Administration* (Chicago: Markham, 1971), pp. 200–201, quoted in Street, Martin, and Gordon, *Welfare Industry*, p. 41.

50 Lipsky, *Street-Level Bureaucracy*, pp. 103–104.

51 Piven and Cloward, "Professional Bureaucracies," p. 219; Irwin Epstein and Kayla Conrad, "The Empirical Limits of Social Work Professionalization," in Sarri and Hasenfeld, eds., *Management of Human Services*, pp. 178–179. See also Neil Tudiver, "Business Ideology and Management in Social Work: The Limits of Cost Control," *Catalyst* 13 (1982): 24–48.

52 See Betty Lou Valentine, *Hustling and Other Hard Work: Life Styles in the Ghetto* (New York: Free Press, 1978); also André Leo, "ADC: Marriage to the State," in Anne Koedt, Ellen Levine, and Anita Rapone, eds., *Radical Feminism* (New York: Quadrangle Books, 1973), pp. 222–227. It is interesting, in light of the role of academic social science in creating and spreading bureaucratic discourse, to note that most social scientific studies of clients' attitudes toward social services indicate a high level of satisfaction. For example, Charles T. Goodsell claims, on the basis of exit interviews with 240 clients in four cities, that "most welfare clients are quite satisfied with the treatment they receive" ("Conflicting Perceptions of Welfare Bureaucracy," *Social Casework: The Journal of Contemporary Social Work* 61 [June, 1980]: 354). Another team of researchers conclude, on the basis of a national survey, that most clients' encounters with bureaucracies are relatively pleasant and satisfying (Daniel Katz, Barbara A. Gutek, Robert L. Kahn, and Eugenia Barton, *Bureaucratic Encounters* [Ann Arbor, Mich.: Institute for Social Research, 1975], p. 114). But in light of the dissatisfaction, hostility, and despair that repeatedly emerges in any in-

depth interview or account of client experiences, these large surveys, methodologically sound though they may be, are shown to be inadequate to their subject matter. People habitually tell the inquiring social scientist what they think they should say, or what they think the social scientist wants to hear. As Barbara Gutek points out in evaluating client alienation studies, "One reason for distrusting measures of satisfaction is simply that people seem to be satisfied with everything that social scientists ask them about" ("Strategies for Studying Client Satisfaction," *Journal of Social Issues* 34 [1978]: 48). She cites various studies that conclude that 85 percent of assembly-line workers are satisfied with their jobs, and that 92 percent of married people are satisfied with their marriages, and that 61 percent of clients are satisfied with their interactions with welfare agencies—this in light of the high rates of absenteeism, turnover, and opposition on the assembly line, the skyrocketing divorce rates, and the widely expressed resentment felt by clients. The inability of large-scale surveys to capture the flavor of individual life experiences recommends in-depth interviewing as a sounder methodological strategy. Further, Goodsell's study may well be correct in suggesting that bureaucrats are not usually unnecessarily nasty toward clients, and that clients are often glad to get the help that is offered. This says nothing, however, about the overall place of welfare in the context of the larger system or in the lives of the poor.

53 Carol Stack, *All Our Kin* (New York: Harper and Row, 1974), p. 124.

54 Valentine, *Hustling*, p. 124.

55 Grønbjerg, Street, and Suttles, *Poverty and Social Change*, pp. 142–143.

56 Street, Martin, and Gordon, *Welfare Industry*, pp. 86, 89.

57 Ralph P. Hummel, *The Bureaucratic Experience* (New York: St. Martin's Press, 1977), p. 17. For supporting evidence from British studies, see Joel E. Mayer and Noel Timms, *The Client Speaks: Working Class Impressions of Casework* (London: Routledge and Kegan Paul, 1970).

58 Gideon Sjoberg, Richard A. Brymer, and Buford Farris, "Bureaucracy and the Lower Class," in Ermer and Strange, eds., *Blacks and Bureaucracy*, pp. 159–171. Sjoberg *et al.* studied Mexican-American families in San Antonio, and find support for their conclusions in studies of other racial groups.

59 Piven and Cloward, *Politics of Turmoil*, p. 23.

60 Peter Berger, Brigitte Berger, and Hansfried Kellner, *The Home-*

less Mind: Modernization and Consciousness (New York: Random House, 1974), pp. 58–59.

61 Lipsky, *Street-Level Bureaucracy*, p. 59.
62 Foucault, *Discipline and Punish*, pp. 128–129.
63 Piven and Cloward, *Politics of Turmoil*, p. 24.
64 Samuel M. Meyers and Jennie McIntyre, *Welfare Policy and Its Consequences for the Recipient Population: A Study of the AFDC Program* (Washington, D.C.: U.S. Government Printing Office, 1969), cited in Katz, Gutek, Kahn, and Barton, *Bureaucratic Encounters*, p. 10. See also B. R. Schiller, "Empirical Studies of Welfare Dependency: A Survey," *The Journal of Human Resources* 8 (1973): 19–32 (supp.); Leonard Goodwin, *Do the Poor Want to Work?* (Washington, D.C.: Brookings Institution, 1972), cited in Katz, Gutek, Kahn, and Barton, *Bureaucratic Encounters*, p. 26. See also Douglas G. Glasgow, *Black Underclass*, for a discussion of work attitudes among street youth; and Ellen I. Rosen, "Between the Rock and the Hard Place: Employment and Unemployment Among Blue Collar Women," unpublished paper, Boston College, Social Welfare Research Institute, Fall, 1981, for evidence that people collecting employment do so for no longer than necessary to find another job.
65 Piven and Cloward, "Professional Bureaucracies," p. 214.
66 Scott Briar, "Welfare from Below: Recipients' View of the Public Welfare System," in Jacobus Ten Broek, ed., *The Law of the Poor* (San Francisco: Chandler, 1966), quoted in Katz, Gutek, Kahn, and Barton, *Bureaucratic Encounters*, p. 10.
67 Donald Arnstine, "The Use of Coercion in Changing the Schools," *Educational Theory* 23 (Fall, 1973): 286.
68 Lipsky, *Street-Level Bureaucracy*, pp. 195, 119, 196, 210–211, 200. Another example of this problem is Dale A. Massi's book *Organizing for Women* (Lexington, Mass.: D. C. Heath, 1981); she criticizes social workers for contributing to the problems of the poor, then looks to them to provide solutions (p. 146).
69 Piven and Cloward, *Regulating the Poor*, p. 348. Piven and Barbara Ehrenreich argue that feminists should take up the call for expanded social services, moving in "where mainstream Democrats fear to tread." While they are right to point to poverty as an important feminist issue, it is naive to believe that pressure to expand social services would result in any radical change in the class structure or in the structure of human service agencies (Francis Fox Piven and Barbara Ehrenreich, "The Left's Best Hope," *Mother Jones* 8 [September/October, 1983]: 26–29).

70 Glasgow, *Black Underclass*, p. 12.

71 *Ibid.*, p. 82.

72 Frank Tripi, "The Inevitability of Client Alienation: A Counter Argument," *Sociological Quarterly* 15 (Summer, 1974): 432–441, and Helene Levens, "Organizational Affiliation and Powerlessness: A Case Study of the Welfare Poor," *Social Problems* 16 (1968): 18–43. Street, Martin, and Gordon also found that activist recipients are more critical toward caseworkers and welfare, more aware of their rights, less embarrassed about receiving welfare, more knowledgeable about it, and more optimistic about changing it than are nonactivists (*Welfare Industry*, pp. 152, 155).

73 In Tripi's study of nine welfare groups, he found that activists constituted less than 1 percent of the total caseload of the agencies ("Inevitability of Client Alienation," p. 433).

74 Francis Fox Piven and Richard Cloward, *Poor People's Movements* (New York: Random House, 1979), make this point well: "First, it was not formal organizations but mass defiance that won what was won in the 1930s and 1960s; industrial workers, for example, forced concessions from industry and government as a result of the disruptive effects of large-scale strikes; defiant blacks forced concessions as a result of the disruptive effects of mass civil disobedience. Second, because they were acutely vulnerable to internal oligarchy and stasis and to external integration with elites, the bureaucratic organizations that were developed within these movements tended to blunt the militance that was the fundamental source of such influence as the movements exerted. And finally, for the most part, the formal organization collapsed as the movement subsided" (pp. xv–xvi).

75 Street, Martin, and Gordon, *Welfare Industry*, pp. 142, 162–164.

76 Piven and Cloward, *Poor People's Movements*, p. 330. A full account of the demise of the NWRO would have to take into account the tapering off of the welfare explosion, the dismantling of the Office of Economic Opportunity, the decline of the civil rights movement, the election of Richard Nixon, and other factors.

Chapter Five

1   Michael Gibbons, "Authority and Politics," Ph.D. dissertation, University of Massachusetts, 1983.

2   Michel Foucault, *Power/Knowledge: Selected Interviews and Other Writings* (New York: Pantheon Books, 1972), p. 81.

3   Michel Foucault, *The History of Sexuality,* I (New York: Random House, 1980), 96.
4   Alan Sheridan, *Michel Foucault: The Will to Truth* (New York: Tavistock Publications, 1980), p. 139.
5   Foucault, *History of Sexuality,* I, 96.
6   Michel Foucault, "The Subject and Power," in Herbert L. Dreyfus and Paul Rabinow, *Michel Foucault: Beyond Structuralism and Hermeneutics* (Chicago: University of Chicago Press, 1982), p. 216.
7   *Ibid.,* p. 211.
8   Foucault, *Power/Knowledge,* p. 82.
9   *Ibid.,* p. 83.
10 *Ibid.*
11 Carol Gilligan, "In a Different Voice: Women's Conception of Self and of Morality," *Harvard Educational Review* 47 (November, 1977): 490.
12 Gilligan, *In a Different Voice* (Cambridge, Mass.: Harvard University Press, 1982), p. 160 *et passim.* Gilligan's research involves, in her own words, "listening to people talk about morality and about themselves" (p. 1). Her book relies on three studies, all based on interviews, through which she explored people's concepts of self, of conflict, of morality, and of choice. In the college student study she interviewed young adults about moral conflicts in their lives. The sample was chosen at random from a group of students who had taken a course on moral and political choice; the students were interviewed in their senior year and again five years after graduation. The abortion decision study interviewed twenty-nine women during the first trimester of a pregnancy while the women were considering abortions. The women ranged in age from fifteen to thirty-three, and were diverse in ethnic identity, class membership, and marital and family status. Twenty-one of the women were interviewed a year later, following their choices concerning their pregnancies. The rights and responsibilities study worked from a total sample of 144 males and females; Gilligan matched them on the variables of age, intelligence, education, occupation, and social class at nine points across the life cycle, ranging from six to sixty years, and interviewed them concerning questions of personal identity and of hypothetical and real-life moral conflicts. The patterns that Gilligan traces in the lives of women and men can also be discerned in a set of interviews done by Ruth Sidel in her book *Urban Survival: The World of Working Class Women* (Boston: Beacon Press, 1978).
13 Nancy Chodorow, "Oedipal Asymmetries and Heterosexual Knots," *Social Problems* 23 (April, 1976): 461.

14 Sandra Harding, "Toward a Strong Program from Epistemology: Clues from Feminist Inquiry," paper presented at the American Political Science Association meetings, New York City, September, 1981.
15 Gilligan, *In a Different Voice*, pp. 163–165.
16 Harding, "Toward a Strong Program," p. 29.
17 *Ibid.*, pp. 28–29.
18 Gilligan, *In a Different Voice*, p. 62.
19 Chodorow, "Oedipal Asymmetries," p. 459; see also Dorothy Dinnerstein, *The Mermaid and the Minotaur* (New York: Harper and Row, 1976), p. 161 *et passim*.
20 Nancy Chodorow, *The Reproduction of Mothering* (Berkeley, Calif.: University of California Press, 1978), p. 176.
21 Harding, "Toward a Strong Program," p. 24.
22 See Gilligan, "Woman's Place in Man's Life Cycle," *Harvard Educational Review* 49 (November, 1979): 435, for a summary of this research.
23 Elizabeth Aries, "Interaction Patterns and Themes of Male, Female, and Mixed Groups," *Small Group Behavior* 7 (1976): 7–18, quoted in Dale Spender, *Man Made Language* (London: Routledge and Kegan Paul, 1980), p. 127.
24 Spender, *Man Made Language*, p. 128.
25 John E. Baird, Jr., "Sex Differences in Group Communication: A Review of Relevant Research," *Quarterly Journal of Speech* 62 (1976): 179–192, and Clarice Stasz Stoll and Paul T. McFarlane, "Sex Differences in Game Strategy," in Stoll, ed., *Sexism: Scientific Debates* (Reading, Mass.: Addison-Wesley, 1973), pp. 74–75, quoted in Spender, *Man Made Language*, p. 127.
26 Thomas K. Uesugi and W. Edgar Vinaki, "Strategy in a Feminine Game," *Sociometry* 26 (1963): 78.
27 *Ibid.*, pp. 79, 80.
28 Gilligan, *In a Different Voice*, p. 41.
29 Selma Kraft, "Cognitive Function and Women's Art," *Women's Art Journal* 4 (Fall, 1983/Winter, 1984): 5.
30 *Ibid.*, p. 6. Kraft points out that these cognitive and perceptual differences point to differences in artistic sensibility, revealing "a particularly female artistic sensibility for patterning, based upon a special ability to see context before content" (p. 8).
31 Gilligan, *In a Different Voice*, p. 173.
32 Spender, *Man Made Language*, pp. 14, 106, *et passim*.
33 *Ibid.*, p. 63.
34 Maggie Scarf, *Unfinished Business* (New York: Ballantine Books, 1980). Scarf's book is a curious one in some respects. She rejects

the feminist claim that women are labeled with negative psychiatric categories for rebelling against the constraints of gender; but many of her own cases are women who are being punished for breaking the rules of appropriate feminine behavior, for being too assertive, too smart, not sufficiently "virtuous" or passive. Scarf's material cries out for a feminist interpretation.

35 Dinnerstein, *Mermaid and the Minotaur*, p. 53.

36 Gilligan, *In a Different Voice*, p. 79.

37 *Ibid.*, pp. 82, 132, 149.

38 *Ibid.*, p. 166.

39 Simone de Beauvoir, *The Second Sex* (New York: Alfred A. Knopf, 1952), p. 133.

40 Gilligan, *In a Different Voice*, p. 171.

41 Jackie St. Joan, "Female Leaders: Who Was Rembrandt's Mother?" in Charlotte Bunche, *et al.*, *Building Feminist Theory: Essays from Quest* (New York: Longman, 1981), p. 230.

42 Sara Ruddick, "Maternal Thinking," *Feminist Studies* 6 (Summer, 1980): 350.

43 Jean Baker Miller, *Toward a New Psychology of Women* (Boston: Beacon Press, 1976), cited in Gilligan, *In a Different Voice*, p. 168.

44 Ruddick recognizes this ("Maternal Thinking," p. 346), but the insight takes a back seat to her emphasis on motherhood. The discussions of mothering in Ruddick, in Chodorow (*The Reproduction of Mothering*), and in Jean Bethke Elshtain ("Antigone's Daughters," *Democracy* 2 [April, 1982]: 45–59) are troubling in that they often attribute universal significance to particular historical patterns of child-rearing. For an excellent analysis of the historical production of mothering, see Linda Nicholson, *Feminism as Political Philosophy*, forthcoming. These discussions are also troubling in that they have little to say about fathering, a task that is often poorly done but that nonetheless has been distinct and crucial to the individual development of many women; many life histories of strong and independent women show the unique and special tie to a father or a male mentor, someone who overcame the mother's fears and helped the girl to loosen the bonds of gender (see Margaret Hennig and Anne Jardin, *The Managerial Woman* [New York: Pocket Books, 1976], pp. 99–132, and Gail Sheehy, *Passages* [New York: E. P. Dutton, 1974], pp. 131–132). Paradoxically, many women learn the values that later make them feminists from their fathers and grandfathers more than from their mothers and grandmothers.

45 Roslyn Wallach Bologh, "Max Weber and the Dilemma of Male Rationality," unpublished manuscript, St. John's University, Octo-

ber 21, 1982, pp. 1–2. See also Elshtain, "Antigone's Daughters," pp. 58–59.

46 For an excellent analysis of the relationship between public citizenship and private life, see Mary G. Dietz, "Citizenship with a Feminist Face: The Problem with Maternal Thinking," paper presented at the Western Political Science Association meetings, Seattle, Wash., March 24–26, 1983.

47 *Ibid.*, p. 36.

48 Martha A. Ackelsberg, "'Sisters' or 'Comrades'? The Politics of Friends and Families," in Irene Diamond, ed., *Families, Politics, and Public Policy* (New York: Longman, 1983), pp. 339–356.

49 *Ibid.*, pp. 342, 344.

50 *Ibid.*, p. 351. Ackelsberg traces her analysis to Aristotle's arguments for civic friendship in the polis.

51 Sheridan, *Michel Foucault*, p. 220.

52 Roland Barthes, *Promesse* 29 (1971): 15, quoted in Rosalind Cavard and John Ellis, *Language and Materialism* (London: Routledge and Kegan Paul, 1977), p. 7.

53 Catherine A. MacKinnon, "Feminism, Marxism, Method and the State: Toward a Feminist Jurisprudence," *Signs* 8 (Summer, 1983): 636.

54 *Ibid.*, pp. 640, 638.

55 *Ibid.*, p. 637 n. 5.

56 Larry Spence, *The Politics of Social Knowledge* (University Park, Pa.: Pennsylvania State University Press, 1978), p. 4.

57 MacKinnon, "Feminism, Marxism, Method and the State," p. 637, n. 5.

58 Harding, "Toward a Strong Program," p. 29.

59 Gilligan, *In a Different Voice*, p. 173.

60 Nancy Hartsock, "Staying Alive," in Bunch, *et al.*, *Building Feminist Theory*, pp. 117–118.

61 Rayna Rapp and Ellen Ross, "It Seems We've Stood and Talked Like This Before," *MS* 11 (April, 1983): 54–59.

62 Foucault, *History of Sexuality*, I, 101–102.

63 Foucault, *Power/Knowledge*, p. 108.

64 For an opposing view of the feminist movement, one that sees feminism as "growing up" from its earlier commitments to sisterhood to an acceptance of "pragmatic politics," see Joyce Gelb and Marian Lief Palley, *Woman and Public Policies* (Princeton, N.J.: Princeton University Press, 1982). Gelb and Palley select for study only groups that have an explicitly reformist strategy, then conclude, not surprisingly, that contemporary feminists "are committed to gaining equal rights within existing society rather than creating a

new society based on new values. In other words, they seek change in institutions instead of new institutions" (p. 38). If Gelb and Palley had canvassed women's health collectives, shelters for battered women, feminist book stores, rape crisis centers, and so forth, instead of the National Organization for Women (NOW), the National Women's Political Caucus (NWPC), the American Association of University Women (AAUW), the Business and Professional Women's Association (BPW), and similar groups, they might well have received different answers.

65 Quoted in Charles Perrow, *Complex Organizations: A Critical Essay* (2nd ed.; Glenview, Ill.: Scott Foresman, 1979), pp. 61–62.

66 Betty Lehan Harragan, *Games Mother Never Taught You: Corporate Gamesmanship for Women* (New York: Warner Books, 1977); Hennig and Jardin, *Managerial Woman*; Marilyn Moats Kennedy, *Office Politics: Seizing Power, Wielding Clout* (New York: Warner Books, 1980). I selected these books from the large number of available success manuals because they are among the most respectable. The authors are clearly intelligent and articulate women. The books have received good reviews from various national publications and are sold in feminist book stores. Since they are less tacky and more substantial than many other such books, they make the "strongest possible case" for their genre. For a brief discussion of other books of this genre, see Suzanne Gordon, "The New Corporate Feminism," *The Nation* 236 (February 5, 1983): 142–147.

67 In *The Radical Future of Liberal Feminism* (New York: Longman, 1981), Zillah Eisenstein makes the opposite argument—she emphasizes the radical potential in liberal feminism, and bases her argument on the fact that liberal feminism acknowledges that "woman's identity as a sexual class" underlies her subordination (p. 4). However, these books' discussions of women's confrontations with bureaucracy show that this insight can easily be stripped of its critical implications.

68 Harragan, *Games Mother Never Taught You*, p. 96.

69 Hennig and Jardin, *Managerial Woman*, pp. 13, 15.

70 Harragan, *Games Mother Never Taught You*, pp. 155, 287; Kennedy, *Office Politics*, p. 221. While this literature frequently recognizes institutionalized racism in organizations, it is completely, and predictably, blind to class.

71 Harragan, *Games Mother Never Taught You*, p. 219; Kennedy, *Office Politics*, p. 218.

72 Yvonne Heather Burry, "The Closet Lady," *Columbus* [Ohio] *Monthly* 7 (November, 1981): 115–122. Carol L. Reed, president of

Executive Image, a wardrobe-consulting/public image improvement business, applies the "dress for success" standards that "established the need for a uniform dress code for business" (p. 116).

73 Harragan, *Games Mother Never Taught You*, p. 55; Hennig and Jardin, *Managerial Woman*, p. 199.

74 Harragan, *Games Mother Never Taught You*, pp. 88–89 (italics in original).

75 *Ibid.*, pp. 216, 228.

76 See Marcia Millman, "Prosperity Training: Hope for the Greedy?" *MS* 11 (October, 1982): 75–79, for a clever and insightful discussion of these seminars.

77 Hennig and Jardin, *Managerial Woman*, p. 33.

78 *Ibid.*, p. 39.

79 Career Track Seminars, Inc., 5370 Manhattan Circle, Suite 205, Boulder, Colo. 80303.

80 Harragan, *Games Mother Never Taught You*, p. 267.

81 Hennig and Jardin, *Managerial Woman*, p. 147.

82 Harragan, *Games Mother Never Taught You*, p. 44 (italics in original).

83 Hennig and Jardin, *Managerial Woman*, p. 46.

84 *Ibid.*, pp. 52–53.

85 *Ibid.*, pp. 51, 52.

86 *Ibid.*, p. 96.

87 For copies of some of the early manifestos, see Anne Koedt, Ellen Levine, and Anita Rapone, eds., *Radical Feminism* (New York: Quadrangle Books, 1973), and Leslie B. Tanner, ed., *Voices from Women's Liberation* (New York: New American Library, 1970).

88 See Joreen, "The Tyranny of Structurelessness," in Koedt, Levine, and Rapone, eds., *Radical Feminism*, pp. 285–300.

89 David Osborne, "My Wife, the Doctor," *Mother Jones* 8 (January, 1983): 20–44; see also Claudia Dreyfus, *Seizing Our Bodies* (New York: Vintage Books, 1977), p. xxx; Naomi Gottlieb, "Women and Health Care," in Gottlieb, ed., *Alternative Social Services for Women* (New York: Columbia University Press, 1980), pp. 61–110.

90 Virginia B. Ermer, "Bureaucratic Clientele Encounters: Female Police Officers and the Public," paper presented at the American Political Science Association meetings, New York City, August 31–September 3, 1978.

91 Harragan, *Games Mother Never Taught You*, p. 307.

92 *Ibid.*, p. 324.

93 Barbara Goldman, an interview with Estelle Ramey, "Different Is Not Lesser: Women in Science," in Barbara L. Forisha and Bar-

bara H. Goldman, eds., *Outsiders on the Inside: Women and Organizations* (Englewood Cliffs, N.J.: Prentice-Hall, 1981), p. 51.
94 Harragan, *Games Mother Never Taught You*, p. 36.
95 Hennig and Jardin, *Managerial Woman*, p. 86.
96 *Ibid.*, p. 230.
97 Foucault, *Discipline and Punish* (New York: Vintage Books, 1979), p. 304.
98 For a summary of the practical distinctions between reforms that challenge the system and those that strengthen it, see Charlotte Bunch, "The Reform Tool Kit," in Bunch, *et al.*, *Building Feminist Theory*, pp. 189–201.
99 MacKinnon, "Feminism, Marxism, Method and the State," p. 643.
100 A good example of the class-based limitations on much affirmative action is the recent case of the Equitable Life Assurance Society, an insurance company whose chair and chief executive officer was saluted by *MS* magazine for supporting feminism by doubling the percentage of women executives and insurance agents in the organization and by eliminating sexist language from business communications. At the same time, Equitable was consulting with a well-known union-busting firm to undermine the organizing drive among its clerical workers. Against the company's continued opposition, the office workers voted to join District 925, the office workers' branch of the Service Employees International Union (Mary Ellen Schoonmaker, "Norman Mailer Was #41," *Mother Jones* 8 [July, 1983]: 8).
101 Tomás Borge, *Women and the Nicaraguan Revolution* (New York: Pathfinder Press, 1982); Sheila Rowbotham, *Women, Resistance and Revolution* (New York: Vintage Books, 1972), pp. 206–220.
102 Terence Ball makes this point well in "Contradiction and Critique in Political Theory," in John S. Nelson, ed., *What Should Political Theory Be Now?* (Albany, N.Y.: State University of New York Press, 1983), p. 138.
103 Cavard and Ellis, *Language and Materialism*, p. 76.
104 I have made this argument about participation in a more detailed way in "Toward a New Anarchism," *Contemporary Crises* 7 (January, 1983): 39–57. See also Jane J. Mansbridge, "The Limits of Friendship," in J. Roland Pennock and John W. Chapman, eds., *Participation in Politics: Nomos XVI* (New York: Lieber-Atherton, 1975).
105 The Women's Encampment for a Future of Peace and Justice at Seneca Falls, N.Y., is an excellent example of such a model. At the encampment, during the summer and fall of 1983, anywhere

from a few dozen to a few thousand women (and children) fed, clothed, housed, and taught themselves in an organizational setting that combined longstanding principles of egalitarian and participatory organization with genuinely creative approaches to both internal and external problems. During my brief stay at the camp I was very impressed with the arrangement for dividing the labor (the work webs) and the procedures for dealing with conflict and negotiating consensus. For a brief discussion of the encampment see Grace Paley, "The Seneca Stories: Tales from the Women's Peace Encampment," *MS* 7 (December, 1983): 54–62. Other examples of nonbureaucratic organizations can be found in the women's health movement. See Elissa Pogue and Cercie Miller, "The Elizabeth Stone House: It Works!" *Radical Therapy* 5 (Spring, 1976): 2–4; and Linda Light, "The Influence of Feminism and Collectivity on the Research Process: The Vancouver Women's Health Collective," *Atlantis: A Women's Studies Journal* 4 (Spring, 1979): 108–120.

106 Roslyn Wallach Bologh, "Beyond Weber's Analysis and Critique of Bureaucracy," paper presented at the First International Conference on the Comparative, Historical, and Critical Analysis of Bureaucracy, Gottlieb Duttweiler Institute, Zurich, Switz., October 4–8, 1982, pt. II, p. 1.

107 Arlie Russell Hochschild, *The Managed Heart* (Berkeley, Calif.: University of California Press, 1983), p. x *et passim*.

108 *Ibid.*, pp. 30–31.

109 Jean Bethke Elshtain and Russell Jacoby have accused radical feminists of collapsing the public realm into the private through the unguarded use of the slogan "the personal is political" (see Elshtain, *Public Man, Private Woman* [Princeton, N.J.: Princeton University Press, 1981], p. 217 *et passim*; and Jacoby, *Social Amnesia* [Boston: Beacon Press, 1975], p. 103). While it is perhaps the case that some of the early radical feminist analyses are guilty of simply identifying the personal with the public, nonetheless one of the major contributions of radical feminism has been to show that the two realms are fundamentally related in ways that have been heretofore disguised by sexist ideology. Elshtain's assertion that radical feminism is fascist, that it tries to destroy all private identity and leave us only with a communitarian public self, is bizarre. She looks only at the weaknesses of early radical feminism, ignoring the contributions this theory made to later feminist analysis, including Elshtain's own work: the idea that the relation between public and private is an important political question; that it is not just women, but women's experience, that

has been excluded from male-dominated public life; that public discourse needs to be reconstituted in a way that takes greater account of female experience; all these arguments owe their origins to early radical feminism.

110 Isaac D. Balbus, *Marxism and Domination* (Princeton, N.J.: Princeton University Press, 1982), p. 312.

111 Robert Michels, "Oligarchy," from Michels, *Political Parties* (New York: Free Press, 1966), pp. 37–54, quoted in Oscar Grusky and George A. Miller, eds., *The Sociology of Organizations* (2nd ed.; New York: Free Press, 1981), p. 51.

112 Katherine Newman, "Incipient Bureaucracy: The Development of Hierarchy in Egalitarian Organizations," in Gerald M. Britan and Ronald Cohen, eds., *Hierarchy and Society* (Philadelphia, Pa.: Institute for the Study of Human Issues, 1980), pp. 143–164.

113 Richard C. Edwards, *Contested Terrain* (New York: Basic Books, 1979), p. 112.

114 Perrow, *Complex Organizations*, p. 213.

115 Henry Etzkowitz, "Over-Determined Technology: The Delegitimation of American Ideology," paper presented at the First International Conference on the Comparative, Historical, and Critical Analysis of Bureaucracy, Gottlieb Duttweiler Institute, Zurich, Switz., October 4–8, 1982.

116 Hartsock, "Staying Alive," p. 118.

117 Jane Dolkart, speaking for the staff of *Quest*, in Bunch, *et al.*, *Building Feminist Theory*, p. xix. The work webs at the Seneca Falls Women's Encampment were based on a vertical division of labor, preserving more of the wholeness of the tasks.

118 Hartsock, "Staying Alive," p. 116.

119 John Dunn, *Western Political Theory in the Face of the Future* (Cambridge, Eng.: Cambridge University Press, 1979), p. 27, n. 69.

120 Ana Gutièrrez Johnson and William Foote Whyte, "The Mondragón System of Worker Production Cooperatives," *Industrial and Labor Relations Review* 31 (October, 1977): 18–30; see also Kirkpatrick Sale, *Human Scale* (New York: Coward, McCann and Geoghegan, 1980). For further discussion of the feasibility of worker-controlled collectives, see Arie Shirom, "The Industrial Relations System of Industrial Cooperatives in the United States, 1880–1935," *Labor History* 13 (Fall, 1972): 533–551; Miriam J. Wells, "Alienation, Work Structures, and the Quality of Life: Can Cooperatives Make a Difference?" *Social Problems* 28 (June, 1980): 548–561; Henrik F. Infield, *Utopia and Experiment: Essays in the Sociology of Cooperation* (New York: Praeger, 1955).

121 Jane J. Mansbridge, *Beyond Adversary Democracy* (New York: Basic Books, 1980). Mansbridge's book provides a thoughtful consideration of the problems that decentralized, participatory organizations face and the possible resolutions they may embrace. Her argument could be developed further if she turned it in a feminist direction. For example, she states that "there is remarkably little evidence on the effect of face-to-face contact on feelings of empathy" (p. 272); there *is* substantial evidence on this question, and it comes from the experience of women in face-to-face relations of care.

122 Jane J. Mansbridge, "Time, Emotion and Inequality: Three Problems of Participatory Groups," *The Journal of Applied Behavioral Science* 9 (1973): 351–368; see also Joan Cassell, *A Group Called Women: Sisterhood and Symbolism in the Feminist Movement* (New York: David McKay, 1977); "The Feminist Workplace," interview with Nancy MacDonald, Washington, D.C., Rape Crisis Center, in Bunch, *et al.*, *Building Feminist Theory*, pp. 251–259; Jo Freeman, "The Women's Liberation Movement: Its Origins, Organizations, Activities, and Ideas," in Jo Freeman, ed., *Women: A Feminist Perspective* (Palo Alto, Calif.: Mayfield, 1979), pp. 557–574.

123 See John Case and Rosemary C. Taylor, eds., *Coops, Communes and Collectives* (New York: Pantheon Books, 1979); *No Bosses Here: A Manual for Working Collectively* (Boston: Vocations for Social Change, 1977); Joyce Rothschild-Whitt, "The Collectivist Organization: An Alternative to Rational-Bureaucratic Models," *American Sociological Review* 44 (August, 1979): 509–527; Daniel Zwerdling, ed., *Workplace Democracy* (New York: Harper and Row, 1978).

124 Sale, *Human Scale*, p. 403.

125 Robert B. Denhardt, "Bureaucratic Socialization and Organizational Accommodation," *Administrative Science Quarterly* 13 (December, 1968): 441–450.

126 Karen Sacks, "Networking: When Potluck Is Political," *MS* 11 (April, 1983): 97–98.

127 Karen S. Louis and Sam D. Sieber, *Bureaucracy and the Dispersed Organization* (Norwood, N.J.: Ablex, 1979).

128 For a discussion of the development of women's studies, see Elaine C. Snyder, ed., *The Study of Women: Enlarging Perspectives on Social Reality* (New York: Harper and Row, 1979); Dale Spender, ed., *Men's Studies Modified* (New York: Pergamon Press, 1981); Elizabeth Langland and Walter Gove, eds., *A Feminist Per-*

spective in the Academy (Chicago: University of Chicago Press, 1981); Hunter College Women's Studies Collective, *Women's Realities, Women's Choices* (Oxford: Oxford University Press, 1983).

129 Newman, "Incipient Bureaucracy," pp. 143–164.

Selected Bibliography

Abbott, Jack. *The Belly of the Beast*. (New York: Random House, 1982).

Abrahamsson, Bengt. *Bureaucracy or Participation: The Logic of Organization*. London: Sage Publications, 1977.

Albritton, Robert B. "Social Amelioration Through Mass Insurgency? A Reexamination of the Piven and Cloward Thesis," *The American Political Science Review* 73 (December, 1979): 1003–1023.

Allan, Peter, and Stephen Rosenberg. *Public Personnel and Administrative Behavior*. Monterey, Calif.: Duxburg Press, 1981.

Arato, Andrew. "Understanding Bureaucratic Centralism," *Telos* 35 (Spring, 1978): 73–87.

Arendt, Hannah. *The Human Condition*. Chicago: University of Chicago Press, 1958.

Arnstine, Donald. "The Use of Coercion in Changing the Schools," *Educational Theory* 23 (Fall, 1973): 271–288.

Aronowitz, Stanley. *False Promises*. New York: McGraw-Hill, 1973.

Balbus, Isaac D. *Marxism and Domination*. Princeton, N.J.: Princeton University Press, 1982.

Ball, Terence. "Contradiction and Critique in Political Theory." In John S. Nelson, ed., *What Should Political Theory Be Now?* pp. 127–150. Albany, N.Y.: State University of New York Press, 1983.

Baptista, José. "Bureaucracy, Political System, and Social Dynamic," *Telos* 22 (Winter, 1974–1975): 66–84.

Bardwick, Judith M. *In Transition*. New York: Holt, Rinehart, and Winston, 1979.

Becker, Howard S., and Anselm L. Strauss. "Careers, Personality and Adult Socialization," *American Journal of Sociology* 62 (November, 1956): 253–263.

Beckman, Norman, and Clyde Christofferson. "Reducing WFA: The Newest Public Administration," *The Bureaucrat* 12 (Fall, 1983): 6–9.

Benello, George. "Wasteland Culture," *Anarchy* 88 (June, 1968): 168–188.

Berberoglu, Berch. "The Essence of Inequality: A Critical Analysis of Classical and Contemporary Theories of Stratification and Inequality," *Social Praxis* 4 (1976–1977): 47–74.

Berger, Peter, Brigitte Berger, and Hansfried Kellner. *The Homeless Mind: Modernization and Consciousness.* New York: Random House, 1974.

Berman, Marshall. *All That Is Solid Melts Into Air.* New York: Simon and Schuster, 1982.

Bernard, Jesse. *The Female World.* New York: Free Press, 1981.

———. *Women and the Public Interest.* Chicago: Aldine, 1971.

Bernstein, Richard J. *The Restructuring of Social and Political Theory.* Philadelphia, Pa.: University of Pennsylvania Press, 1976.

Blanchard, Kenneth, and Spencer Johnson. *The One-Minute Manager.* New York: Berkly Books, 1981.

Blau, Peter. *Formal Organizations.* London: Routledge and Kegan Paul, 1963.

Bologh, Roslyn Wallach. "Beyond Weber's Analysis and Critique of Bureaucracy," paper presented at the First International Conference on the Comparative, Historical, and Critical Analysis of Bureaucracy, Gottlieb Duttweiler Institute, Zurich, Switz., October 4–8, 1982.

———. "Max Weber and the Dilemma of Male Rationality," unpublished manuscript, St. John's University, October 21, 1982.

Bookchin, Murray. "Beyond Neo-Marxism," *Telos* 36 (Summer, 1978): 5–28.

———. "Self-Management and the New Technology," *Telos* 41 (Fall, 1979): 5–16.

Borge, Tomás. *Women and the Nicaraguan Revolution.* New York: Pathfinder Press, 1982.

Boyatzis, Richard E. *The Competent Manager.* New York: John Wiley and Sons, 1982.

Braverman, Harry. *Labor and Monopoly Capital.* New York: Monthly Review Press, 1974.

Britan, Gerald M., and Ronald Cohen, eds. *Hierarchy and Society.* Philadelphia, Pa.: Institute for the Study of Human Issues, 1980.

Bruner, Dick. "Why White Collar Workers Can't Be Organized." In Sigmund Nosow and William H. Form, eds., *Man, Work, and Society*, pp. 188–196. New York: Basic Books, 1962.

Bryant, Dorothy. *The Kin of Ata Are Waiting for You.* New York: Moon Books, 1971.

Budd, John. *The Fast Track: How to Survive in the Corporate Labyrinth.* New York: St. Martin's Press, 1982.

Bunch, Charlotte, *et al. Building Feminist Theory: Essays from Quest.* New York: Longman, 1981.

Burry, Yvonne Heather. "The Closet Lady," *Columbus [Ohio] Monthly* 7 (November, 1981): 115–122.

Caiden, Gerald E., and Heinrich Siedentopf, eds. *Strategies for Administrative Reform.* Lexington, Mass.: D. C. Heath, 1982.

Case, John, and Rosemary C. Taylor, eds. *Coops, Communes and Collectives.* New York: Pantheon Books, 1979.

Cassell, Joan. *A Group Called Women: Sisterhood and Symbolism in the Feminist Movement.* New York: David McKay, 1977.

Cavard, Rosalind, and John Ellis. *Language and Materialism.* London: Routledge and Kegan Paul, 1977.

Cavendish, Ruth. *Women on the Line.* London: Routledge and Kegan Paul, 1982.

Chamberlain, Judi. *On Our Own.* New York: Hawthorn Books, 1978.

Chodorow, Nancy. "Oedipal Asymmetries and Heterosexual Knots," *Social Problems* 23 (April, 1976): 454–468.

———. *The Reproduction of Mothering.* Berkeley, Calif.: University of California Press, 1978.

Clawson, Dan. *Bureaucracy and the Labor Process.* New York: Monthly Review Press, 1980.

Clegg, Stewart, and David Dunkerley. *Critical Issues in Organizations.* London: Routledge and Kegan Paul, 1977.

Cohen, Jean. "Max Weber and the Dynamics of Rationalized Domination," *Telos* 14 (Winter, 1972): 63–86.

Collins, Randall. *The Credential Society.* New York: Academic Press, 1979.

Connolly, William E. *Appearance and Reality in Politics.* Cambridge, Eng.: Cambridge University Press, 1981.

Connolly, William E., and Glen Gordon, eds. *Social Structure and Political Theory.* Lexington, Mass.: D. C. Heath, 1974.

Conover, Pamela Johnston, and Virginia Gray. "Political Activists and the Conflict Over Abortion and the ERA," paper presented at the Midwest Political Science Association meetings, Cincinnati, Ohio, 1981.

Cook, James. "The X-Rated Economy," *Forbes* 122 (September 18, 1978): 81–89.

Davies, Margery, "Women's Place Is at the Typewriter: The Feminization of the Clerical Force," *Radical America* 8 (1974): 1–28.

Davis, Margaret R. *Families in a Working World: The Impact of Organizations on Domestic Life.* New York: Praeger, 1982.

de Beauvoir, Simone. *The Second Sex.* New York: Alfred A. Knopf, 1952.

Delaney, Doris. "Before the Robots," *UAW Solidarity*, December 16–31, 1981, p. 10.

Denhardt, Robert B. "Bureaucratic Socialization and Organizational Accommodation," *Administrative Science Quarterly* 13 (December, 1968): 441–450.

————. *In the Shadow of Organization*. Lawrence, Kan.: Regents Press of Kansas, 1981.

Denhardt, Robert B., and Jan Perkins. "The Coming Death of Administrative *Man*," *Women in Public Administration* 36 (July/August, 1976): 379–384.

Densford, John P. "This, Then, Is Existentialism," *Religious Humanism* 2 (Spring, 1968): 53–60.

Deukmejian, George. "Welfare Reform in California," *The Bureaucrat* 12 (Fall, 1983): 10–11.

Diamond, Irene, ed. *Families, Politics, and Public Policy*. New York: Longman, 1983.

Dietz, Mary G. "Citizenship with a Feminist Face: The Problem with Maternal Thinking," paper presented at the Western Political Science Association meetings, Seattle, Wash., March 24–26, 1983.

Dinnerstein, Dorothy. *The Mermaid and the Minotaur*. New York: Harper and Row, 1976.

DiTomaso, Nancy. "The Problem of Organizing: Ends versus Means," unpublished paper, Northwestern University, January, 1981.

————. "Sexuality in the Workplace: Discrimination versus Harassment," paper presented at the Society for Social Problems meetings, San Francisco, September, 1982.

Douglas, Ann. *The Feminization of American Culture*. New York: Alfred A. Knopf, 1977.

Douglas, Mary. *Purity and Danger*. London: Routledge and Kegan Paul, 1966.

Downs, Anthony. *Inside Bureaucracy*. Boston: Little, Brown, 1967.

Dreyfus, Claudia. *Seizing Our Bodies*. New York: Vintage Books, 1977.

Dreyfus, Herbert L., and Paul Rabinow. *Michel Foucault: Beyond Structuralism and Hermeneutics*. Chicago: University of Chicago Press, 1982.

Dunn, John. *Western Political Theory in the Face of the Future*. Cambridge, Eng.: Cambridge University Press, 1979.

Dworkin, Andrea. *Pornography*. New York: Perigee Books, 1979.

Edelman, Murray. "The Political Language of the Helping Professions," *Politics and Society* 4 (1964): 295–310.

Edwards, Richard C. *Contested Terrain*. New York: Basic Books, 1979.

Ehrenreich, Barbara, and Francis Fox Piven. "The Left's Best Hope," *Mother Jones* 8 (September/October, 1983): 26–29.

Eisenstein, Zillah R., ed. *Capitalist Patriarchy and the Case for Socialist Feminism*. New York: Monthly Review Press, 1979.

Eisenstein, Zillah R. *The Radical Future of Liberal Feminism*. New York: Longman, 1981.

Elgin, Duane S., and Robert A. Bushnell. "The Limits to Complexity: Are Bureaucrats Becoming Unmanageable?" *Futurist* 11 (December, 1977): 337–349.

Ellul, Jacques. *The Technological Society*. New York: Alfred A. Knopf, 1964.

Elshtain, Jean Bethke. "Antigone's Daughters," *Democracy* 2 (April, 1982): 45–59.

———. *Public Man, Private Woman*. Princeton, N.J.: Princeton University Press, 1981.

Erie, Stephen P. "Two Faces of Ethnic Power: Comparing the Irish and Black Experiences," *Polity* 13 (Winter, 1980): 261–284.

Ermer, Virginia B. "Bureaucratic Clientele Encounters: Female Police Officers and the Public," paper presented at the American Political Science Association meetings, New York City, August 31–September 3, 1978.

Ermer, Virginia, B., and John H. Strange, eds. *Blacks and Bureaucracy*. New York: Thomas Y. Crowell, 1972.

Etzioni, Amitai. *A Comparative Analysis of Complex Organizations*. New York: Free Press, 1961.

Etzkowitz, Henry. "Over-Determined Technology: The Delegitimation of American Ideology," paper presented at the First International Conference on the Comparative, Historical, and Critical Analysis of Bureaucracy, Gottlieb Duttweiler Institute, Zurich, Switz., October 4–8, 1982.

Ewen, Stuart. *Captains of Consciousness: Advertising and the Social Roots of the Consumer Culture*. New York: McGraw-Hill, 1976.

Fanon, Frantz. *Studies in a Dying Colonialism*. New York: Monthly Review Press, 1965.

Ferguson, Charles A., and Shirley Brice Heath, eds. *Language in the U.S.A.* Cambridge, Eng.: Cambridge University Press, 1981.

Ferguson, Kathy E. *Self, Society and Womankind: The Dialectic of Liberation*. Westbury, Conn.: Greenwood Press, 1980.

———. "Toward a New Anarchism," *Contemporary Crises* 7 (January, 1983): 39–57.

Ferrarotti, Franco. "The Struggle of Reason Against Total Bureaucratization," *Telos* 9 (Spring, 1976): 157–169.

Firestone, Shulamith. *The Dialectic of Sex*. New York: Bantam Books, 1970.

Forisha, Barbara L., and Barbara H. Goldman, eds. *Outsiders on the Inside: Women and Organizations*. Englewood Cliffs, N.J.: Prentice-Hall, 1981.

Foucault, Michel. *The Archaeology of Knowledge*. New York: Pantheon, 1972.

———. *The Birth of the Clinic*. New York: Vintage Books, 1975.

———. *Discipline and Punish*. New York: Vintage Books, 1979.

———. "An Exchange with Michel Foucault," *The New York Review of Books* 30 (letters to the editor) (March 31, 1983): 42–43.

———. "History, Discourse and Discontinuity," *Salmagundi* 20 (Summer/Fall, 1972): 223–248.

———. *The History of Sexuality*. Vol. I. New York: Random House, 1980.

———. *The Order of Things*. New York: Vintage Books, 1973.

———. *Power/Knowledge: Selected Interviews and Other Writings*. New York: Pantheon Books, 1972.

Freeman, Jo, ed. *Women: A Feminist Perspective*. 2nd ed. Palo Alto, Calif.: Mayfield, 1979.

Friedan, Betty. *The Second Stage*. New York: Summit Books, 1981.

Gannon, Martin J. *Organizational Behavior*. Boston: Little, Brown, 1979.

Gardner, B. B., and W. F. Whyte. "The Man in the Middle: Position and Problems of the Foreman," *Applied Anthropology (Human Organization)* 2 (1945): 1–28.

Gardner, Neely. "Power Diffusion in the Public Sector: Collaboration for Democracy," *The Journal of Applied Behavioral Science* 10 (1974): 367–372.

Garskoff, Michele H., ed. *Roles Women Play*. Belmont, Calif.: Brooks/Cole, 1971.

Garson, Barbara. *All the Livelong Day*. New York: Doubleday, 1975.

Geertz, Clifford. *Negara: The Theatre-State in Nineteenth Century Bali*. Princeton, N.J.: Princeton University Press, 1981.

Gelb, Joyce, and Marian Lief Palley, *Women and Public Policies*. Princeton, N.J.: Princeton University Press, 1982.

Gibbons, Michael. "Authority and Politics," Ph.D. dissertation, University of Massachusetts, 1983.

Giele, Janet Zollinger. *Women and the Future*. New York: Free Press, 1978.

Gilligan, Carol. *In a Different Voice*. Cambridge, Mass.: Harvard University Press, 1982.

———. "In a Different Voice: Women's Conception of Self and of Morality," *Harvard Educational Review* 47 (November, 1977): 481–517.

———. "Woman's Place in Man's Life Cycle," *Harvard Educational Review* 49 (November, 1979): 431–446.

Gilman, Charlotte P. *Herland*. New York: Pantheon Books, 1979.

Glasgow, Douglas G. *The Black Underclass*. New York: Vintage Books, 1980.

Glennon, Lynda M. *Women and Dualism*. New York: Longman, 1979.

Goffman, Erving. *Asylums*. Garden City, N.Y.: Anchor, 1961.

———. *Presentation of Self in Everyday Life*. New York: Doubleday, 1959.

Goldman, Paul. "The Organization Caste System and the New Working Class," *Insurgent Sociologist* 3 (Winter, 1973): 41–52.

Goldman, Paul, and Donald R. Van Houten. "Managerial Strategies and the Worker: A Marxist Analysis of Bureaucracy," *Sociological Quarterly* 18 (Winter, 1977): 108–125.

Golembiewski, Robert T. *Public Administration as a Developing Discipline*. New York: Marcel Dekker, 1977.

Goodman, Robert. *After the Planners*. New York: Simon and Schuster, 1971.

Goodsell, Charles T. "Client Evaluation of Three Welfare Programs," *Administration and Society* 12 (August, 1980): 123–136.

———. "Conflicting Perceptions of Welfare Bureaucracy," *Social Casework: The Journal of Contemporary Social Work* 61 (June, 1980): 354–360.

Goodstadt, Barry, and Larry A. Hjelle, "Power to the Powerless: Focus of Control and the Use of Power," *Journal of Personality and Social Psychology* 27 (1973): 190–196.

Goodstadt, Barry, and David Kipnis. "Situational Influences on the Use of Power," *Journal of Applied Psychology* 54 (1970): 201–207.

Gordon, George. *Public Administration in America*. 2nd ed. New York: St. Martin's Press, 1982.

Gordon, Suzanne. "The New Corporate Feminism," *The Nation* 236 (February 5, 1983): 129–147.

Gornick, Vivian and Barbara K. Moran, eds. *Woman in Sexist Society*. New York: Basic Books, 1971.

Gottlieb, Naomi, ed. *Alternative Social Services for Women*. New York: Columbia University Press, 1980.

Gouldner, Alvin. "Metaphysical Pathos and the Theory of

Bureaucracy." In Lewis A. Coser and Bernard Rosenburg, eds. *Sociological Theory*, pp. 500–510. New York: Macmillan, 1964.
————. "Stalinism: A Study of Internal Colonialism," *Telos* 34 (Winter, 1977–1978): 5–48.

Gray, J. Glenn. "Winds of Thought," *Social Research* 44 (Spring, 1977): 44–62.

Gray, Thomas, and Cynthia Roberts-Gray. "Structuring Bureaucratic Rules to Enhance Compliance," *Psychological Reports* 45 (October, 1979): 579–589.

Green, Philip. *The Pursuit of Inequality*. New York: Pantheon Books, 1981.

Greenwald, Carol S. *Women in Management*. Scarsdale, N.Y.: Work in America Institute, 1980.

Grønbjerg, Kristen, David Street, and Gerald D. Suttles. *Poverty and Social Change*. Chicago: University of Chicago Press, 1978.

Gross, Bertrand. *Friendly Fascism*. New York: M. Evans, 1980.

Grusky, Oscar, and George A. Miller, eds. *The Sociology of Organizations*. 2nd ed. New York: Free Press, 1981.

Gutek, Barbara A. "Strategies for Studying Client Satisfaction," *Journal of Social Issues* 34 (1978): 44–55.

Habermas, Jurgen. "Hannah Arendt's Communications Concept of Power," *Social Research* 44 (Spring, 1977): 3–24.

Handrahan, Laura A. "Teachers Increasingly Become Targets of Violence," *Albany Times Union*, March 29, 1983, p. 1.

Harding, Sandra. "Toward a Strong Program for Epistemology: Clues from Feminist Inquiry," paper presented at the American Political Science Association meetings, New York City, September 1981.

Harmon, Michael M. *Action Theory for Public Administration*. New York: Longman, 1983.

Harragan, Betty Lehan. *Games Mother Never Taught You: Corporate Gamesmanship for Women*. New York: Warner Books, 1977.

Hartsock, Nancy. "Political Change: Two Perspectives on Power," *Quest* 1 (1974): 3–19.

Hearn, Francis. "Rationality and Bureaucracy: Maoist Contributions to a Marxist Theory of Bureaucracy," *Sociological Quarterly* 19 (Winter, 1978): 37–54.

Heclo, Hugh. *Government of Strangers*. Washington, D.C.: Brookings Institution, 1977.

Heilbrun, Caroline. *Reinventing Womanhood*. New York: W. W. Norton, 1979.

Hellbriegel, Don, and John W. Slocum, Jr. *Organizational Behavior*. 2nd ed. St. Paul, Minn.: West, 1979.

Henley, Nancy. *Body Politics: Power, Sex, and Nonverbal Communication.* Englewood Cliffs, N.J.: Prentice-Hall, 1977.

Hennig, Margaret, and Anne Jardin. *The Managerial Woman.* New York: Pocket Books, 1976.

Heydebrand, Wolf. "Organizational Contradictions in Public Bureaucracies: Toward a Marxian Theory of Organizations," *Sociological Quarterly* 18 (Winter, 1977): 83–107.

Hochschild, Arlie Russell. *The Managed Heart.* Berkeley, Calif.: University of California Press, 1983.

Hodges, Donald C. *The Bureaucratization of Socialism.* Amherst, Mass.: University of Massachusetts Press, 1981.

Howard, Robert. "Strung Out at the Phone Company: How AT&T's Workers Are Drugged, Bugged, and Coming Unplugged," *Mother Jones* 6 (August, 1981): 39–59.

Hummel, Ralph P. *The Bureaucratic Experience.* New York: St. Martin's Press, 1977.

Hunter College Women's Studies Collective. *Women's Realities, Women's Choices.* Oxford: Oxford University Press, 1983.

Infield, Henrik F. *Utopia and Experiment: Essays in the Sociology of Cooperation.* New York: Praeger, 1955.

Inzerilli, Giorgio. "The Organization-Client Relationship as an Aspect of Interorganizational Analysis," *Human Relations* 32 (1979): 419–437.

Jacoby, Henry. *The Bureaucratization of the World.* Berkeley, Calif.: University of California Press, 1973.

Jacoby, Russell. *Social Amnesia.* Boston: Beacon Press, 1975.

Jacques, Elliott. *A General Theory of Bureaucracy.* New York: Halssed Press, 1976.

Jaggar, Alison M. "Human Biology and Feminist Politics," unpublished paper, University of Cincinnati, 1981.

Jaggar, Alison M., and Paula Rothenberg Struhl, eds. *Feminist Frameworks.* New York: McGraw-Hill, 1978.

Janeway, Elizabeth. *Between Myth and Morning: Women Awakening.* New York: William Morrow, 1975.

———. *Man's World, Woman's Place.* New York: Delta Books, 1971.

Jansen, Robert B. *The ABCs of Bureaucracy.* Chicago: Nelson Hall, 1978.

Jennings, Edward T., Jr. "Social Amelioration Through Mass Insurgency Revisited: Another Look at the Welfare Consequences of Urban Riots," paper presented at the Midwest Political Science Association meetings, Cincinnati, Ohio, April 16–18, 1981.

Johnson, Ana Guitèrrez, and William Foote Whyte, "The Mondragón

System of Worker Production Cooperatives," *Industrial and Labor Relations Review* 31 (October, 1977): 18–30.

Jonas, Hans. "Acting, Knowing, Thinking: Gleanings from Hannah Arendt's Philosophical Work," *Social Research* 44 (Spring, 1977): 25–43.

Kanter, Rosabeth Moss. *Men and Women of the Corporation.* New York: Basic Books, 1977.

Kanter, Rosabeth Moss, and Barry Stein, eds. *Life in Organizations.* New York: Basic Books, 1979.

Katz, Daniel, Barbara A. Gutek, Robert L. Kahn, and Eugenia Barton. *Bureaucratic Encounters.* Ann Arbor, Mich.: Institute for Social Research, 1975.

Kennedy, Marilyn Moats. *Office Politics: Seizing Power, Wielding Clout.* New York: Warner Books, 1980.

Kerber, Linda K., and Jane de Hart Matthews. *Women's America.* New York: Oxford University Press, 1982.

Kessler, Suzanne J., and Wendy McKenna. *Gender: An Ethnomethodological Approach.* New York: John Wiley and Sons, 1978.

Kharasch, Robert N. *The Institutional Imperative.* New York: Charterhouse Books, 1973.

Killens, John. *Black Man's Burden.* New York: Trident Press, 1965.

Knowles, James. "The Rockefeller Family Group." In Ralph L. Andreano, ed., *Superconcentration/Supercorporation*, pp. 1–59. New York: Irvington, 1974.

Knowles, Louis, and Kenneth Prewitt, eds. *Institutional Racism in America.* Englewood Cliffs, N.J.: Prentice-Hall, 1969.

Koedt, Anne, Ellen Levine, and Anita Rapone, eds. *Radical Feminism.* New York: Quadrangle Books, 1973.

Kontos, Alkis, ed. *Domination.* Toronto: University of Toronto Press, 1975.

Kovel, Joel. "Rationalization and the Family," *Telos* 37 (Fall, 1978): 5–21.

Kraft, Selma. "Cognitive Function and Women's Art," *Women's Art Journal* 4 (Fall, 1983/Winter, 1984): 5–9.

Kramer, Fred. *The Dynamics of Public Bureaucracy.* 2nd ed. Cambridge, Mass.: Winthrop, 1981.

Kramnick, Isaac. "Joseph Priestly—English Philosophe," paper presented to the Columbia University Seminar on Political and Social Thought, December 16, 1982.

Kuhn, Thomas. *The Structure of Scientific Revolutions.* 2nd ed. Chicago: University of Chicago Press, 1970.

Kvale, Steinar. "Examinations: From Ritual Through Bureaucracy to Technology," *Social Praxis* 3 (1975): 187–206.

Ladd, John. "Morality and the Ideal of Rationality in Formal Organizations," *Monist* 54 (October, 1970): 488–517.

Ladner, Joyce. *Tomorrow's Tomorrow: The Black Woman.* New York: Doubleday, 1971.

Lakoff, Robin. *Language and Woman's Place.* New York: Harper and Row, 1975.

Langland, Elizabeth, and Walter Gove, eds. *A Feminist Perspective in the Academy.* Chicago: University of Chicago Press, 1981.

Lefort, Claude. "What Is Bureaucracy?" *Telos* 22 (Winter, 1974–1975): 31–65.

Leiss, William. *The Domination of Nature.* New York: George Braziller, 1972.

Levens, Helene. "Organizational Affiliation and Powerlessness: A Case Study of the Welfare Poor," *Social Problems* 16 (1968): 18–43.

Levi, Margaret. *Bureaucratic Insurgency: The Case of Police Unions.* Lexington, Mass.: Lexington Books, 1977.

Lewis, Eugene. *American Politics in a Bureaucratic Age.* Cambridge, Mass.: Winthrop, 1977.

———. *Public Entrepreneurship: Toward a Theory of Bureaucratic Political Power.* Bloomington, Ind.: Indiana University Press, 1980.

Light, Linda. "The Influence of Feminism and Collectivity on the Research Process: The Vancouver Women's Health Collective," *Atlantis: A Women's Studies Journal* 4 (Spring, 1979): 108–120.

Lindsey, Robert. "California Weighs Plan to Curb Welfare Fraud," *The New York Times*, February 27, 1983, p. 26.

Lipsky, Michael. *Street-Level Bureaucracy.* New York: Russell Sage, 1980.

Louis, Karen S., and Sam D. Sieber. *Bureaucracy and the Dispersed Organization.* Norwood, N.J.: Ablex, 1979.

Luke, Timothy W. "Culture and Politics in the Age of Artificial Negativity," *Telos* 35 (Spring, 1978): 55–72.

———. "Regulating the Haven in a Heartless World: The State and Family Under Advanced Capitalism," *New Political Science* 2 (Fall, 1981): 51–74.

Lukes, Stephen. *Power: A Radical View.* London: Macmillan, 1974.

MacDonald, Kenneth W. "A Class Analysis of Perception and Explanations of Opportunity in America: An Empirical Test of William Ryan's *Blaming the Victim* Thesis," Ph.D. dissertation, Northeastern University, 1983.

MacKinnon, Catherine A. "Feminism, Marxism, Method and the

State: Toward a Feminist Jurisprudence," *Signs* 8 (Summer, 1983): 635–658.

Mallet, Serge. *Bureaucracy and Technocracy in the Socialist Countries.* Nottingham, Eng.: Bertrand Russell Peace Foundation, 1974.

Mandell, Betty Reid. *Welfare in America: Controlling the Dangerous Classes.* Englewood Cliffs, N.J.: Prentice-Hall, 1975.

Mansbridge, Jane J. *Beyond Adversary Democracy.* New York: Basic Books, 1980.

―――. "The Limits of Friendship." In J. Roland Pennock and John W. Chapman, eds., *Participation in Politics: Nomos XVI,* New York: Lieber-Atherton, 1975, pp. 246–275.

―――. "Time, Emotion and Inequality: Three Problems of Participatory Groups," *The Journal of Applied Behavioral Science* 9 (1973): 351–368.

Manson, Grace E. "Occupational Interests and Personality Requirements of Women in Business and the Professions," *Michigan Business Studies* 3 (April, 1931): 281–409.

Marcus, Philip M., and James S. House. "Exchange Between Superiors and Subordinates in Large Organizations," *Administrative Science Quarterly* 18 (1973): 209–222.

Marcuse, Herbert. *One-Dimensional Man.* Boston: Beacon Press, 1964.

Marglin, Stephen A. "What Do Bosses Do? The Origins and Functions of Hierarchy in Capitalist Society," *Review of Radical Political Economy* 6 (Summer, 1974): 60–112.

Mariolis, Peter. "Interlocking Directorates and Control of Corporations," *Social Science Quarterly* 56 (December, 1975): 425–439.

Marks, Elaine, and Isabelle de Courtivron, eds. *New French Feminisms.* Amherst, Mass.: University of Massachusetts Press, 1980.

Massi, Dale A. *Organizing for Women.* Lexington, Mass.: D. C. Heath, 1981.

Matthaei, Julie A. *An Economic History of Women in America.* New York: Schocken, 1983.

Mayer, Joel E., and Noel Timms. *The Client Speaks: Working Class Impressions of Casework.* London: Routledge and Kegan Paul, 1970.

McCleary, Richard. "On Becoming a Client," *Journal of Social Issues* 34 (1978): 57–75.

McDonell, Donald J. "On Foucault's Philosophical Method," *Canadian Journal of Philosophy* 7 (September, 1977): 537–553.

Mead, Margaret. *Sex and Temperament in Three Primitive Societies.* New York: William Morrow, 1935.

Meehanic, David. "Sources of Power of Lower Participants in Complex Organizations," *Administrative Science Quarterly* 7 (December, 1962): 349–364.

Melanson, Philip H., ed. *Knowledge, Politics, and Public Policy: Introductory Readings in American Politics.* Cambridge, Mass.: Winthrop, 1973.

Melossi, Dario, and Massimo Parvarini, *The Prison and the Factory.* Totowa, N.J.: Barnes and Noble, 1981.

Merton, Robert K. "Bureaucratic Structure and Personality." In Merton, *Social Theory and Social Structure*, pp. 249–260. New York: Free Press, 1968.

Meyer, Marshall W., and associates, eds. *Environments and Organizations.* San Francisco: Jossey-Bass, 1978.

Meyer, Marshall W., and M. Craig Brown. "The Process of Bureaucratization," *American Journal of Sociology* 83 (September, 1977): 364–385.

Millet, Kate. *Sexual Politics.* New York: Avon Books, 1970.

Millman, Marcia. "Prosperity Training: Hope for the Greedy?" *MS* 11 (October, 1982): 75–79.

Millman, Marcia, and Rosabeth Moss Kanter, eds. *Another Voice.* New York: Doubleday, 1975.

Mintz, Beth, Peter Freitag, Carol Hendricks, and Michael Schwartz. "Problems of Proof in Elite Research," *Social Problems* 23 (February, 1976): 314–324.

Molloy, John T. *Dress for Success.* New York: Warner Books, 1975.
————. *The Woman's Dress for Success Book.* New York: Warner Books, 1977.

Mosher, Frederick C. *Democracy and the Public Service.* New York: Oxford University Press, 1968.

Mouzelis, Nicos P. *Organization and Bureaucracy.* Chicago: Aldine, 1968.

Nelson, Bryce. "Bosses Face Less Risk than the Bossed," *The New York Times* April 3, 1983, p. 16E.

Nicholson, Linda. *Feminism as Political Philosophy.* Forthcoming.

No Bosses Here: A Manual for Working Collectively. Boston: Vocations for Social Change, 1977.

Norton, Mary Beth. *Liberty's Daughters.* Boston: Little, Brown, 1980.

O'Donnell, Guillermo. "Reflections on the Patterns of Change in the Bureaucratic-Authoritarian State," *Latin American Research Review* 13 (1978): 13–38.

Offe, Claus. "Advanced Capitalism and the Welfare State," *Politics and Society* 2 (Summer, 1972): 479–488.

———. "Political Authority and Class Structure," *International Journal of Sociology* 2 (Spring, 1972): 73–107.

Ollman, Bertell. *Social and Sexual Revolution.* Boston: South End Press, 1979.

O'Neil, John, ed. *On Critical Theory.* New York: Seabury Press, 1976.

Ortner, Sherry B., and Harriet Whitehead, eds. *Sexual Meanings.* Cambridge, Eng.: Cambridge University Press, 1981.

Osborne, David. "My Wife, the Doctor," *Mother Jones* 8 (January, 1983): 20–44.

Paley, Grace. "The Seneca Stories: Tales from the Women's Peace Encampment," *MS* 7 (December, 1983): 54–62.

Patten, Thomas H., Jr., ed. *Classics of Personnel Management.* Oak Park, Ill.: Moore, 1979.

Perrow, Charles. *Complex Organizations: A Critical Essay.* 2nd ed. Glenview, Ill.: Scott Foresman, 1979.

———. "A Framework for the Comparative Analysis of Organizations," *American Sociological Review* 32 (1967): 194–208.

Pesić-Golucović, Zagorka. "Socialist Ideas and Reality," *Praxis* 7 (1971): 399–421.

Piercy, Marge. *Woman on the Edge of Time.* New York: Fawcett, 1981.

Piven, Francis Fox, and Richard Cloward. *The New Class War.* New York: Pantheon Books, 1982.

———. *The Politics of Turmoil.* New York: Random House, 1965.

———. *Poor People's Movements.* New York: Random House, 1979.

———. *Regulating the Poor.* New York: Random House, 1971.

Piven, Francis Fox, and Barbara Ehrenreich. "The Left's Best Hope," *Mother Jones* 8 (September/October, 1983): 26–29.

Plattel, Martin. "Critical Theory and Contemporary Society," *Humanities* 11 (February, 1975): 5–14.

Pogue, Elissa, and Cercie Miller, "The Elizabeth Stone House: It Works!" *Radical Therapy* 5 (Spring, 1976): 2–4.

Polsky, Andrew J. "The Administered Citizen," paper presented at the American Political Science Association meetings, Chicago, Ill., September 1–4, 1983.

Pranger, Robert J. *The Eclipse of Citizenship: Power and Participation in Contemporary Politics.* New York: Holt, Rinehart and Winston, 1968.

Presthus, Robert. *The Organizational Society.* New York: Alfred A. Knopf, 1962.

Pulliam, John D. "Alienation and the College Professor," *Journal of Thought* 9 (April, 1974): 84–90.

Rader, Melvin. "The Artist as an Outsider," *Journal of Aesthetics and Art Criticism* 16 (March, 1958): 306–318.

Ransford, H. Edward, and Jon Miller. "Race, Sex and Feminist Outlooks," *American Sociological Review* 48 (February, 1983): 46–59.

Rapp, Rayna, and Ellen Ross. "It Seems We've Stood and Talked Like This Before," *MS* 11 (April, 1983): 54–59.

Rich, Adrienne. "Privilege, Power, and Tokenism," *MS* 8 (September, 1979): 42–44.

Rittersporn, Gabor T. "The State Against Itself: Socialist Tensions and Political Conflict in the USSR, 1936–1938," *Telos* 41 (Fall, 1979): 87–104.

Rosen, Ellen I. "Between the Rock and the Hard Place: Employment and Unemployment Among Blue Collar Women," unpublished paper, Boston College, Social Welfare Research Institute, Fall, 1981.

Rossi, Alice. "A Biosocial Perspective on Parenting," *Daedalus* 106 (Spring, 1977): 1–31.

Roszak, Theodore. *The Making of a Counterculture.* New York: Anchor Books, 1969.

———. *Where the Wasteland Ends.* New York: Doubleday, 1972.

Rothschild-Whitt, Joyce. "The Collectivist Organization: An Alternative to Rational-Bureaucratic Models," *American Sociological Review* 44 (August, 1979): 509–527.

Rowbotham, Sheila. *Women, Resistance and Revolution.* New York: Vintage Books, 1972.

Rubin, Lillian Breslow. *Worlds of Pain.* New York: Basic Books, 1976.

Ruble, Diane N., and E. Tory Higgins. "Effects of Group Sex Composition on Self-Presentation and Sex-Typing," *Journal of Social Issues* 32 (1976): 125–132.

Ruddick, Sara. "Maternal Thinking," *Feminist Studies* 6 (Summer, 1980): 342–367.

Rudolph, Lloyd I., and Susanne H. Rudolph. "Authority and Power in Bureaucratic and Patrimonial Administration: A Revisionist Interpretation of Weber on Bureaucracy," *World Politics* 3 (January, 1979): 195–227.

Sacks, Karen. "Networking: When Potluck Is Political," *MS* 11 (April, 1983): 97–98.

Saffioti, Heleieth B. *Women in Class Society.* New York: Monthly Review Press, 1978.

Salaman, Graeme, and Kenneth Thompson, eds. *Control and Ideology in Organizations.* Cambridge, Mass.: MIT Press, 1980.

Sale, Kirkpatrick. *Human Scale.* New York: Coward, McCann and Geoghegan, 1980.

Sanday, Peggy Reeves. *Female Power and Male Dominance.* London: Cambridge University Press, 1981.

Sarri, Rosemary C., and Yeheskel Hasenfeld, eds. *The Management of Human Services.* New York: Columbia University Press, 1978.

Sayers, Dorothy. *Are Women Human?* Grand Rapids, Mich.: Eerdmans, 1971.

Scarf, Maggie. *Unfinished Business.* New York: Ballantine Books, 1980.

Schoonmaker, Mary Ellen. "Norman Mailer Was # 41," *Mother Jones* 8 (July, 1983): 8.

Schuman, David. *The Ideology of Form.* Lexington, Mass.: D. C. Heath, 1978.

Schutz, Alfred. *Collected Papers.* The Hague: Martinus Nijhoff, 1964.

Scott, William G., and David K. Hart. *Organizational America.* Boston: Houghton Mifflin, 1979.

Seidman, Steven, and Michael Gruber. "Capitalism and Individuation in the Sociology of Max Weber," *British Journal of Sociology* 28 (December, 1977): 498–508.

Sennett, Richard. *Authority.* New York: Alfred A. Knopf, 1980.

———. *The Fall of Public Man.* New York: Vintage Books, 1978.

Sennett, Richard, and Jonathan Cobb. *The Hidden Injuries of Class.* New York: Vintage Books, 1972.

Shafritz, Jay M., Walter L. Balk, Albert C. Hyde, and David H. Rosenbloom. *Personnel Management in Government.* New York: Marcel Dekker, 1978.

Shapiro, Michael J. *Language and Political Understanding.* New Haven, Conn.: Yale University Press, 1981.

Sheridan, Alan. *Michel Foucault: The Will to Truth.* New York: Tavistock Publications, 1980.

Sheriff, Peter E. "Unrepresentative Bureaucracy," *Sociology* 8 (September, 1974): 447–462.

Shirom, Arie. "The Industrial Relations System of Industrial Cooperatives in the United States, 1800–1935," *Labor History* 13 (Fall, 1972): 533–551.

Shorris, Earl. *The Oppressed Middle: The Politics of Middle Management.* New York: Anchor/Doubleday, 1981.

Sibley, Mulford Q. *Nature and Civilization: Some Implications for Politics.* Itasca, Ill.: F. E. A. Peacock, 1977.

Sidel, Ruth. *Urban Survival: The World of Working Class Women.* Boston: Beacon Press, 1978.

Siebert, Rudolph. "Horkheimer's Sociology of Religion," *Telos* 30 (Winter, 1976–1977): 127–144.

Silver, Murray, and Daniel Gelber. "On the Irrelevance of Evil: The Organization and Individual Action," *Journal of Social Issues*, 34 (1978): 125–136.

Smith, Roy C. "How to Be a Good Subordinate," *The New York Times*, November 25, 1979, p. 16F.

Snyder, Elaine C., ed. *The Study of Women: Enlarging Perspectives on Social Reality*. New York: Harper and Row, 1979.

Spangler, Eve, Marsha A. Gordon, and Ronald M. Pipkin. "Token Women: An Empirical Test of Kanter's Hypothesis," *American Journal of Sociology* 84 (1978): 160–170.

Spence, Larry. *The Politics of Social Knowledge*. University Park, Pa.: Pennsylvania State University Press, 1978.

Spencer, Charles. *Blue Collar*. Chicago: Lakeside Charter Books, 1977.

Spender, Dale. *Man Made Language*. London: Routledge and Kegan Paul, 1980.

———, ed. *Men's Studies Modified*. New York: Pergamon Press, 1981.

Stack, Carol. *All Our Kin*. New York: Harper and Row, 1974.

Steus, Richard M. *Introduction to Organizational Behavior*. Glenview, Ill.: Scott, Foresman, 1981.

Stever, James A. *Diversity and Order in State and Local Politics*. Columbia, S.C.: University of South Carolina Press, 1980.

Stewart, Douglas J. "Pornography, Obscenity and Capitalism," *Antioch Review* 35 (Fall, 1977): 389–398.

Stockman, Norman. "Habermas, Marcuse, and the *Aufhebung* of Science and Technology," *Philosophy of Social Science* 8 (March, 1978): 15–35.

Stone, Clarence, and Kathy Reynolds, "Complexity and Democratic Theory: Administrative Accountability in Post-Industrial Society," paper presented at the Midwest Political Science Association meetings, Cincinnati, Ohio, April 16–18, 1981.

Street, David, George T. Martin, Jr., and Laura Kramer Gordon. *The Welfare Industry*. Beverly Hills, Calif.: Sage Publications, 1979.

Sturrock, John, ed. *Stucturalism and Science*. Oxford: Oxford University Press, 1979.

Sullivan, Robert R. "Public Authority, Technology, Speech, and Language," *Polity* 14 (Summer, 1982): 585–602.

Sullivan, Timothy. "The Educational Bureaucracy's Credibility Gap," *Social Work Journal of Philosophy* 3 (Winter, 1972): 85–91.

Tanner, Leslie B., ed. *Voices from Women's Liberation.* New York: New American Library, 1970.

Thayer, Frederick C. "Organization Theory, Political Theory, and the International Arena: Some Hope but Very Little Time," paper presented at the International Studies Association meetings, March, 1981.

Tripi, Frank. "The Inevitablity of Client Alienation: A Counter Argument," *Sociological Quarterly* 15 (Summer, 1974): 432–441.

Tudiver, Neil. "Business Ideology and Management in Social Work: The Limits of Cost Control," *Catalyst* 13 (1982): 24–48.

————. "Quality of Work Life: The New Shape of Employer Paternalism," paper presented at the First International Conference on the Comparative, Historical, and Critical Analysis of Bureaucracy, Gottlieb Duttweiler Institute, Zurich, Switz., October 4–8, 1982.

Turnbull, Colin. *The Mountain People.* New York: Simon and Schuster, 1972.

Uesugi, Thomas K., and W. Edgar Vinaki. "Strategy in a Feminine Game," *Sociometry* 26 (1963): 75–88.

Unger, Roberto M. *Knowledge and Politics.* New York: Free Press, 1975.

Valentine, Betty Lou. *Hustling and Other Hard Work: Life Styles in the Ghetto.* New York: Free Press, 1978.

Vash, Carolyn L. *The Burnt-out Administrator.* New York: Springer, 1980.

Vetterling-Braggin, Mary, Frederick A. Elliston, and Jane English, eds. *Feminism and Philosophy.* Totowa, N.J.: Littlefield, Adams, 1977.

Vocino, Thomas, and Richard Heimovics, eds. *Public Administration Education in Transition.* New York: Marcel Dekker, 1982.

Vocino, Thomas, and Jack Rabin. *Contemporary Public Administration.* New York: Harcourt, Brace, Jovanovich, 1981.

Vogt, Paul W. "The Theory of the Credentialed Class," *The Review of Education* 7 (Spring, 1981): 135–151.

Vollbrath, Ernst. "Hannah Arendt and the Method of Political Thinking," *Social Research* 44 (Spring, 1977): 160–182.

Wack, Jeffrey, and Judith Rodin. "Nursing Homes for the Aged: The Human Consequences of Legislation-Shaped Environments," *Journal of Social Issues* 34 (1978): 7–21.

Walker, Pat, ed. *Between Labor and Capital.* Boston: South End Press, 1979.

Watson, Bill. "Counter Planning on the Shop Floor," *Radical America* 5 (1971): 1–10.

Weber, Max. *The Theory of Social and Economic Organizations*, trans. A. M. Henderson and Talcott Parsons. New York: Free Press of Glencoe, 1964.

Weinstein, Deena. *Bureaucratic Opposition*. New York: Pergamon Press, 1979.

Weinstein, Deena, and Michael A. Weinstein. "An Existential Approach to Society: Active Transcendence," *Human Studies* 1 (1978): 38–47.

———. "Self, Society, and Social Control: An Existential Perspective," *Humanity and Society* 1 (Summer, 1977): 104–115.

Weinstein, Michael A. *Meaning and Appreciation: Time and Modern Political Life*. West Lafayette, Ind.: Purdue University Press, 1978.

———. "Philosophical Mentality and the Public Situation," *Review of Social Theory* 2 (May, 1974): 134–142.

———. *Structure of Human Life: A Vitalist Ontology*. New York: New York University Press, 1979.

Wells, Miriam J. "Alienation, Work Structures, and the Quality of Life: Can Cooperatives Make a Difference?" *Social Problems* 28 (June, 1980): 548–561.

White, Hayden V. "Foucault Decoded: Notes from Underground," *Historical Theory* 12 (1973): 23–54.

White, Orion F. "Improving the Prospects for Heterodoxy in Organization Theory: A Review of *Sociological Paradigms and Organizational Analysis* by Gibson Burrell and Gareth Morjan," *Administration and Society* 15 (August, 1983): 257–272.

Whyte, William F., and Burleigh Gardner. "The Man in the Middle," *Applied Anthropology* 2 (1945): 1–28.

Whyte, William H., Jr. *The Organization Man*. New York: Doubleday, 1957.

Wilcox, Herbert G. "The Culture Trait of Hierarchy in Middle Class Children," *Public Administration Review* 28 (May/June, 1968): 222–235.

Wilensky, Harold L. *Organizational Intelligence*. New York: Basic Books, 1967.

———. "The Professionalization of Everyone?" *American Journal of Sociology* 70 (September, 1965): 137–158.

Wolin, Sheldon S. "Hannah Arendt and the Ordinance of Time," *Social Research* 44 (Spring, 1977): 91–105.

Wright, J. Patrick, with John De Lorean. *On a Clear Day You Can See General Motors*. New York: Avon Books, 1979.

Yates, Douglas. *Bureaucratic Democracy*. Cambridge, Mass.: Harvard University Press, 1982.

Zwerdling, Daniel, ed. *Workplace Democracy*. New York: Harper and Row, 1978.

Index

Bureaucracy(ies), opposition (*cont.*):
121, 180, 208–212; and power,
x, 5, 18, 79, 89–90, 98, 101,
203; and public/private life, 4,
8, 49–53, 57, 91; and race, 7,
106–108; and recruitment,
101–104, 106–107, 115–116;
as resources, 39–41, 70, 81,
125, 132–133, 134; roles within, 13, 22, 36–37, 42–44, 78,
84, 137, 157; norms and rules
of, 9–10, 12, 14, 19, 21, 103,
109, 144, 145; and sexuality,
13, 54–57; subordinates in,
108, 110; "tokens" in, 107–108
Bureaucrat(s), 94; attitude of, toward clients, 14–16, 139–142,
144–145; attitude of, toward
conflict, 104–105, 120; attitude of, toward rules, 9–10;
attributes of, 99–102, 104,
106, 107, 109–111, 116; resistance by, 17, 19, 101, 102,
116–117; similarity of, to clients, 92, 98–99, 128, 130, 142,
145, 148, 153; street-level,
127, 129, 134, 136, 139, 149
Bureaucratic capitalism, 8, 40,
154–170, 182, 193, 195, 198;
double bind of, 157; resistance
to, 202, 203, 205, 208–212;
service organizations in, 123–
124, 128–136, 139
Bureaucratic discourse, xi, xii,
16, 37, 39–40, 72–73, 77–79,
103, 107, 116; and clients,
136–137, 151, 152; competing
dimensions of, 22–23, 30; definition of, 6, 59–62; and feminist discourse, 196, 204, 207,
209; and legal discourse, 35,
38–39, 138, 181–182; and lib-

eral feminism, 184, 187, 192–
193; and political theory, 79–82
Bureaucratization, 37; effects of,
117; incompleteness of, 22, 30,
56, 57, 90; of education, 43–
46, 61–62, 78, 225 n. 35; of the
family, 46–53; pervasiveness
of, 20, 30, 51, 58; and political
theory, 79–82; of politics, 83,
99; as a process, 6–7, 9, 30; of
sexuality, 13, 54–57, 138–139;
of society, xi, 9, 56–57, 91, 99;
of work, 11, 13, 84–90
Burke, Edmund, 32, 80

Capitalism: and bureaucracy, 8,
11, 31, 35–36, 38, 40, 56–57,
84–85, 135, 148; ethic of, 93;
and rationalization of consumption, 48, 51. *See also* Bureaucratic capitalism
Caretaking, x, 24–26, 28, 158,
161, 166, 170–175, 197, 198
Carson, Cindy, 118–119
Carson, Phil, 119
Children, 161–162; as clients,
38–39
Chodorow, Nancy, 161–162
Class: and bureaucracy, 7, 8, 11,
38, 106–108, 192, 195; definition of, 84–86; and education,
43–44; and gender, 93, 97,
160, 175, 177, 234–235 n. 24;
and human service organizations, 135, 148
Clawson, Dan, 11, 19
Clerical work, 87, 88, 98,
111–112
Client(s), 14–16, 123–125, 128,
190; as "case," 38, 137, 138,
141, 144, 149; as constituency,
134, 152; and dependency,

Unions, and bureaucratic organizations (*cont.*):
40–41, 209, 210, 237 n. 60; and confrontation with management, 118–119; of welfare clients, 149, 151
Universalism, 34

Valentine, Bettylou, 143

Weber, Max, 31, 38; definition of bureaucracy, 7
Welfare programs, 124, 128–130, 135, 136, 138–145, 147, 150; and legal discourse, 39, 138; and welfare rights organizations, 139, 149, 150–153. *See also* Bureaucracy(ies), street-level; Human service organizations
Welfare rights activists, 139, 149, 150–153
Whyte, William H., 81, 104
Wilcox, Herbert, 46
Wilensky, Harold, 100
Women: and biology, 28; career advice to, 94, 184, 186; as caretakers, x, 24–26, 28, 158, 161, 166, 170–175, 197, 198; and class, 58, 93, 97, 160, 175, 177; and conformity, 29, 184; and dependence, 25, 98, 167–168; experiences of, x, 24–27, 93–95, 97–98, 154, 157–159, 166–168, 170–171, 174–175, 196–204; language of, 95–96, 154, 163–166; liberation of, 83, 94, 122; as managers, 98, 107, 121, 192, 209; as a marginal group, 23–24, 177–178; and mothering, 161–163, 171–172; and political/legal reforms, 28, 181, 193–195; and public/private split, 27–28, 47, 94–95, 172–174; and race, 92, 97, 158, 175, 214 n. 1, 234–235 n. 24; and resistance, 155–157, 180, 208–212; and self-identity, 157–160, 162–165, 167, 169; and sexuality, 54–55, 165; submerged discourse of, xiii, 23–24, 155–157; subordination of, 24, 26, 28, 92–96, 166–170; and success, ix, 183–189; as victims, 24, 26, 166–167; and work, 47–48, 97. *See also* Family
Women's movement: first wave, 3, 50, 58, 181; second wave, 3
Work: and clerical workers, 87–89, 111–113; and disciplinary control, 89; and health and safety issues, 85–87; and industrial workers, 85–87, 89, 112–116; and job satisfaction, 113; and "new working class," 84–85, 87; and workplace sabotage, 113